# PowerPoint® 4 for Windows™
# SmartStart

DAN SPEERS

QUE COLLEGE

## PowerPoint 4 for Windows SmartStart

### Copyright © 1995 by Que® Corporation.

Library of Congress Catalog No.: 94-068012

ISBN: 1-56529-795-4

98  97  96          4  3

Interpretation of the printing code: the rightmost double-digit number is the year of the book's printing; the rightmost single-digit number, the number of the book's printing. For example, a printing code of 95-1 shows that the first printing of the book occurred in 1995.

Screens reproduced in this book were created using Collage Plus from Inner Media, Inc., Hollis, NH.

*PowerPoint 4 for Windows SmartStart* is based on Version 4 of PowerPoint for Windows.

**Publisher:** David P. Ewing

**Associate Publisher:** Paul Boger

**Book Designer:** Paula Carroll

**Production Team:** Michael Dietsch, Cynthia Drouin, DiMonique Ford, Aren Howell, Debra A. Kincaid, Steph Mineart, G. Alan Palmore, Victor Peterson, Clair Schweinler,  Kris Simmons, Michael Thomas, Tina Trettin, Donna Winter

Composed in *Stone Serif* and *MCPdigital* by Que Corporation.

# About the Author

**Dan Speers** is a consultant and trainer with an extensive background in computer programming. He specializes in developing interactive tutorials, multimedia sales training systems, and activity-based courseware. His software and educational materials have been widely used by both universities and Fortune 500 companies.

**Publishing Manager**

Chris Katsaropoulos

**Series Editor**

Mary-Terese Cozzola

**Developmental Editor**

Ellen Camm

**Managing Editor**

Sheila B. Cunningham

**Senior Editor**

Jeannine Freudenberger

**Copy Editor**

Beth Hux

**Editorial Coordinator**

Elizabeth D. Brown

# Acknowledgments

Que College is grateful for the assistance provided by the following reviewers: Tom Farrell, South Dakota State University, and Fredi Griggs, Monsanto State University. A special thanks also to our technical editors, Marsha Lawson, Middlesex Community College, and Samantha Penrod, Purdue University—Calumet. Thanks also to figure specialist, Ron Holmes.

## Trademark Acknowledgments

# Contents at a Glance

# Table of Contents

## 6 Converting Existing Information into a Presentation    127

## 7 Embellishing a Presentation with Text Effects    161

## 8 Illustrating a Presentation            187

## 9 Communicating with Graphs — 213

## 10 Creating a Professional Presentation — 231

# Preface

Que College is the educational publishing imprint of Macmillan Computer Publishing, the world's leading computer book publisher. Macmillan Computer Publishing books have taught over 20 million people how to be productive with their computers.

This expertise in producing high-quality computer tutorial and reference books is evident in every Que College title we publish. The same tried and true authoring and product development process that makes Macmillan Computer Publishing books bestsellers is used to ensure that every Que College textbook has the most accurate and most up-to-date information. Experienced and respected college instructors write and review every manuscript to provide class-tested pedagogy. Quality-assurance editors check every keystroke and command in Que College books to ensure that instructions are clear and precise.

Above all, Macmillan Computer Publishing and, in turn, Que College have years of experience in meeting the learning demands of computer users in business and at home. This "real-world" experience means that Que College textbooks help students understand how the skills they learn will be applied and why these skills are important.

## A Smart Start to Learning PowerPoint 4 for Windows

*PowerPoint 4 for Windows SmartStart* provides a hands-on approach to one of the most popular presentation programs available. The design of the text is flexible enough to meet a wide variety of needs. The text includes both basic and advanced features of PowerPoint 4 for Windows. This text can introduce a student to presentations, or it can supplement a student's previous learning. An abundance of step-by-step, hands-on tutorials enable students to learn either independently or within a large lab setting.

Prior to presenting the step-by-step tutorials, *PowerPoint 4 for Windows SmartStart* explains the purpose and practical use of each software feature. Within this context, students quickly learn how to use the software. The explanations and abundance of tutorials enable students to remember how to apply the particular skill and to transfer their knowledge easily to other software applications. This approach ensures that students will use their skills in a practical manner.

## Organization

*PowerPoint 4 for Windows SmartStart* uses a logical, simple-to-complex organization. Features that are easy to use and understand are presented first. The student can quickly master basic features and develop a framework for learning more complicated features. In addition, software features that students can use to improve efficiency as they are learning are introduced very early in the text.

Each chapter contains many hands-on tutorials, tables, and screen illustrations to facilitate learning. Learning objectives are listed after the introduction and then repeated at the appropriate points within the chapter. Each chapter ends with a summary to help the student absorb and remember the chapter skills. The end-of-chapter exercises include objective questions and hands-on projects to help students check and apply their skills.

## Distinctive Features

*PowerPoint 4 for Windows SmartStart* provides many distinctive features to ensure students success, including the following:

- For convenience and easy reference, key terms are defined in the margin where a new term is first used.

- Each tutorial consists of concise, clear steps. These steps are highlighted in the book design for ease of use and later reference.

- Notes, tips, shortcuts, cautions, and other helpful hints provide additional information to enhance learning.

- Each project is realistic and designed to appeal to a wide variety of business skills and interests.

- The end-of-chapter exercises focus on developing and applying critical thinking skills—not rote memorization.

- Continuing projects are provided throughout the text. The continuing projects help learners "pull the pieces together."

- A glossary is provided.

- An alphabetical index helps users quickly locate information.

## To the Student:

Although this SmartStart provides a step-by-step approach, it is much more than a button-pushing book. In response to your requests, we have included a short explanation of the purpose for each software feature. Our focus is on teaching you to use the software effectively rather than on simply listing the software's features. We want to make certain that you remember how to apply your knowledge of PowerPoint 4 for Windows long after you have taken this course.

You will not spend a great deal of time simply typing documents. We have provided your instructor with a data disk containing example information for many of the hands-on projects. You can then spend your time completing interesting projects with real-life scenarios.

## To the Instructor:

As a result of your feedback, this SmartStart includes several improvements over previous books in the SmartStart series. The number of screen illustrations has been increased to help students move through the steps more quickly. The new end-of-chapter exercises do not test rote memorization; they do reinforce practical knowledge. Each chapter has enough end-of-chapter exercises to ensure that all objectives have been fully addressed.

The instructor's manual includes a Curriculum Guide to help you plan class sessions and assignments. Each chapter in the instructor's manual contains teaching tips, answers to "Checking Your Skills" questions, transparency masters, and test questions and answers. The manual also offers advice on what to teach when time is short or when the students have a specific need. Additional project ideas and suggestions also are included.

Look for the following additional SmartStarts:

| | |
|---|---|
| *Access 2 for Windows SmartStart* | 1-56529-874-8 |
| *BASIC SmartStart* | 1-56529-402-5 |
| *dBASE III Plus SmartStart* | 1-56529-410-6 |
| *dBASE IV SmartStart* | 1-56529-251-0 |
| *Excel 4 for Windows SmartStart* | 1-56529-202-2 |
| *Excel 5 for Windows SmartStart* | 1-56529-794-6 |
| *Lotus 1-2-3 SmartStart* (covers 2.4 and below) | 1-56529-245-6 |
| *Lotus for Windows SmartStart* | 1-56529-404-1 |
| *MS-DOS SmartStart* | 1-56529-249-9 |
| *Novell NetWare SmartStart* | 1-56529-411-4 |
| *Paradox SmartStart* | 1-56529-406-8 |
| *Personal Computing SmartStart* | 1-56529-455-6 |
| *Quattro Pro DOS SmartStart* | 1-56529-408-4 |
| *Quattro Pro for Windows 1.0 SmartStart* | 1-56529-409-2 |
| *Windows 3.1 SmartStart* | 1-56529-203-0 |
| *Word for Windows SmartStart* | 1-56529-204-9 |
| *Word 6 for Windows SmartStart* | 1-56529-796-2 |
| *WordPerfect 5.1 SmartStart* | 1-56529-246-4 |
| *WordPerfect 6 SmartStart* | 1-56529-407-6 |
| *WordPerfect for Windows SmartStart* | 1-56529-403-3 |
| *Works for DOS SmartStart* | 1-56529-396-7 |
| *Works for the Mac SmartStart* | 1-56529-395-9 |
| *Works for Windows SmartStart* | 1-56529-394-0 |

For more information call:

**1-800-428-5331**

# Introduction

In today's world of information overload, the ability to present data in a quick, concise, and effective format is an important skill. To that end, presentation of information has become a major concern in businesses. PowerPoint has always been at the forefront of Windows presentation packages. PowerPoint enables people to present information easily and quickly through a variety of methods, such as on-screen slide shows, 35mm slides, and handouts.

In this new version of PowerPoint, Microsoft has even further enhanced a great product. The developers have added many new features and have improved most of the old ones. PowerPoint now shares the same look and many of the features of Microsoft Excel and Word for Windows. You can also copy objects from one windows application to another, subject to certain limitations.

This book, *PowerPoint 4 for Windows SmartStart*, takes you into PowerPoint and teaches you how to get started with this program. This book teaches you the basics and gives you a few pointers along the way. New and improved features for this version are one of the main focuses of this book. Many illustrations are included to help clarify the text and the program.

## Who Should Use This Book

*PowerPoint 4 for Windows SmartStart* is a tutorial developed with easy-to-follow, step-by-step instructions. Because *PowerPoint 4 for Windows SmartStart* concisely covers only the most important concepts, your time on the learning curve is greatly reduced. Each chapter begins with a set of objectives. You learn by following the hands-on tutorials in each chapter. Exercises and questions at the end of a chapter give you a chance to practice what you have learned and to check your understanding of the objectives.

If you are a new PowerPoint user, *PowerPoint 4 for Windows SmartStart* will help you become productive quickly. If you are an experienced computer user who is new to the Windows environment, *PowerPoint 4 for Windows SmartStart* will give you a head start on learning other Windows applications, such as Microsoft Word for Windows, Microsoft PowerPoint, Aldus PageMaker, or any of the many other Windows applications you might use.

**Note:** *In order to complete all the tutorials in this book, you must also use Microsoft Word 6 and Excel.*

# How This Book Is Organized

Each chapter in this book relates to a particular PowerPoint procedure or procedures. The basic composition of *PowerPoint 4 for Windows SmartStart* reflects the normal operations of someone creating a presentation. This book starts by familiarizing you with the look of and use of the components of PowerPoint. Then the text progresses through creating text slides, using the drawing tools, and adding clip art and other objects. The book also covers creating full multislide presentations and getting the final output.

Chapter 1, "Getting Started," introduces you to PowerPoint and presents an overview of the program's special features. You learn how to start the program and then how to navigate the PowerPoint screen and use the toolbars, buttons, menus, views, and dialog boxes. You are also introduced to PowerPoint's Help features.

Chapter 2, "Creating a Presentation," introduces you to the AutoContent Wizard by guiding you through the steps of creating a new presentation. You learn how to plan a presentation. You work in both Outline view and Slide view and then save your presentations for future use.

In Chapter 3, "Adding Impact to a Presentation," you start with the basic presentation and make it more effective. You learn to open and copy presentations. You add and delete individual slides. You learn to choose among PowerPoint's many layouts and to add graphics, clip art, and tables. Finally, you enhance the text of your presentation with many special effects.

Chapter 4, "Making Effective Presentations," teaches you more about the actual delivery of your presentations. You learn about PowerPoint's Notes Pages feature. You use the Slide Sorter view, add transitions between slides, and add hidden slides for backup. You also rehearse and present your slide show.

Chapter 5, "Planning and Building a Presentation," deals with the presentation process. You learn to use the PowerPoint templates, work with the Slide Master, and edit individual slides.

Chapter 6, "Converting Existing Information to a Presentation," teaches you how to take text from other Microsoft applications and turn it into a PowerPoint presentation. You work with both Word and Excel documents in PowerPoint.

Chapter 7, "Embellishing a Presentation with Text Effects," takes you into more advanced enhancements of your presentation. You create and work with text objects. Then you change text styles, colors, and alignment. You learn to group objects, to find and replace text, and to spell check your text.

Chapter 8, "Illustrating a Presentation," introduces you to PowerPoint's drawing capabilities. You use the drawing tools, AutoShapes, and the FreeForm tool. You edit your lines and shapes; add various enhancements; and learn the usefulness of guides, grids, and rulers. Finally, you are introduced to PowerPoint's color capabilities.

Chapter 9, "Communicating with Graphs," introduces PowerPoint's graphic capabilities. You work with charts and datasheets to create attractive slides that present data in clear, attractive graphs.

Chapter 10, "Creating a Professional Presentation," ties together all you have learned in the first nine chapters. Here, you add the final touches to make your presentations truly professional. You learn the basic principles of working with color schemes; you practice your presentation skills. You learn to do on-screen drawings, create branched presentations, print various components of your presentation, and use the PowerPoint Viewer.

Appendix A, "Working with Windows," is written for the user who is new to Microsoft Windows. In this appendix, you learn the basic skills you need to work in any Windows program.

Appendix B, "Sending and Routing Presentation Files on Mail Systems," tells you exactly how to send your presentations to other users through electronic mail systems.

Finally, the Glossary provides an alphabetized list of all the key terms defined in the text.

## Conventions Used in This Book

This book uses a number of conventions to help you learn the program quickly.

Step-by-step tutorials are given a light screened background to set them off from the rest of the text. Information you are asked to type is printed in **boldface and teal** in the tutorials and in **boldface** elsewhere. Menu letters you type to activate a command appear in boldface and teal in tutorials, review exercises, and projects—**V**iew—and in boldface elsewhere—**V**iew. Keys you press are shown as keyboard icons—⏎Enter—and in teal icons in tutorials, review exercises, and projects—⏎Enter. Keys you press together are joined by a plus sign—Alt+F2.

Exact quotations of words that appear on-screen are spelled as they appear on-screen and printed in a special typeface.

# CHAPTER 1

# Getting Started

**Presentation graphics program**
A software application used for creating presentations.

**Presentation**
A collection of slides that are displayed in a timed sequence to convey information.

**Electronic slide show**
A presentation created and displayed on a computer.

One of the most powerful ways to present an idea, plan, or report to a group is to use a series of slides that illustrate the important points. PowerPoint provides the tools you need to create dynamic and colorful presentations, complete with slides, charts, and special effects. PowerPoint is a *presentation graphics program*. It provides features and tools for creating a *presentation* consisting of a collection of slides. You display these slides, which contain text, charts, and graphics, in a timed sequence to convey or illustrate information.

This type of presentation is also known as an *electronic slide show*. You can combine a wide variety of type sizes and styles with illustrations, charts, and documents (such as spreadsheets and financial statements) to build convincing and dynamic visual presentations.

Beginning with an overview of PowerPoint's uses and capabilities, this chapter introduces the tools you use to access the many features of the program. This chapter also introduces the extensive help and tutorial features that provide explanations and assistance as you create your own presentations.

## Objectives

By the time you have finished this chapter, you will have learned to

1. Understand PowerPoint's Special Features
2. Start PowerPoint
3. Use the PowerPoint Screen
4. Use Toolbars and Buttons
5. Use the Menus
6. Use the View Buttons
7. Get Help
8. Exit PowerPoint

# Objective 1: Understand PowerPoint's Special Features

PowerPoint contains the same basic Windows features as other Windows applications, and many of the capabilities and commands are the same as those found in Microsoft Word, Excel, and Access. These features include ToolTips, which display toolbar button functions; the status bar, which provides messages and instructions; shortcut menus, which are accessed by clicking the right mouse button; customizable toolbars; and context-sensitive help. Document window sizing and manipulation and the application control menus are also familiar functions.

Although the features peculiar to PowerPoint are specialized for building and enhancing presentations, all features follow the standard Windows conventions. In PowerPoint, you drag and drop, use specialized dialog boxes, click and double-click the mouse to select or initiate an action, and work with drawing tools.

**Wizard**

A utility that asks a series of questions and produces a presentation based on the answers.

Many Microsoft Windows applications provide *wizards*, which ask a series of questions and then produce a document based on your answers. One of the most powerful features of PowerPoint is the AutoContent Wizard, which suggests slide types, content, and structure. By following the steps provided by this wizard, you can easily turn an idea into a convincing presentation.

Among the other capabilities of PowerPoint are the following:

- You can take information written in other Windows programs and turn it into or include it in presentations. The Present It button turns a Word for Windows 6.0 document or outline into a PowerPoint presentation. You can incorporate text from Word or an ASCII file directly into a slide.

- You can import spreadsheets, charts, and data graphs directly from Excel.

- You can insert into a slide show illustrations from Corel Draw!, PC Paintbrush, Harvard Graphics, and other similar programs.

- You can use the new Media Player to include multimedia effects, such as AVI movie files and WAV sound files.

- You can use the ClickSlides function to create more than 21 different types of slides.

- You can edit and spell check text slides with a built-in word processor and the Spelling Checker, and you can enhance your slides with special text effects and color.

- You can add graphic images both through freehand drawing and by using an AutoShapes tool that provides 24 customizable, quick diagram shapes. A charting tool offers more than 100 types of graphs.

- For technical presentations, an Equation Editor simplifies the presentation of mathematical, engineering, and scientific equations.

- During a presentation, you can draw lines, circles, and other freehand illustrations to emphasize important points.

- You can incorporate scripts, timing between slides, and speaker's notes directly into the presentation.

- You can print speaker's notes, handouts, and outline pages for review or distribution.

- Presentations can be electronically mailed to other users, distributed on disk, or converted to 35mm slides.

The major difference between PowerPoint and most other Windows applications is that in PowerPoint some commands and operations can be done only with a mouse. A mouse is desirable in other applications, but it is required for PowerPoint.

# Objective 2: Start PowerPoint

PowerPoint must operate with Windows and requires the use of a mouse. PowerPoint 4.0 icons, like those for Word 6.0 and Excel 5.0, are usually installed in the Microsoft Office group window.

## Starting PowerPoint

This tutorial assumes that you are starting Windows and PowerPoint from the MS-DOS prompt. If your computer automatically loads Windows when booting, skip step 1, and go directly to step 2. To start PowerPoint, follow these steps:

**1** Type **win** at the MS-DOS prompt.

The Program Manager appears and displays either the Microsoft Office icon or the Microsoft Office group window. If the Microsoft Office group window is not open, double-click the Microsoft Office icon. When open, the Microsoft Office group window should resemble the window shown in figure 1.1.

**Figure 1.1**
The Microsoft
Office group.

**PowerPoint icon**

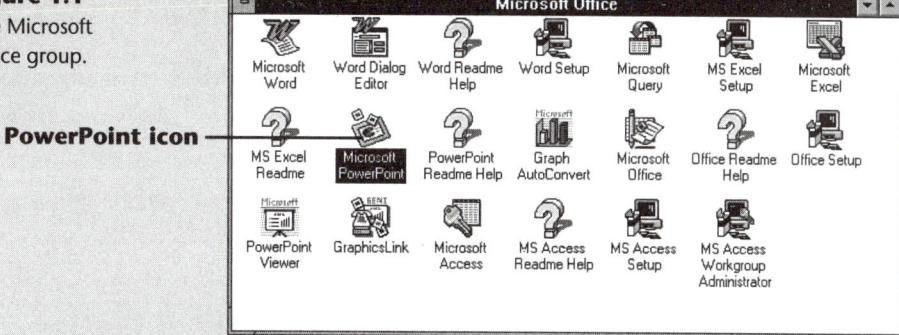

(continues)

## Starting PowerPoint (continued)

❷ Double-click the PowerPoint icon.

The PowerPoint program starts and displays the Tip of the Day dialog box (see figure 1.2). If you don't want to view a tip each time you start PowerPoint, deselect the check box at the bottom left of the dialog box.

**Figure 1.2**
The Tip of the Day dialog box.

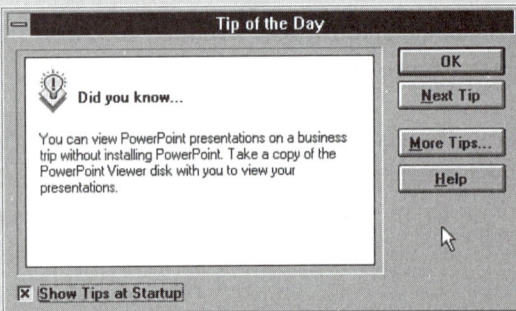

❸ Read the tip, and click OK in the Tip of the Day dialog box.

The PowerPoint start-up dialog box appears (see figure 1.3). In later tutorials, you use this dialog box to create new presentations. (If you have been working on another presentation and now want to start a new one, the dialog box is called the New Presentation dialog box.)

**Figure 1.3**
The PowerPoint start-up dialog box, also called the New Presentation dialog box.

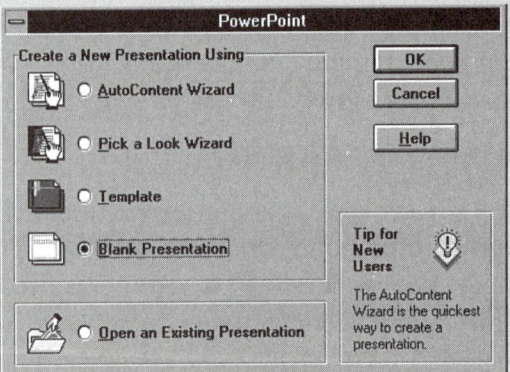

❹ Click Cancel in the PowerPoint start-up dialog box.

The PowerPoint application window appears (see figure 1.4).

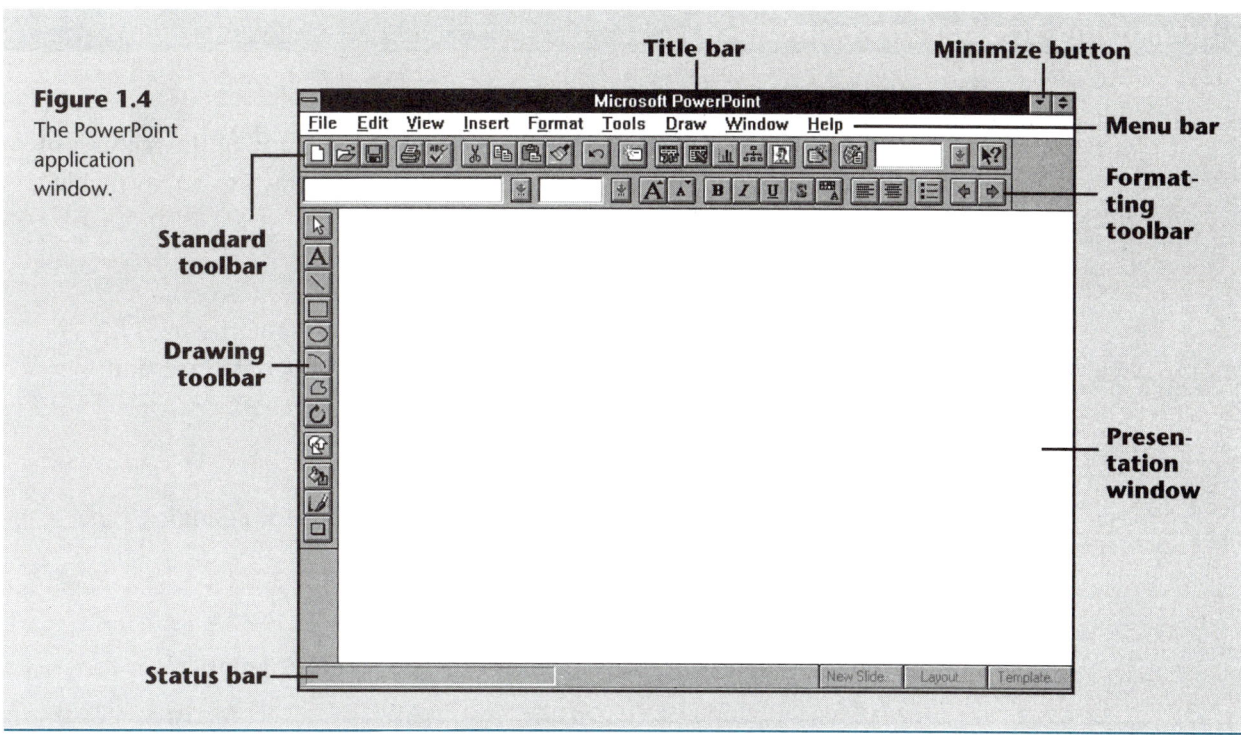

**Figure 1.4**
The PowerPoint application window.

## Objective 3: Use the PowerPoint Screen

The PowerPoint presentation window contains many of the same elements as other Windows applications. Standardizing these elements among the various Windows applications makes learning and using new applications easier.

Like other Windows applications, the PowerPoint window contains a title bar, menu bar, Standard toolbar, Formatting toolbar, status bar, Minimize and Maximize buttons, and application control menus.

### Identifying Screen Parts

Refer to figure 1.4 to identify the currently displayed parts of the PowerPoint window.

❶ Locate the title bar.

The title bar displays the program name.

(continues)

## Identifying Screen Parts (continued)

**❷** Locate the menu bar.

PowerPoint provides drop-down menus from which many of the features of the program can be accessed. Features that appear in gray are not available in the current mode.

**❸** Locate the Standard toolbar.

The Standard toolbar gives quick access to the most frequently used file functions; quick printing; cutting, copying and pasting; data insertion; selected wizards; zoom; and help.

**❹** Locate the Formatting toolbar.

The Formatting toolbar provides controls and buttons for changing type fonts, sizes, display attributes, and color.

**❺** Locate the Drawing toolbar.

This toolbar provides buttons for inserting text or quick graphics.

The presentation window is the blank workspace in the center of the PowerPoint screen. This area is where you create your presentations.

## Learning the Parts of the Presentation Window

To initiate a presentation and display the parts of the presentation window, do the following:

**❶** Choose **F**ile on the menu bar, or click the New button on the Standard toolbar.

**❷** Choose **N**ew from the **F**ile menu.

The New Presentation dialog box appears.

**❸** Select **B**lank Presentation, and click the OK button.

The New Slide dialog box appears (see figure 1.5).

**Figure 1.5**
The New Slide dialog box.

**AutoLayout list box**

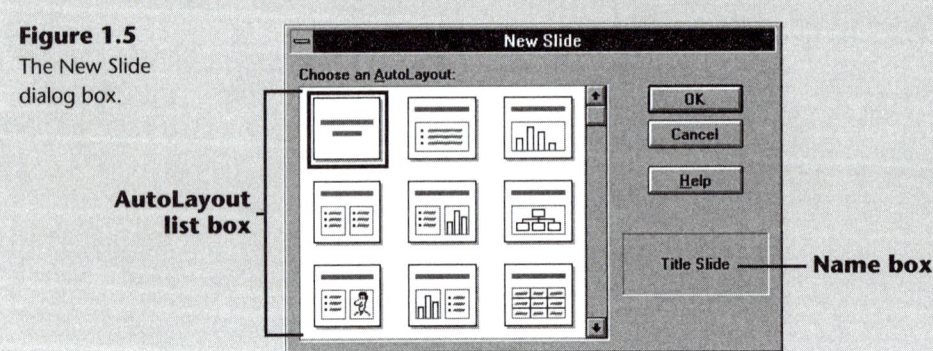

**4** If the first slide template in the AutoLayout list box is not highlighted (the slide is surrounded by a black outline and the words, `Title Slide`, appear in the name box on the right side of the dialog box), click this slide template to select it.

**5** With the Title Slide template selected, click OK.

A new presentation slide appears in the presentation window (see figure 1.6). The control buttons on the status bar at the lower right of the window are now black, indicating that these commands are available.

**Figure 1.6**
The PowerPoint presentation window.

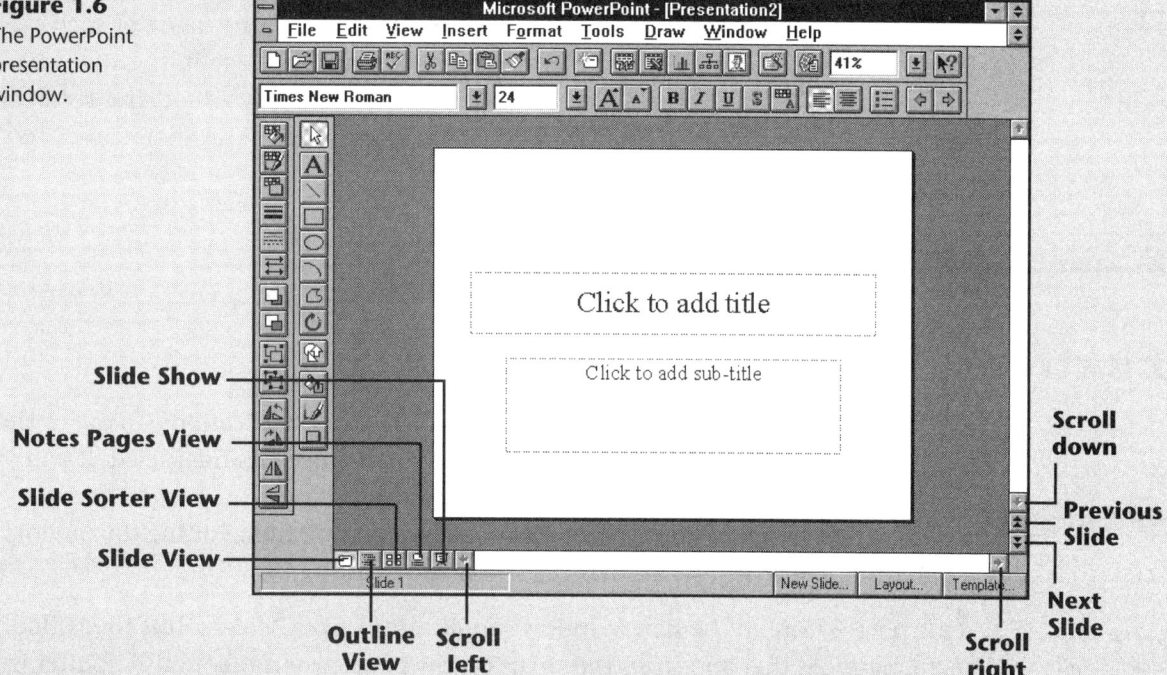

**6** Locate the presentation title bar.

The presentation title bar contains the name of the current presentation.

**7** Locate the status bar.

If no buttons or menu commands are selected, the status bar shows the current slide number.

**8** Locate the vertical scroll bar.

Located at the right of the presentation window, the vertical scroll bar contains scrolling buttons. The buttons with single arrows scroll the current slide. The buttons with double arrows access either the next or preceding slide.

(continues)

### Learning the Parts of the Presentation Window (continued)

**⑨** Position the mouse pointer over the lowest button with a double arrow on the vertical scroll bar, and wait until a message appears in a small yellow box.

The words `Next Slide` appear in the box. Moving the mouse pointer up to next button produces the message `Previous Slide`. Also notice the messages that appear in the status bar.

**⑩** Locate the Slide View and Notes Pages View buttons.

These buttons are located at the lower left of the presentation window. Position the mouse pointer over each button in turn; the name of each button appears in a yellow box with a contextual message in the status bar. The first button is the Slide View button, which displays the current slide in the presentation window. You edit individual slides in the Slide view. The Notes Pages view displays the notes pages that are associated with the slides.

## Objective 4: Use Toolbars and Buttons

As Microsoft has released new versions of its Windows applications, many of the toolbars, buttons, and customization functions have been standardized. If you are familiar with another Microsoft Windows application, you already know many of the standard PowerPoint buttons for accessing files, editing documents, formatting documents and their contents, and printing.

**ToolTip**
A small yellow box that displays the name of a tool when the mouse pointer is over that button.

One new feature in the new Windows applications from Microsoft is the balloon help messages that appear in the small yellow boxes when the mouse pointer is positioned over a button for a few seconds. These balloon help messages are known as *ToolTips*. When a ToolTip message appears, an additional help message also appears in the status bar.

As in other applications, toolbars can be selected, moved about the screen to other locations, customized for a particular application, and deselected when not needed for a particular project.

### Viewing the Standard Toolbar

The Standard toolbar contains buttons for the most commonly accessed functions in PowerPoint (see figure 1.7). This toolbar is called the Standard toolbar because of its similarity in a variety of Microsoft Windows programs. Table 1.1 shows the buttons available on this toolbar and summarizes their functions.

**Figure 1.7**
The Standard toolbar.

## Table 1.1   Standard Toolbar Buttons

| Button | Button Name | Function |
|---|---|---|
| | New | Creates a new presentation. |
| | Open | Opens an existing presentation. |
| | Save | Saves the active presentation to a file. |
| | Print | Prints the current presentation. |
| | Spelling | Checks the spelling in the current presentation. |
| | Cut | Copies the selection to the Clipboard and removes the selection from the presentation. |
| | Copy | Copies the selection to the Clipboard without removing it from the presentation. |
| | Paste | Inserts the contents of the Clipboard at the insertion point location. |
| | Format Painter | Copies the selected format to another object. |
| | Undo | Reverses the latest command or action. |
| | Insert New Slide | Inserts new slide after the current slide. |
| | Insert Word Table | Adds a Microsoft Word table to the current slide. |
| | Insert Excel Sheet | Adds a Microsoft Excel worksheet to the current slide. |
| | Insert Graph | Adds a Microsoft graph to current slide. |
| | Insert Org Chart | Adds an organizational chart to current slide. |
| | Insert Clip Art | Adds image from Clip Art library to slide. |
| | Pick a Look Wizard | Design a "look" for current presentation. |
| | Report It | Transfers contents of current presentation to Microsoft Word. |
| | Zoom Control | Changes the size of the screen image. |
| | Help | Provides context-sensitive help about different areas of the PowerPoint screen. |

### Viewing the Formatting Toolbar

You use the Formatting toolbar to select type fonts and sizes and to change the appearance of selected text (see figure 1.8). Table 1.2 shows the buttons and summarizes their functions on this toolbar.

**Figure 1.8**
The Formatting
toolbar.

| Table 1.2 | Formatting Toolbar Buttons | |
|---|---|---|
| **Button** | **Button Name** | **Function** |
| Times New Roman | Font list box | Lists available type fonts. |
| 24 | Font Size | Selects the type size. |
| A | Increase Font Size | Incrementally increases selected font size. |
| A | Decrease Font Size | Incrementally decreases selected font size. |
| B | Bold | Boldfaces the current type selection. |
| I | Italic | Italicizes the current type selection. |
| U | Underline | Underlines the current type selection. |
| S | Text Shadow | Adds shadow highlight to type selection. |
| A | Text Color | Selects a color for text selection. |
| | Left Align | Left-aligns current text selection. |
| | Center Align | Centers the current text selection. |
| | Bullet On/Off | Adds bullets to selected text. |
| ⇦ | Promote (Indent Less) | Moves selected text to the left. |
| ⇨ | Demote (Indent More) | Moves selected text to the right. |

## Viewing the Drawing Toolbar

The Drawing toolbar provides tools for selecting objects, drawing, and adding text to slides (see figure 1.9). Table 1.3 shows the buttons and summarizes their functions on this toolbar.

**Figure 1.9**
The Drawing
toolbar.

| Table 1.3 | Drawing Toolbar Buttons | |
| Button | Button Name | Function |
| --- | --- | --- |
| | Selection tool | Picks up tool for selecting and editing an object. |
| | Text tool | Adds text object. |
| | Line tool | Adds lines to slide. |
| | Rectangle tool | Adds rectangles to slide. |
| | Ellipse tool | Adds an ellipse to slide. |
| | Arc tool | Adds an arc to slide. |
| | FreeForm tool | Allows free-form drawing or adding polygons. |
| | Free Rotate tool | Rotates a selected object. |
| | AutoShapes | Toggles (shows or hides) the AutoShapes toolbar. |
| | Fill On/Off | Toggles fill on or off. |
| | Line On/Off | Toggles line on or off. |
| | Shadow On/Off | Toggles shadowing on or off. |

## Examining the Buttons on a Toolbar

One of the easiest ways to become familiar with the buttons on a toolbar is to use the ToolTips feature and at the same time read the messages on the status bar. Using tables 1.1 through 1.3, complete the following steps, comparing the messages in the status bar with the descriptions listed under Function in the tables.

**Note:** *Because you do not have data in the new presentation on-screen, some of the messages will be different from the functions given in the tables.*

❶ Position and hold the mouse pointer over each button on the Standard toolbar, and compare the status bar message with the function description listed for that button in table 1.1.

❷ Position and hold the mouse pointer over each button on the Formatting toolbar, and compare the status bar message with the function description listed for that button in table 1.2.

❸ Position and hold the mouse pointer over each button on the Drawing toolbar, and compare the status bar message with the function description listed for that button in table 1.3.

# Objective 5: Use the Menus

Recent Windows applications released by Microsoft as part of its Office Suite provide relatively standardized menu structures. The small differences among the menu bars relate to the types of application. For example, Word 6.0 has a T**a**ble option, and PowerPoint has a **D**raw option.

When, for example, you choose the **F**ile menu in PowerPoint, the drop-down menu that appears contains many of the same items that are found in the Word 6.0 **F**ile menu (see figure 1.10). If you are familiar with any of the other Microsoft Windows applications' menus, you already know many of the PowerPoint menu items.

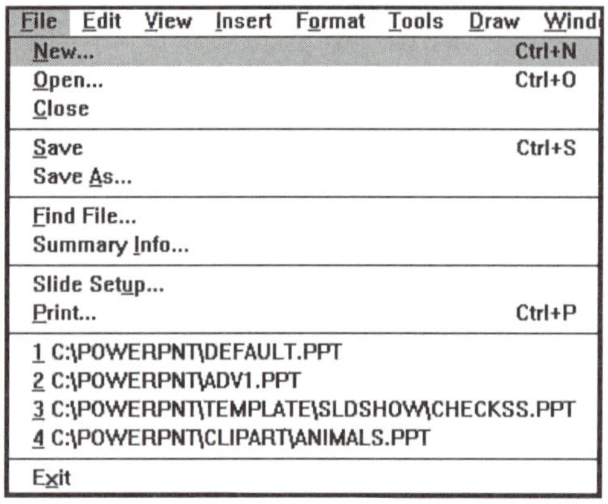

**Figure 1.10**

The drop-down File menu.

| File | Edit | View | Insert | Format | Tools | Draw | Wind|
|------|------|------|--------|--------|-------|------|-----|
| **New...** | | | | | | | Ctrl+N |
| **O**pen... | | | | | | | Ctrl+O |
| **C**lose | | | | | | | |
| **S**ave | | | | | | | Ctrl+S |
| Save **A**s... | | | | | | | |
| **F**ind File... | | | | | | | |
| Summary **I**nfo... | | | | | | | |
| Slide Set**u**p... | | | | | | | |
| **P**rint... | | | | | | | Ctrl+P |
| **1** C:\POWERPNT\DEFAULT.PPT | | | | | | | |
| **2** C:\POWERPNT\ADV1.PPT | | | | | | | |
| **3** C:\POWERPNT\TEMPLATE\SLDSHOW\CHECKSS.PPT | | | | | | | |
| **4** C:\POWERPNT\CLIPART\ANIMALS.PPT | | | | | | | |
| E**x**it | | | | | | | |

**Select**

To highlight a menu item as a possible choice.

**Choose**

To initiate a command or option.

When you *select* a menu item, you are highlighting that item as a possible choice. Selected menu items are always accompanied by a descriptive message in the status bar. When you *choose* a menu item, you are initiating the action that is implemented by that item.

## Selecting and Choosing a Menu Item

Complete the following steps to explore the different methods of selecting and choosing menu items, as well as to discover the purpose of each selection:

**❶** Click the **F**ile choice on the menu bar.

Note that a description of the first choice on this menu now appears in the status bar.

**❷** Use → to move the highlight to each menu bar selection, reading the description message in the status bar for each menu's first selection in turn.

**❸** Use ← to move the highlight back to the **F**ile selection on the menu bar, and press ↓.

**❹** Use ↓ and ↑ to move the highlight to each selection on the drop-down menu.

As the highlight moves to a new selection, the message in the status bar changes to describe the selected item.

⑤ Highlight the **O**pen choice, and press `↵Enter`.

The Open dialog box appears (see figure 1.11). This dialog box is explained in detail in a later chapter.

**Figure 1.11**
The Open dialog box.

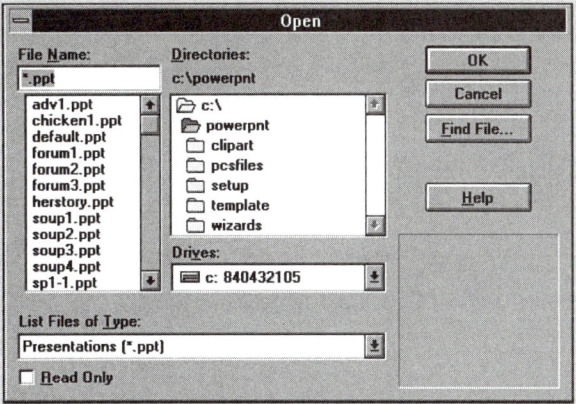

⑥ In the **D**irectories list box, click the directory that contains the PowerPoint program files (if necessary), and then double-click the SAMPLES subdirectory.

⑦ In the File **N**ame list box, click the CALENDAR.PPT presentation.

⑧ Click OK.

The presentation, CALENDAR, now appears in the Presentation window.

## Exploring the Shortcut Menus

Shortcut menus provide a quick way to access certain features or functions in PowerPoint. To display a shortcut menu, position the mouse pointer in a particular area of the screen, and press the right mouse button.

**Note:** *The shortcut menus may look different in different views. If your menus do not match the figures exactly, don't worry. The shortcut menu always matches what you are doing.*

To explore several shortcut menus, complete the following steps:

❶ Position the mouse pointer in one of the toolbars, and press the right mouse button.

The Toolbar menu appears (see figure 1.12). Items with a check mark are currently displayed toolbars. You select or deselect a toolbar by clicking the name of the toolbar.

(continues)

## Exploring the Shortcut Menus (continued)

**Figure 1.12**
The Toolbar
shortcut menu.

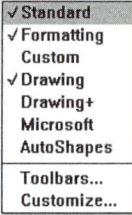

2 Click the left mouse button anywhere outside the shortcut menu to remove it.

3 Position the mouse pointer on the white space inside the presentation window, and click the right mouse button.

The Edit shortcut menu appears (see figure 1.13).

**Figure 1.13**
The Edit
shortcut menu.

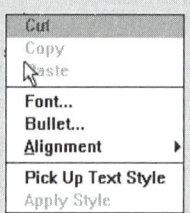

4 Press Esc to remove the Edit menu.

# Objective 6: Use the View Buttons

**View**
The perspective
from which you
look at a presenta-
tion.

PowerPoint provides several different ways to view a presentation; each way has particular advantages for the work being done. For example, you work with only a single slide in the Slide view while entering text or other data, but you use the Slide Sorter button when you want to view all the slides in a presentation. *Views* enable you to look at the presentation from a variety of perspectives.

The View buttons are located at the bottom of the presentation window at the left end of the horizontal scroll bar (refer to figure 1.6). In addition to the Slide and Slide Sorter views, PowerPoint provides two other important views: Notes Pages, which enables you to enter and review notes associated with the presentation, and Outline, which displays the headings and text of all the slides in a presentation.

## Examining View Buttons and Linked Functions

In addition to changing the view of the current presentation, holding down ⇧Shift while clicking a view button accesses certain related functions. Complete the following steps to explore these options:

**1** Position and hold the mouse pointer over each view button, and read the corresponding status bar message (refer to figure 1.7).

The Slide Show button (the farthest right of the view buttons) runs the current presentation. You use this view to see how the presentation will appear as a slide show.

**2** Click the Slide Show button.

The CALENDAR electronic slide show starts.

**3** Click the left mouse button, or press ↵Enter to advance from slide to slide.

**4** Press Esc to exit the slide show and return to the presentation window.

# Objective 7: Get Help

**Cue cards**

Boxed descriptions of various PowerPoint procedures, which you can display while completing the procedure.

Many Help functions are available in PowerPoint; these Help functions range from animated tutorials to electronic manuals, to simple contextual help on a selected command, to *cue cards*, which provide step-by-step instructions for accomplishing a specific task.

You have already used the ToolTips Help function and the short, descriptive messages that appear in the status bar to explore the buttons on the toolbars. These Help functions are known as context-sensitive help because the messages relate to a selected position on-screen or a selected command on the menu bar.

Another way to get contextual help is to use the Help button at the far right of the Standard toolbar. This button has a question mark and an arrow that represents the mouse pointer. When you click that button, a question mark attaches itself to the mouse pointer. You can then click any other button, menu item, or Window component, such as a scroll bar, and a Help window will open (see figure 1.14).

This Help window contains a menu bar from which you can select various options, including printing a copy of the Help topic. The Help buttons below the menu bar enable you to access more complete Help functions, including contents, a subject index, and a search option.

**Figure 1.14**
A Help information
window.

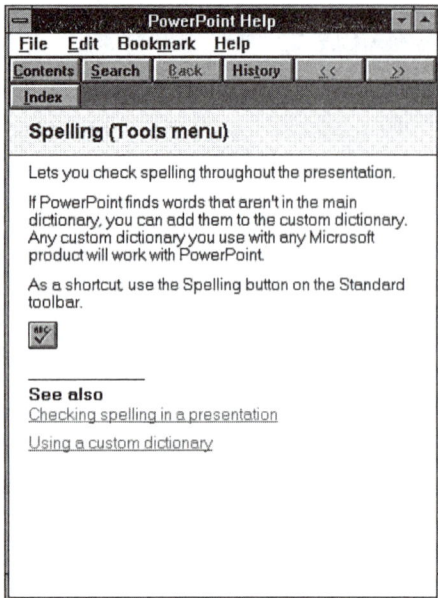

Selecting the **H**elp menu item on the application menu bar produces the Help
menu, from which various help options may be selected. For example, to access
the full PowerPoint Help facility, you choose **C**ontents from the **H**elp menu.
Then you choose Using PowerPoint from the Help window (see figure 1.15).

**Figure 1.15**
The PowerPoint
Help window.

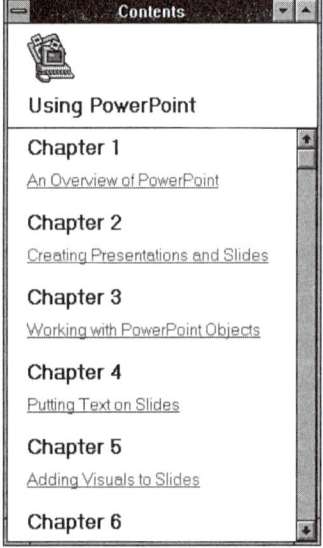

Other options on the **H**elp menu include **S**earch, **I**ndex, **Q**uick Preview, and Ti**p**
of the Day.

## Using the Help Button

To use the Help button, follow these steps:

❶ Click the Help button on the Standard toolbar.

A question mark attaches itself to the mouse pointer.

**2** Position the mouse pointer with the attached question mark over the first button on the Standard toolbar, and click the left mouse button.

The Help window appears for the New button.

**3** Choose Exit from the File menu on the Help window to close the window.

**4** Repeat steps 1, 2, and 3, but this time, position the mouse pointer over the vertical scroll bar on the presentation window.

You can also use the menu bar and the drop-down Help menu to access the Help features.

## Using the Help Menu

To use the **H**elp menu, follow these steps:

**1** Choose **H**elp from the menu bar.

The drop-down **H**elp menu appears.

**2** Choose **S**earch for Help On from the **H**elp menu.

The Search dialog box appears.

**3** Type the word **tool** in the text box.

**4** Highlight the subject Toolbars in the Search list box.

**5** Click the **S**how Topics button.

A list of topics appears in the topics list box.

**6** Click the topic About the Drawing Toolbars in the topics list box.

**7** Click the **G**o To button.

A Help window appears.

**8** Click the Tip button at the bottom of the Help window.

You may have to scroll down the window to see the Tip selection. When the pointer is over the Tip button, the pointer changes to a hand with a pointing finger.

**9** After reading the tip, click the right mouse button, or choose Exit from the File menu to remove the Help window.

The Cue Cards option produces the Cue Cards menu, which provides step-by-step instructions for completing selected functions.

## Using Help Cue Cards

To use the Help Cue Cards, follow these steps:

**1** Choose Cue Cards from the Help menu.

The Cue Cards menu appears (see figure 1.16).

**Figure 1.16**
The Cue Cards menu.

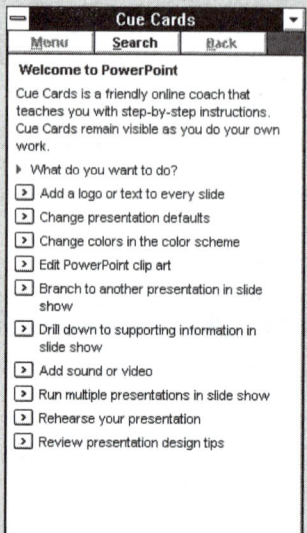

**2** Click the first menu item: Add a Logo or Text to Every Slide.

A cue card that contains other buttons appears.

**3** Click the first button.

Another cue card appears.

**4** Click the Back button to return to the preceding cue card.

**5** Repeat steps 3 and 4 for the remaining buttons.

**6** With a cue card on-screen, click anywhere on the presentation window outside the cue card area.

The cue card remains on-screen, enabling you to continue your work in the presentation window. When you complete the task described in the cue card, you can remove it by choosing Close from Cue Card control menu.

**7** Click the small, gray square in the upper-left corner of the cue card.

The Cue Card control menu appears.

**8** Choose Close from the Cue Card control menu.

The Cue Card is removed from the screen.

# Objective 8: Exit PowerPoint

To exit the PowerPoint application, you choose E**x**it from the **F**ile menu. If you have made changes to the current presentation, PowerPoint prompts you to save or ignore the changes, a topic that is covered in Chapter 2.

### Exiting PowerPoint

Because you have the sample presentation, CALENDAR, on-screen, you need to close the presentation without saving any changes you may have made. To exit PowerPoint, follow these steps:

**1** From the **F**ile menu, choose **C**lose to close the CALENDAR.PPT presentation.

If prompted to save any changes, choose **N**o.

**2** From the **F**ile menu, choose E**x**it.

PowerPoint closes.

# Chapter Summary

In this chapter, you have been introduced to PowerPoint, a program you use to create electronic slides to accompany presentations. You have learned how to start PowerPoint and explored the elements of the PowerPoint screen that you use to create the individual slides. You have examined the toolbars and the buttons that provide access to commonly used functions, the view buttons that change the perspective, and the menu commands available from the menu bar and from shortcut menus. You have learned how to use the extensive Help features of the program. You opened and ran a sample presentation. The chapter concludes with exiting and closing instructions.

# Checking Your Skills

### True/False Questions

For each of the following statements, circle *T* or *F* to indicate whether the statement is true or false.

T  F  **1.** PowerPoint must operate with Windows and requires the use of a mouse.

T  F  **2.** Features that appear in gray on a menu are not available in the current mode.

T  F  **3.** The Drawing toolbar provides buttons only for tools that insert quick graphics.

T  F   **4.** The Slide Sorter button enables you to view the presentation from a variety of perspectives.

T  F   **5.** You can keep cue cards on-screen so that you don't have to remember what the cue card says while completing the function described on the card.

## Multiple-Choice Questions

In the blank provided, write the letter of the correct answer for each of the following questions.

___ **1.** The New button on the Standard toolbar is used to _____.

   **a.** start a Quick Preview tutorial for a new user

   **b.** insert a new slide

   **c.** create a new presentation

   **d.** change a selected type style to a new style

___ **2.** The Bullet On/Off button is normally found on the _____.

   **a.** Drawing toolbar

   **b.** Formatting toolbar

   **c.** Office toolbar

   **d.** Standard toolbar

___ **3.** AutoShapes is a _____.

   **a.** term used in preparing presentations on automobile designs

   **b.** toggle button that shows or hides the AutoShapes toolbar

   **c.** Drawing toolbar button that inserts a variety of shapes

   **d.** Drawing toolbar button that allows free-form drawing

___ **4.** To edit a single slide, you most probably will use the _____.

   **a.** Slide view

   **b.** Outline view

   **c.** Notes Pages view

   **d.** Slide Sorter view

___ **5.** One way to obtain contextual help is to _____.

   **a.** choose the appropriate Help menu command

   **b.** use the Search feature on the Help menu

   **c.** click the status bar

   **d.** use the Help button on the Standard toolbar

### Fill-in-the-Blank Questions

In the blank provided, write the correct answer for each of the following questions.

1. By default, the PowerPoint window also contains a _____ toolbar (the vertical toolbar at the left of the window).

2. If no buttons or menu commands are selected, the status bar shows the current _____.

3. You use the _____ toolbar to select type fonts and sizes and to change the appearance of selected text.

4. The _____ view displays the headings and text of all the slides in a presentation.

5. To exit the PowerPoint application, choose E**x**it from the _____ menu.

# Applying Your Skills

## Review Exercises

### Exercise 1: Using Quick Preview
Choose the **Q**uick Preview item from the **H**elp menu, and complete the on-line tutorial program.

### Exercise 2: Examining More Toolbars
In this chapter, you examined the default toolbars, that is, those that normally appear on the screen. PowerPoint contains several other toolbars that are used for special operations. Use the Toolbar shortcut menu to select these other toolbars, and then use ToolTips and the status bar messages to learn the names and purposes of associated buttons.

### Exercise 3: Exploring the Menus
Select various menus from the menu bar, and highlight the menu items. Based on the introductory material in this chapter and your knowledge of Windows and other Microsoft Windows applications, can you guess what each menu selection does if you actually choose the selection?

## Continuing Projects

### Project 1: Understanding Presentation Programs
Review "Objective 1" of this chapter, and list some of the benefits or uses of the itemized features of PowerPoint. For example, why is it useful to have the capability to convert word processing documents or outlines into a presentation?

### Project 2: Understanding Presentation Approaches
Workers are often called on to conduct presentations. A presentation may be a reorganization plan for a company division, a marketing plan for a new product, or a sales plan for an extensive real estate development. The approach used in a presentation often depends on the audience and the purpose of the presentation. Here is an example of a presentation for an advertising campaign:

| Presentation: | Advertising campaign |
| Audience: | Client company |
| Purpose: | To outline a new advertising concept |
| Possible approach: | A series of drawings that illustrate scenes in a proposed commercial |

What ideas for possible approaches would you consider for each of the following:

1. A presentation to your boss on why you are entitled to a raise and promotion.

2. A presentation to your sales force on a new product that you are introducing in a highly competitive market.

3. A presentation that outlines your proposal for a new company; the presentation is given to a group of investment bankers.

# CHAPTER 2

# Creating a Presentation

Creating a presentation need not be a frustrating task involving countless hours of planning, designing, and formatting your materials. PowerPoint has a built-in tool, the AutoContent Wizard, that prompts you for answers to a series of questions and then creates a template you can edit.

The AutoContent Wizard is a fast and effective way to create a presentation. Starting with a title slide, the wizard guides you through choosing a presentation category and provides an outline with sample text that shows where and how to enter your own text. In this chapter, you learn how to create and refine a presentation by using the AutoContent Wizard.

## Objectives

By the time you have finished this chapter, you will have learned to

1. Start Your Presentation with the AutoContent Wizard
2. Pick the Presentation Type
3. Determine the Major Points
4. Replace Suggested Content
5. Use the Outline View
6. Use the Slide View
7. Save the Presentation

# Objective 1: Start Your Presentation with the AutoContent Wizard

The primary purpose for creating a presentation is to convey an idea clearly and convincingly. Although each situation has its own ground rules—a business plan for starting a new company requires different supporting documentation than does an internal reorganization of the shipping department—the general steps for preparing any presentation are similar:

1. Make sure that the presentation fits the situation.

2. State the problem or premise.

3. Determine the major points to be covered.

4. Add supporting data.

5. Supply a solution or plan.

6. Conclude with an easy-to-understand summary.

You will be following these steps throughout this book to create and refine presentations involving a typical company, Mom's Home Cookin' Chicken Soup Company, known affectionately to its employees as "Mom's."

Scientists at the laboratory kitchens at Mom's have developed a no-fat, no-cholesterol chicken soup. As the marketing manager for the chicken soup division, your first job is to convince the company directors that the soup has a sufficient sales potential for them to invest the money required to bring the product to market.

**AutoContent Wizard**
A tool that guides a planner through the steps of a proposed presentation.

Because your biggest competitor, Dad's Homebrew Soups, is rumored to have developed a similar product, you have to move quickly. Fortunately, the other members of your team have developed the manufacturing data, financials, and research demographics; and you will be using PowerPoint's *AutoContent Wizard*, a built-in scripting tool, to create a quick, but effective presentation. This wizard guides you though the steps of planning a presentation by suggesting slide types, formats, and contents.

## Using the Wizard to Begin Your Presentation

To begin preparation for your presentation, follow these steps:

❶ Start PowerPoint, and proceed to the New Presentation (start-up) dialog box for creating a new presentation (see figure 2.1).

**Figure 2.1**
The PowerPoint
New Presenta-
tion dialog box.

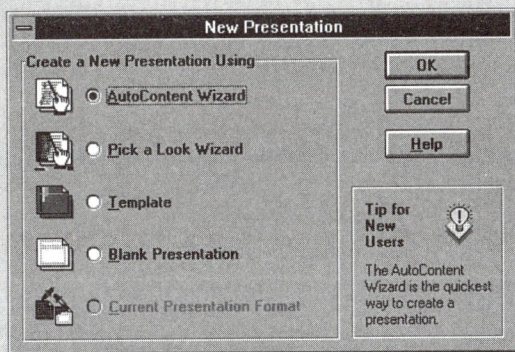

**Note:** *If you have deselected the Tip of the Day window, the start-up (New Pre-sentation) dialog box appears as soon as the PowerPoint application loads. If PowerPoint is already loaded, choose **N**ew from the **F**ile menu to produce the New Presentation dialog box.*

**2** Select the **A**utoContent Wizard.

The selected option contains a black dot in the center of the selection circle.

**3** Click OK.

The AutoContent Wizard Step 1 of 4 dialog box appears (see figure 2.2).

**Figure 2.2**
The
AutoContent
Wizard - Step 1
of 4 dialog box.

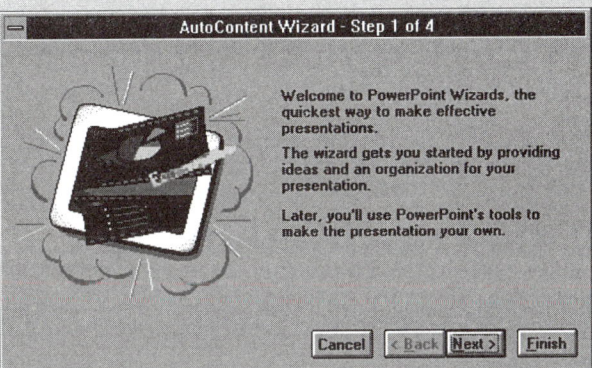

**4** Click the **N**ext button.

The AutoContent Wizard Step 2 of 4 dialog box appears.

**Note:** *In this tutorial, be sure to type the words exactly as given; you will learn to correct spelling errors in a later chapter.*

**5** Type the words **Thik 'N' Thin Chik'N Soup**, in the text box beneath the question What are you going to talk about?

**6** Click the What is your name? text box, and type your name.

(continues)

**Using the Wizard to Begin Your Presentation (continued)**

**7** Type the following in the Other information you'd like to include text box:

**Thick Chunky Chicken Goodness without Fat, without Chloresterol**

The dialog box now contains the required information for the title slide (see figure 2.3).

**Figure 2.3**
The completed AutoContent Wizard - Step 2 of 4 dialog box.

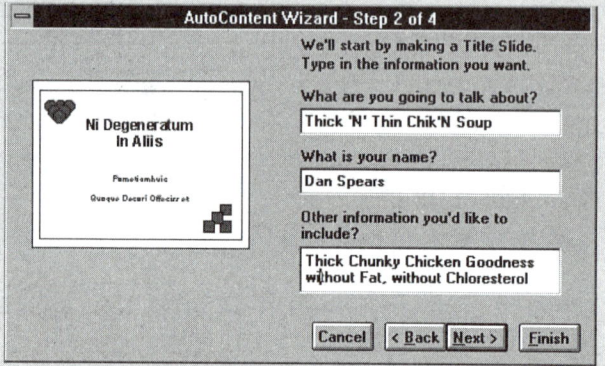

**8** Click the **N**ext button.

The AutoContent Wizard Step 3 of 4 dialog box appears. You learn how to use this dialog box in the next tutorial.

**Note:** *Because the tutorials are continued through the chapter, you need not worry about closing or saving your work at this point.*

# Objective 2: Pick the Presentation Type

**Presentation type**
A classification of a presentation according to the situation or circumstances.

Any presentation must fit the situation. To help you achieve this goal, PowerPoint enables you to choose the *presentation type*; you have the following choices:

- Recommending a Strategy
- Selling a Product, Service or Idea
- Training
- Reporting Progress
- Communicating Bad News
- General

When you select one of the Wizard's categories in the Step 3 dialog box, a suggested content list appears in the list box at the left of the dialog box.

## Evaluating the Presentation Types

To learn the differences of the presentation types, work through the following steps:

**1** Select each of the presentation types offered by the AutoContent Wizard Step 3 dialog box by clicking each choice in turn.

The suggested content of the selected presentation type appears in the Contents list box (see figure 2.4).

**Figure 2.4**
The AutoContent Wizard - Step 3 of 4 dialog box.

**Contents List box** ——

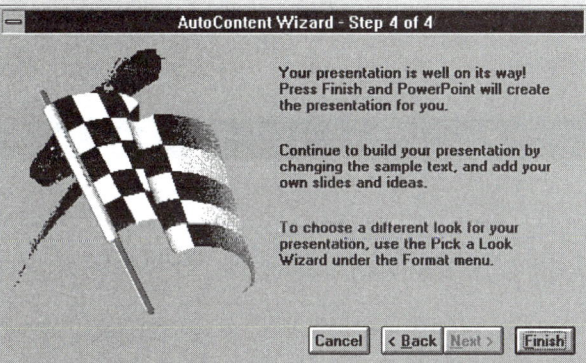

**2** Select the type `Selling a Product, Service or Idea`.

**3** Click the **N**ext button.

The AutoContent Wizard Step 4 of 4 dialog box appears (see figure 2.5).

**Figure 2.5**
The AutoContent Wizard - Step 4 of 4 dialog box.

**4** Read the information displayed in the Step 4 dialog box, and click the **F**inish button.

**Note:** *If you are not satisfied with your responses or the format, click the **B**ack button to return to a prior dialog box. After you click the **F**inish button, you will have to restart the AutoContent Wizard to choose a different presentation format.*

(continues)

**Evaluating the Presentation Types (continued)**

The hourglass mouse pointer appears while PowerPoint creates the basic presentation. Then you see the cue card "Tips for Working in PowerPoint" displayed over the presentation window (see figure 2.6).

**Figure 2.6**
The "Tips for Working in PowerPoint" cue card.

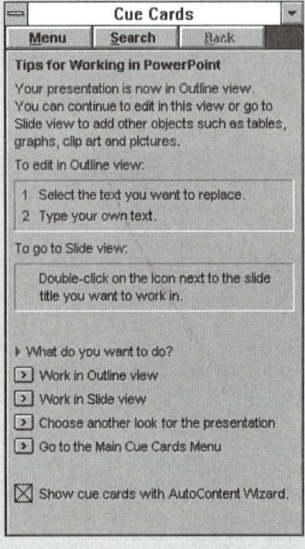

**Outline view**
A view of a presentation in which the text is shown in outline form.

The basic presentation that you have prepared thus far appears in the *Outline view*. You can edit the presentation directly in the Outline view or switch to the Slide view to edit one slide at a time.

**Using the Cue Cards**

The "Tips for Working in PowerPoint" cue card that appears with the presentation window provides suggestions for the activities that you can do next. To read these suggestions, do the following:

❶ Click each menu button under the caption What do you want to do?, and read the resulting cue card. Figure 2.7 shows one cue card.

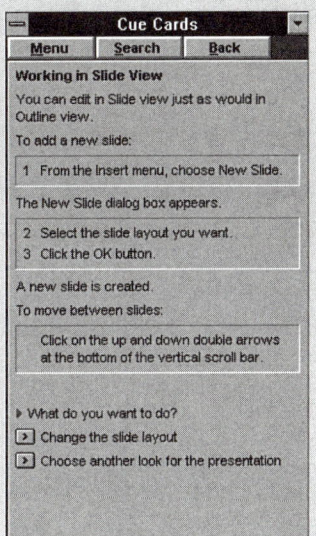

**Figure 2.7**
The "Working in Slide View" cue card.

❷ To return to the main cue card, click the **B**ack button.

❸ Press Esc to remove the main cue card from the screen. Choose **C**lose from the control menu.

# Objective 3: Determine the Major Points

**Objective**
The goal of a presentation; another way of defining a problem or premise.

Before you can consider the major points of a presentation, you must determine the problem or premise for the presentation. PowerPoint uses the term *objective* in the opening slide to suggest that a presentation should begin with a statement that defines the goal of presentation.

As an employee of Mom's, your objective is to convince the board to invest the capital required to market the new chicken soup. The premise for this objective is that the soup is a new and exciting product, that customer demand is substantial, and that the company can manufacture the soup at a reasonable cost and sell it at a price that generates a substantial profit for the company.

The one annoying factor is that Dad's Homebrew Soup may be introducing a competing product. If Mom's can beat Dad's to the market, however, Dad's will have an up-hill battle to seize a market share.

## Adding the Major Points to the Presentation

To add the major points to the presentation, follow these steps:

**1** Highlight the word Objective, next to the slide 2 icon (see figure 2.8).

**Figure 2.8**
The basic presentation window prepared by the AutoContent Wizard.

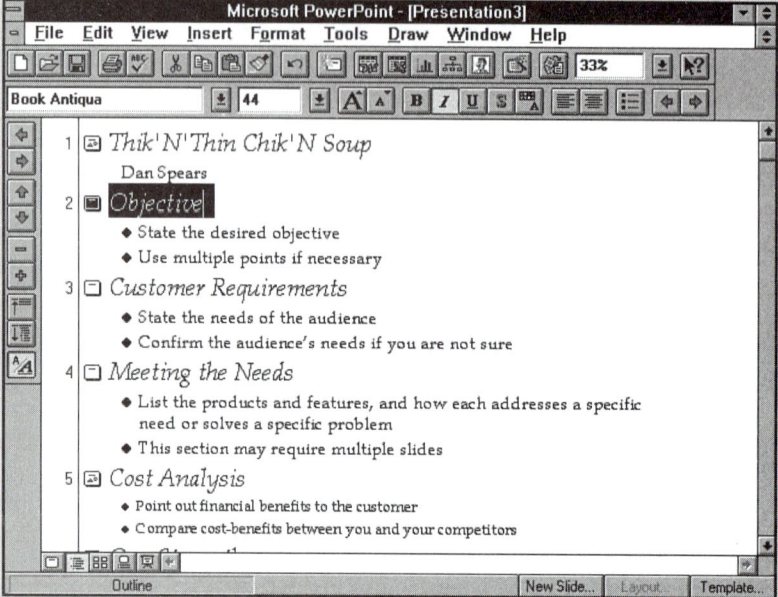

Highlighting text is the same thing as selecting text. Position the mouse pointer to the immediate left of the first letter in the word or words you want to select. The mouse pointer changes to an I-beam. Press and hold the left mouse button, and drag the highlight to the last character that will be included in the selection.

**2** Type the word **Introducing**.

The new word, Introducing, replaces the word Objective.

**3** Starting with the I-beam to the immediate left of the letter S, drag to highlight the entire phrase State the desired objective.

**4** Type the new phrase

**No-Fat, No-Chloresterol Chicken Soup**

**5** Position the mouse pointer over the black diamond in front of the phrase Use multiple points if necessary.

The mouse pointer changes to a four-headed arrow.

**6** Click the left mouse button.

The entire phrase is highlighted (white letters on a black background).

**7** Position the mouse pointer over the Demote button on the Formatting toolbar. This button has a small green arrow pointing to the right and is located at the far right of the toolbar.

The ToolTip `Demote (Indent more)` appears.

**8** Click the Demote button.

The highlighted line is reduced in type size and indented to the right.

**9** With the line still highlighted, type the line

### Substantial customer demand

The new line replaces the old.

**10** Press `↵Enter`, and type the phrase

### Low manufacturing cost

**11** Press `↵Enter`, and type the phrase

### High profitability

**12** Press `↵Enter`, and type the phrase

### First to market

Your screen should now look like figure 2.9.

**Figure 2.9**
The objectives of the presentation.

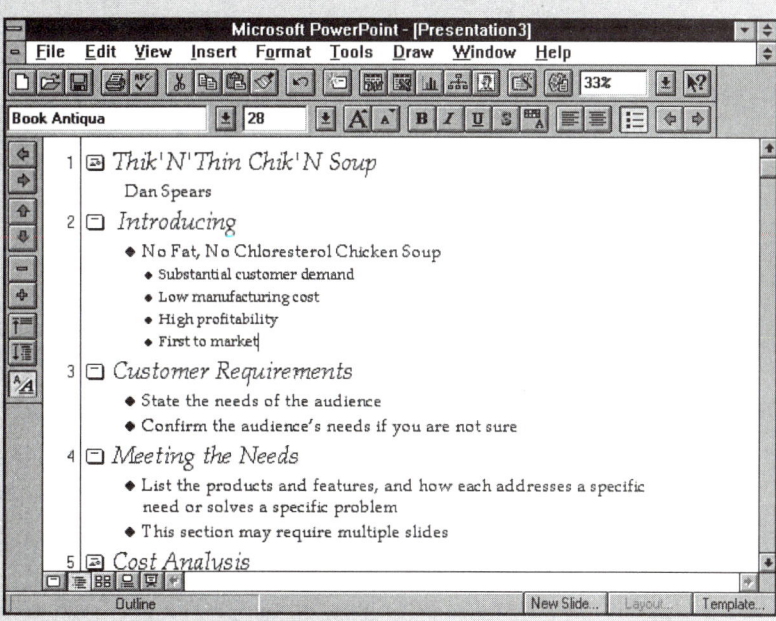

At this point, checking what you have accomplished would be useful. You can view the results of your work by running the initial presentation.

**Running the Initial Presentation**

To run the slide show, follow these steps:

**1** Position the mouse pointer in the title line of slide 1, and click the left mouse button to ensure that the slide show starts with slide 1.

**2** Click the Slide Show button.

The slide show begins by displaying the title screen.

**Note:** *The mouse pointer is hidden when a new slide appears during a slide show. Moving the mouse slightly shows the mouse pointer.*

**3** Move the mouse slightly so that the mouse pointer appears on-screen; the pointer is in the form of an arrow. Click the left mouse button.

The title slide is now replaced by the slide completed in the preceding tutorial (see figure 2.10). Review the slide, and continue clicking the left mouse button until the Outline view of the presentation returns.

**Figure 2.10**
The completed slide entitled "Introducing."

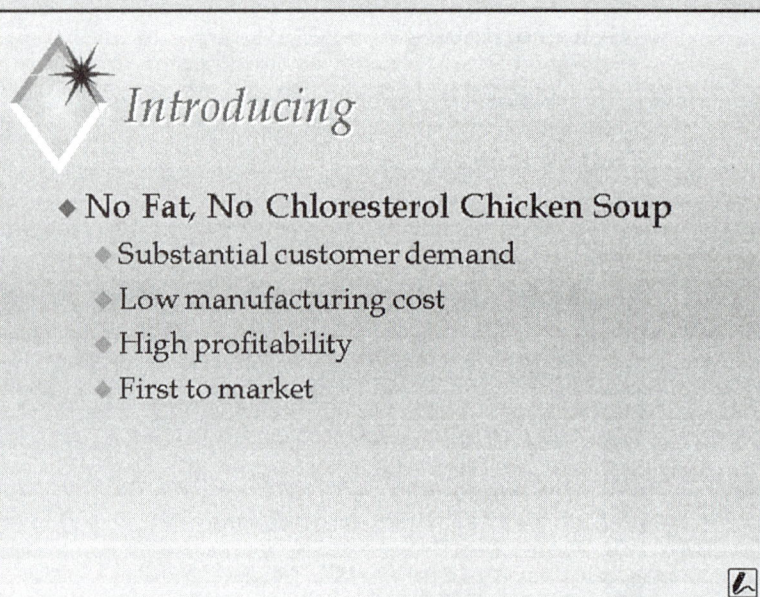

**Note:** *Do not click the small microphone icon that appears at the bottom right of the screen. This icon normally indicates the vocal part of the presentation. Clicking this box produces a pen you can use to draw on the current screen during a presentation. This feature is covered in a later chapter.*

# Objective 4: Replace Suggested Content

Viewing the presentation by using the Slide Show button during the initial preparation helps many people visualize the material in context. With the title and objective slides forming the foundation for the presentation, you can replace with information pertaining to your project the content suggested by the AutoContent Wizard.

Mom's marketing research department commissioned a national telephone survey on a 2,000-base sample to determine to what degree the average American is concerned or worried about weight and cholesterol. Research also commissioned an in-store survey to determine the number of shoppers who purchased soup on any given day and to conduct random interviews of soup purchasers. This survey was followed by a Soup-Tasting Focus Group.

At the same time, the manufacturing group conducted a cost analysis and provided the results to the accounting department who, in turn, produced the financials.

In the following tutorials, you use this information to create your presentation.

**2**

## Changing Content

To include this research data in the presentation, follow these steps:

**1** Position the insertion point to the immediate left of the word Requirements in the heading Customer Requirements of slide 3 (refer to figure 2.8).

**2** Press Del repeatedly until the word Requirements is deleted.

**3** Type the word **Profile**.

**4** Replace the line that reads State the needs of the audience with a line that reads

**47% of Americans concerned about weight**

**5** Replace the line that reads Confirm the audience's needs if you are not sure with a line that reads

**53% of Americans worry about chloresterol**

**6** With the insertion point to the immediate right of the second letter l in the word chloresterol, press ↵Enter.

A new bulleted line is generated.

**7** Add this line after the new bullet:

**31% of sample purchase a chicken soup variety**

**8** Add the following lines to this slide:

**22% of shoppers purchase soup**

**77% would purchase a no-fat, no-chloresterol chicken soup**

Now continue the process by editing the remaining slides. Note that in steps 9 and 10, the first line you type is the slide title.

(continues)

## Changing Content (continued)

**9** Change slide 4, "Meeting the Needs," to read as follows:

**Focus Group**

**322 tasters**

**68% could not distinguish Thik 'N' Thin from regular varieties**

**22% preferred Thik 'N' Thin**

**29% would purchase based on weight concerns**

**31% would purchase based on no chloresterol**

**10** Change slide 5, "Cost Analysis," to read as follows:

**Cost Analysis**

**Cost-of-Goods Sold: $234,000**

**First-year Sales: $2.2 m**

**Operating Expenses: $1.3 m**

**Contribution Income: $666,000**

**Return-on-Investment: 31%**

Figure 2.11 shows the completed slide 5.

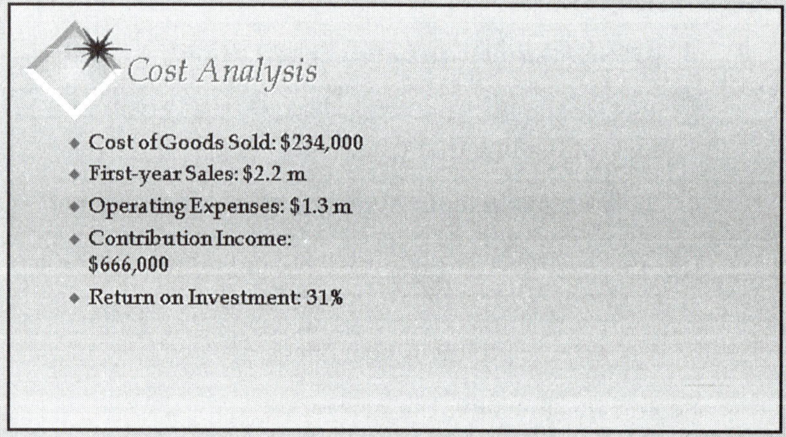

**Figure 2.11**
The completed "Cost Analysis" slide 5.

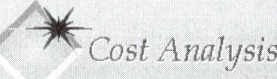

- Cost of Goods Sold: $234,000
- First-year Sales: $2.2 m
- Operating Expenses: $1.3 m
- Contribution Income: $666,000
- Return on Investment: 31%

Thus far, the presentation has met the steps outlined in slide 2: showing that customer demand is substantial (slides 3 and 4), that the manufacturing cost is low (slide 5), and that profitability is high (the last bulleted line on slide 5). At this point, however, reinforcing the profitability section would be useful. You can add more lines and slides to the presentation.

## Adding New Slides and New Lines

To add a new slide, do the following:

**1** Point to the number 5 in the outline, and click the left mouse button.

The contents of slide 5, "Cost Analysis," are highlighted.

**2** Click the New Slide button on the status bar.

A new slide with number 6 is inserted after the current slide, slide 5.

**3** With the insertion point to the right of the icon for slide 6, type the phrase **ROI: Five-Year Plan**, and press `↵Enter`.

A new slide, slide 7, is generated. You can demote the new slide to become a line of text on slide 6.

**4** Select slide 7, and click the Demote button on the Formatting toolbar.

The slide is demoted to a bulleted line on slide 6.

**5** Add the following lines to slide 6:

**Year 1: 31%**

**Year 2: 33%**

**Year 3: 37%**

**Year 4: 39%**

**Year 5: 40%**

Figure 2.12 shows the completed slide 6.

**Figure 2.12**
The completed
"ROI" slide 6.

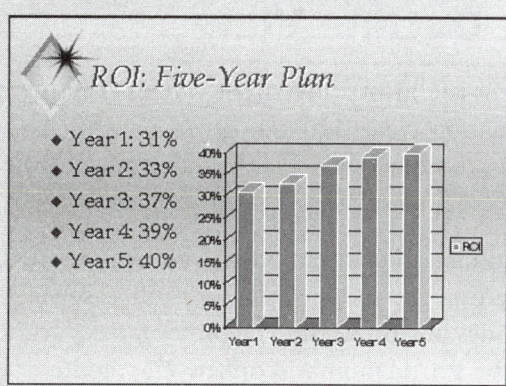

(continues)

**Adding New Slides and New Lines (continued)**

❻ Add the following lines to slide 7, "Our Strengths":

**Largest Soup Manufacturer in America**

**Reputation for Quality**

**First to Market**

**Key Image: Mom and Chicken Soup**

❼ Change slide 8, "Key Benefits," to read as follows:

**Competitive Analysis**

**No current competition in no-fat, no-chloresterol soups**

**Dad's Homebrew Soup developing own product**

**No cannibalization of existing product**

❽ Change slide 9, "Next Steps," to read as follows:

**Recommendations**

**Allocate pilot plant resources for initial product introduction**

**Set up test market locations**

**Launch introductory advertising campaign**

**Authorize engineering to begin plant site feasibility study**

# Objective 5: Use the Outline View

The Outline view is the most convenient way of entering text information and modifying information created by one of the wizards. You can change the font, size, and attributes (boldface, italic, and so on) but not the color or special effects such as shading.

In addition to adding and changing text, you can use the Outline view to re-arrange the content of the slides or the slides themselves. To review an outline, click the Show Slides button to run the presentation, and to print a hard copy of the outline, use the **P**rint command on the **F**ile menu.

## Rearranging Text on a Slide

You can move letters and blocks of text within phrases, delete them, or add them to other lines. You can also move text on a single slide or to another slide. To move a line of text on a slide, do the following.

**❶** Position the mouse pointer over the bullet in front of the line 22% of grocery shoppers purchase soup on slide 3, "Customer Profile" (see figure 2.13).

**Figure 2.13**
Outline view showing text line before move.

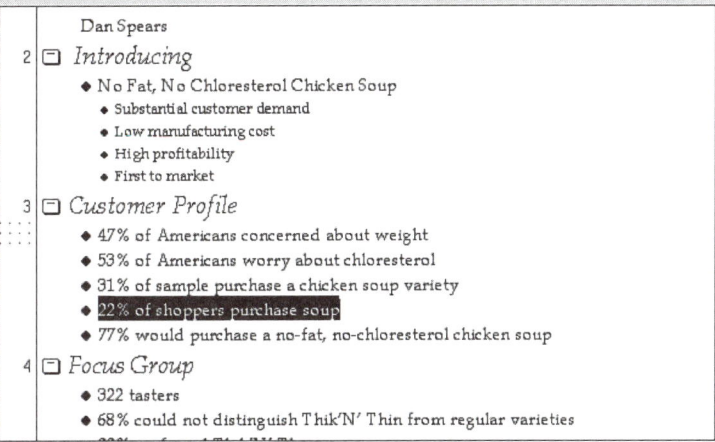

The mouse pointer changes to a four-headed arrow.

**❷** Press and hold down the left mouse button, and without releasing the mouse button, move the mouse pointer up until a line appears between the two bulleted statements that begin with *53%* and *31%*.

The line indicates where the highlighted sentence will be moved.

**❸** Release the left mouse button.

The highlighted line is inserted in the new position (see figure 2.14).

**Figure 2.14**
The line of text after repositioning.

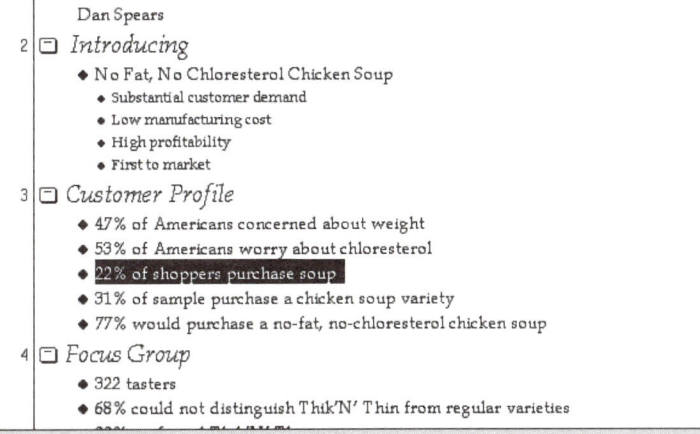

You can also move an entire slide to a new location. This task is simple when you are using the Outline view.

## Moving a Slide

To move a slide in the Outline view, do the following:

**1** Position the mouse pointer over the icon for slide 8, "Competitive Analysis."

**2** Press and hold down the left mouse. Do not release the mouse button.

All the text of the slide is highlighted (see figure 2.15).

**Figure 2.15**
The highlighted "Competitive Analysis" slide contents.

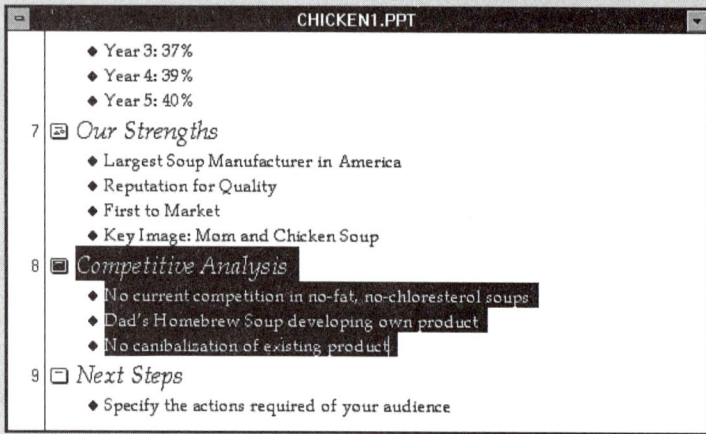

**3** Drag the icon to just above slide 6 until a horizontal line indicates where slide 8 will be repositioned.

**4** Release the left mouse button.

The former slide 8 is now slide 6 in the new location, and all the slides from this point down are renumbered (see figure 2.16).

**Figure 2.16**
The renumbered slide positions after a move.

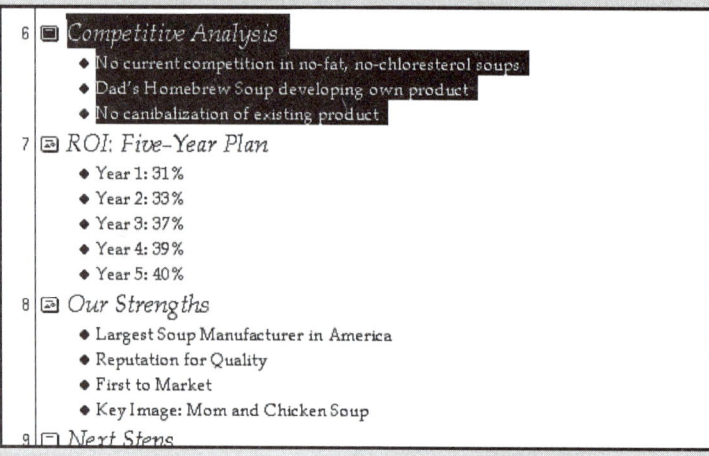

A printout of an outline of the presentation is useful for reviewing the contents and for sketching in proposed changes.

## Printing an Outline

To print a hardcopy of the Outline view, do the following:

**❶** Choose **P**rint from the **F**ile menu.

The print dialog box appears (see figure 2.17).

**Figure 2.17**
The Print dialog box.

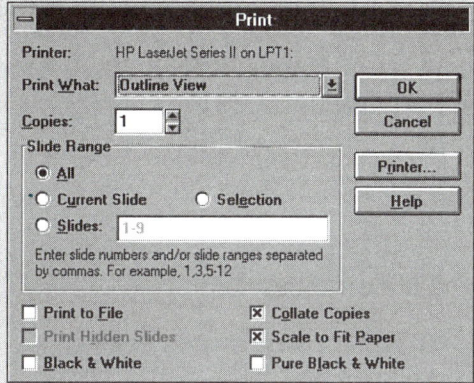

**❷** Click the down-arrow button on the Print **W**hat list box.

The Print **W**hat list box displays the options for printing presentations (see figure 2.18).

**Figure 2.18**
The Print What drop-down list box.

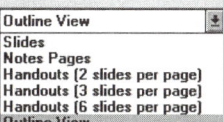

**❸** Select Outline View.

**Note:** *You also can print individual Slides, Notes Pages, and three choices of Handouts.*

**❹** Indicate the number of copies desired in the **C**opies box.

**❺** Select **A**ll under Slide Range to print the entire outline.

**❻** Click the OK button.

A printed copy of the outline results.

# Objective 6: Use the Slide View

**Slide view**
A view in which slides display one at a time.

**Clip art**
Small pictures or illustrations.

The *Slide view* presents one slide at a time. Text can be added or deleted and formatted in this view just as in the Outline view. The Slide view, however, also enables you to draw graphics and add graphs, pictures, and *clip art* (small predrawn pieces of artwork). You can also change the color and add special effects to text.

## Switching to and Navigating in the Slide View

To switch to the Slide view and move from slide to slide in it, follow these steps:

❶ In the Outline view, position the insertion point in slide 6. Click the Slide View button, the leftmost button on the horizontal scroll bar.

The presentation changes to the Slide view. The current slide is the slide that was current in the Outline view.

❷ To return to the title slide, point to the elevator box on the vertical scroll bar, press and hold the left mouse button.

A Slide Number text box appears; it reads `Slide 6`.

❸ While continuing to hold down the left mouse button, drag the box to the top of the scroll bar. Release the left mouse button when the Slide Number text box reads `Slide 1`.

The title slide is now displayed.

Now you can move from slide to slide.

❹ Click the Next Slide button at the bottom of the vertical scroll bar.

The presentation display advances to the next slide, slide 2.

❺ Click the Previous Slide button, which is immediately above the Next Slide button.

The presentation display returns to the preceding slide, the title slide.

You can also use the Slide view to edit the text of your slides.

## Editing the Text of a Slide

To change the text in a slide, do the following:

❶ Position the mouse pointer to the left of the first letter of your name on slide 1, and click the left mouse button.

A text box appears around the lines of text on the slide, and the insertion point is placed before your name.

**2** Press Del until your name is removed, and type the words **Mom's Home Cookin' Soup**.

**3** Highlight the words Mom's Home Cookin' Soup, and click the Font drop-down menu list on the Formatting toolbar.

**4** Click the choice Brush Script. Use the scroll bar if necessary.

**Note:** *If your font choices do not include Brush Script, select any script or other fancy font.*

**5** With the phrase still highlighted, click the **S**ize drop-down list on the Formatting toolbar, and select the size 48 (points).

**6** With the phrase still highlighted, click the Bold button on the Formatting toolbar.

**7** Click anywhere on the presentation window outside the text box to remove the text box border.

The resulting slide should resemble the slide in figure 2.19.

**Figure 2.19**
The title slide with edited text.

**Datasheet**
A small spreadsheet in a Datasheet dialog box that is used to produce graphs.

As you build a slide using various objects such as graphs, clip art, and illustrations, you may decide that you no longer need an object. You can remove an object, change an object, or replace it with another object, such as a *datasheet*. A datasheet is a miniature spreadsheet that appears in a Datasheet dialog box; you use the datasheet for entering numbers to produce various graphs.

## Deleting and Inserting Objects

To remove an object from a slide and then insert a datasheet on another slide, do the following:

**1** Go to slide 5, using the scroll bar or Next Slide button.

An Insert Graph object appears on this slide. If you wanted to insert a graph on this slide, you would double-click the Insert Graph icon.

(continues)

## Deleting and Inserting Objects (continued)

**2** Click once inside the Graph box to select the Insert Graph object. Click the Cut button on the Standard toolbar.

**3** Go to slide 7, and click the Insert Graph button on the Standard toolbar.

A Datasheet dialog box appears.

**Note:** *Several of the following steps involve changes to the datasheet. When you have completed those changes, the datasheet will look like the completed datasheet in figure 2.20.*

**4** Select rows 2 and 3 on the datasheet by dragging the mouse pointer over the row headings.

**5** Press Del.

**6** Click the cell containing the word East, and type the letters **ROI**.

**7** In the label cells, which are the cells immediately below the column headings in a row that is not numbered, type **Year 1** in column A, **Year 2** in column B, **Year 3** in column C, **Year 4** in column D, and **Year 5** in column E.

**Note:** *You make a cell active by clicking that cell. You move from cell to cell by pressing Tab to move to the right and Shift+Tab to move to the left.*

**8** In the cells in row 1 corresponding to the years, type the following percentages:

| Year 1 | Year 2 | Year 3 | Year 4 | Year 5 |
|--------|--------|--------|--------|--------|
| **31%** | **33%** | **37%** | **39%** | **40%** |

Your completed datasheet should look like figure 2.20.

**Figure 2.20**
The Datasheet dialog box with ROI data.

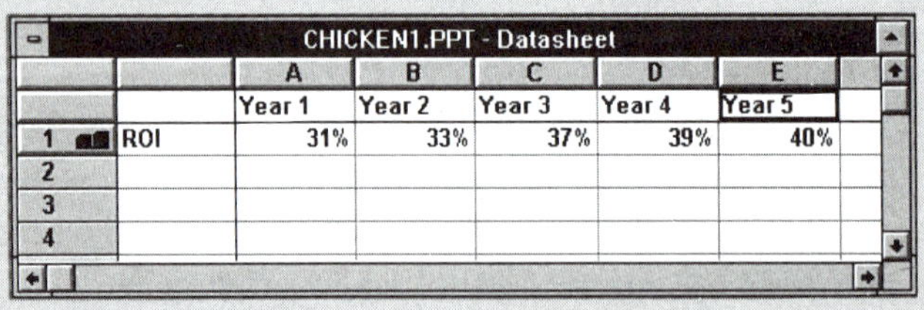

| | A | B | C | D | E |
|---|---|---|---|---|---|
| | Year 1 | Year 2 | Year 3 | Year 4 | Year 5 |
| 1 ROI | 31% | 33% | 37% | 39% | 40% |
| 2 | | | | | |
| 3 | | | | | |
| 4 | | | | | |

CHICKEN1.PPT - Datasheet

**9** Click the dialog box control menu button at the far left of the Datasheet dialog box title bar, and choose Close from the drop-down menu.

**Handles**

Small black sizing boxes located between and on the corners of a high-lighted border or frame of an object.

The Datasheet dialog box closes, and the new graph appears on slide 7 enclosed by a highlighted border. At each corner of the border and midway between the corners are small black sizing boxes called *handles*. When the mouse pointer is positioned over a handle, the mouse pointer changes to a double-headed arrow indicating the directions in which the graph can be sized.

You can change the height and width of any graph or picture by dragging the handles on the sides of the highlighted border. When the mouse pointer is positioned over a corner handle, the mouse pointer changes to an angled, double-headed arrow. When a corner handle is dragged, the highlighted object is sized proportionately in the direction in which the border is dragged.

**2**

## Changing the Size of a Graph

To change the size of the inserted graph, follow these steps:

1 Position the mouse pointer over the middle handle on the right border. Click and drag the right border to a point near the right border of the slide.

2 Position the mouse pointer over the middle handle on the left border. Click and drag the left border to the right until it is aligned directly below the hyphen in the words Five-Year.

3 Continue adjusting the size of the graph if necessary so that no bulleted text line is concealed.

4 Click anywhere outside the graph (or text box) on the slide to deselect the graph.

To move a graph, picture, or text box, you follow the same procedures.

## Moving a Graph

To move a graph, do the following:

1 Select the graph on slide 7 by double-clicking the graph.

2 When the sizing handles appear, position the mouse pointer directly between any two handles, and press and hold down the left mouse button.

3 Drag the frame to a new location, and release the left mouse button.

4 Repeat steps 2 and 3 to adjust the position of the graph on the slide.

The area on a slide where you enter text is called a text box. When you position your pointer inside a text area and click the mouse button, the text area is framed by a box. You can select the box, change its size, and move it to another location on the slide.

## Sizing a Text Box

To size a text box, follow these steps:

**❶** Click the Previous button twice to go to slide 5, "Cost Analysis."

**❷** Position the mouse pointer inside a bulleted text area, and click the left mouse button to show the text box.

**❸** Click the border of the text box to select the text box. The sizing handles appear.

**❹** Drag the sizing handle midway on the right border to the right to expand the text box horizontally and provide enough room that no text on a bulleted line runs over to the next line.

# Objective 7: Save the Presentation

When you save a presentation to a file, you are making a copy that you can retrieve later, make additional copies of, and use slides from in other presentations. You use the Save **A**s command when you save a presentation for the first time or when you change the name, drive, or directory of a saved presentation; you use the **S**ave command to save a previously saved presentation with the same name, drive, and directory.

## Saving a Presentation

This tutorial requires that you have a formatted disk in drive A. To save this presentation, do the following:

**❶** Choose Save **A**s from the **F**ile menu.

The Save As dialog box appears (see figure 2.21).

**Figure 2.21**
The Save As dialog box.

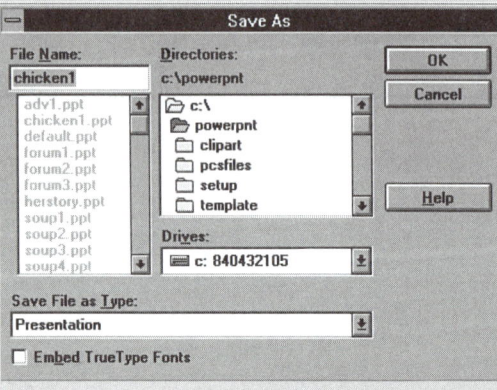

**2** Select a: from the Drives list box to specify that the presentation file be saved on drive A.

**3** Type the name **chicken1**, in the File Name text box.

PowerPoint automatically adds the PPT extension.

**4** Click OK.

When the file is saved, the Summary Info dialog box appears (see figure 2.22). You use this dialog box to record information about the presentation; you can use some of this information later for file retrieval and searches.

**Figure 2.22**
The Summary Info dialog box with information filled in.

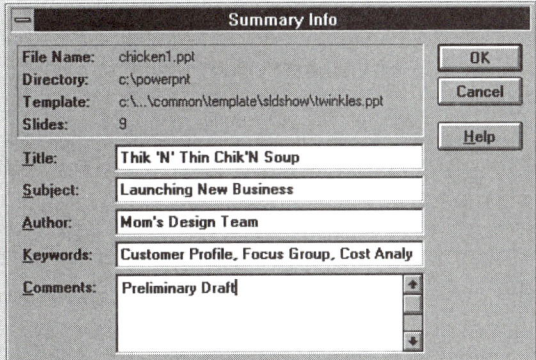

**5** Complete the Summary Info dialog box as shown in figure 2.22, and click the OK button.

In the future, when you want to save this presentation, you can either choose **S**ave from the **F**ile menu or click the Save button on the Standard toolbar. You are now ready to complete your presentation and leave PowerPoint.

## Completing the Presentation and Closing the Program

To complete this presentation, do the following:

**1** Click the Slide Show button to run the presentation and review the slides.

Congratulations! You have completed your first presentation.

**2** Choose E**x**it from the **F**ile menu.

This step closes PowerPoint.

# Chapter Summary

You can now create a presentation by starting the AutoContent Wizard, entering a title, and choosing a presentation type. You can work with the major points of the presentation to replace the content suggested by the wizard, move lines of text, and reposition slides in order to improve the presentation. You can use the Outline and Slide views to add information and graphs. You can run the slide show to see the changes and improvements to the presentation. You know how to save the presentation to a file and add summary information that further describes the presentation.

# Checking Your Skills

## True/False Questions

For each of the following statements, circle *T* or *F* to indicate whether the statement is true or false.

T  F  **1.** One of the important reasons for creating a presentation is to avoid writing a report.

T  F  **2.** The AutoContent Wizard guides a planner through various steps of a proposed presentation by suggesting a title, presentation type, data requirements for graphs, and financial analysis.

T  F  **3.** The objective of a presentation is to define a problem or premise.

T  F  **4.** A handle is a small black box attached to the mouse pointer and is used to resize a graph, text box, or picture.

T  F  **5.** The Slide view is the most convenient format for entering large amounts of data.

## Multiple-Choice Questions

In the blank provided, write the letter of the correct answer for each of the following questions.

___  **1.** To add a line of bulleted text to a new slide in the Outline view, you _____.

   **a.** press ⏎Enter after typing the title line for that slide

   **b.** choose **L**ine from the **I**nsert menu

   **c.** insert a new slide and then demote it

   **d.** insert a new slide and then promote it

___  **2.** The Outlining toolbar appears _____.

   **a.** when you select **A**utoContent Wizard

   **b.** below the presentation window

    **c.** to the left of the presentation window in the Outline view

    **d.** when you edit in the Slide view text that was entered in the Outline view

___ **3.** If you enter text in the Outline view, _____.

    **a.** the text must be changed in the Slide view

    **b.** you can edit the text in either the Outline or the Slide view

    **c.** you can move text using a text box in the Outline view

    **d.** you cannot delete text in that view

___ **4.** The presentation type classifies a presentation _____.

    **a.** as a strategy

    **b.** according to the situation or circumstances

    **c.** according to the type of business plan or general information to be displayed

    **d.** according to the type of people who are expected to view the presentation

___ **5.** The _____ dialog box is used to record information on the presentation, some of which can be used later for file retrieval and searches.

    **a.** Save As

    **b.** Summary Info

    **c.** Datasheet

    **d.** Create New

## Fill-in-the-Blank Questions

In the blank provided, write the correct answer for each of the following questions.

**1.** To return to the main cue card after reading a tip on a subordinate cue card, click the _____ button on the menu bar.

**2.** To advance from slide to slide, click the _____ button at the bottom of the vertical scroll bar.

**3.** To move from the back to the front of a presentation, click the _____ button at the bottom of the vertical scroll bar.

**4.** The _____ and _____ buttons are used to create various indent levels.

**5.** You can modify the appearance of selected text by changing the _____ , size, or style.

# Applying Your Skills

## Review Exercises

### Exercise 1: Modifying a Slide in a Presentation

Your division manager says that the "Cost Analysis" slide is too cluttered with the numbers immediately following the colons. He suggests that you can make this slide clearer by lining up the numbers in a single column. Using the Outline view, insert spaces before the numbers on slide 5 of the CHICKEN1 presentation to align the numbers in a visually pleasing way.

### Exercise 2: Adding a Slide to a Presentation

The company business manager has been told by the president of the company that all future presentations must include a cost breakdown of the amount of money invested in the research and development of any new product. Add the following slide to the CHICKEN1 presentation as slide 3:

### Cost of Development

| | |
|---|---|
| **Cooking Labs Expense:** | **$76,340** |
| **Marketing Survey:** | **$36,800** |
| **Administrative Costs:** | **$27,926** |
| **Total Sunk Costs:** | **$141,066** |

### Exercise 3: Adding a New Slide and Graph

Vice President M. T. Graves has requested a price comparison of the no-fat, no-cholesterol soup with the other chicken soup varieties manufactured by the company. Here are suggested retail prices:

| | |
|---|---|
| Thik 'N' Thin Chik'N Soup | .49 |
| Mom's Own Chicken Dumplings | .78 |
| Mom's Hot Lunch Chicken Noodle | .39 |
| Mom's Chunky Chicken and Rice | .49 |
| Mom's Clear Chicken Broth | .35 |
| Mom's Mother-Loving Good Chicken Stew | .59 |

Your task is to create one or more slides that convey this information clearly by using a graph. Use the CHICKEN1 presentation in either the Outline or Slide view. Choose a slide format suitable for this information and insert the new slide(s) in front of the "Our Strengths" slide.

## Continuing Projects

### Project 1: Creating a New Look

Changing the presentation type changes the focus of a presentation. Using the information in this chapter for creating the CHICKEN1 presentation and the AutoContent Wizard, design your own presentation using the presentation type

Recommending a Strategy on the Step 3 of 4 AutoContent dialog box. Name your presentation, **CHIXSTRAT.PPT**. Although you will be using the same information that is in CHICKEN1, you will be emphasizing different points as you create a strategy for developing and marketing the product.

**Project 2: Building a General Business Presentation**

The presentation type General in the AutoContent Wizard allows for the creating of a wide variety of presentations. Your task is to create a presentation that illustrates and explains one of the following activities:

1. You are to evaluate the effect on productivity and morale of a four-day work week for company employees (pro or con). Prepare a presentation for the CEO.

2. Management is considering instituting a smoke-free environment in all company workplaces. Your presentation must explain the benefits to company employees.

3. You have decided to seek another position and you have a brilliant idea. You will include with your resume a computer disk that contains a presentation about yourself, your education and training, and your major accomplishments. Create an electronic resume about yourself.

**2**

# CHAPTER 3

# Adding Impact to a Presentation

The AutoContent Wizard enables you to create a presentation quickly; you can make that presentation more effective by adding visual enhancements to capture and hold your audience's attention. In this chapter, you learn how to open an existing presentation and how to modify the presentation with new slides.

## Objectives

By the time you have finished this chapter, you will have learned to

1. Open and Copy an Existing Presentation
2. Delete or Add Slides
3. Choose the Layout
4. Add Graphs
5. Add Organization Charts
6. Add Clip Art
7. Add Tables
8. Add Special Text Effects

## Objective 1: Open and Copy an Existing Presentation

To open an existing presentation, you follow the standard Windows procedures with the familiar Open and Search dialog boxes. However, PowerPoint does have a dialog box that is unique to this program—the PowerPoint dialog box, which you have used in the preceding chapters. You see this dialog box when you start PowerPoint and close the Tip of the Day dialog box.

You can also open a presentation by choosing **O**pen from the **F**ile menu or by choosing the Open button from the Standard toolbar. Both methods produce the Open dialog box. You can access both the Search and Advanced Search dialog boxes from the Open dialog box by choosing **F**ind File.

**Summary tab**
In Advanced Search dialog box for entering summary information.

**Location tab**
In Advanced Search dialog box for entering drive and directory information.

**Timestamp**
In Advanced Search dialog box for entering information about last time presentation was saved.

The Advanced Search dialog box has three tabs. These tabs open sections of the dialog box where you enter specific information about the presentation for which you are searching. You use the **Summary tab** selection to enter summary information to locate a presentation file. You use the **Location tab** to enter drive and directory information. You use the *Timestamp tab* to enter information about the last time a file was saved.

The board of Mom's Home Cookin' Soup Company liked the initial presentation you prepared to launch a new business to manufacture and sell Thik 'N' Thin Chik'N Soup. Before giving final approval, however, the board wants to review the business structure, marketing strategy, and advertising plans.

The downside to this news is that the board wants to see the presentation in two days. The upside is that all the departments involved have made the furnishing of pertinent information a Number One priority. Because of the time constraints, you should probably use the CHICKEN1 presentation (prepared earlier) as the starting point for the new presentation.

## Starting PowerPoint and Opening a Presentation

To load an existing presentation when starting PowerPoint, follow these steps:

**1** Start PowerPoint, and click OK in the Tip of the Day dialog box.

The PowerPoint dialog box appears (see figure 3.1). You used this same dialog box to select the AutoContent Wizard to prepare the original presentation.

**Figure 3.1**
The PowerPoint dialog box.

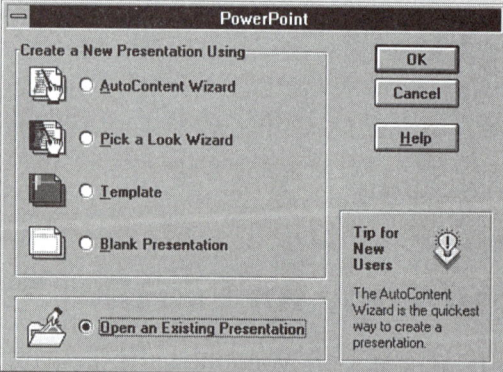

**2** Select the **O**pen an Existing Presentation option, and click OK.

**3** The Open dialog box appears.

Normally, you would select the presentation you want to open at this point, but your boss calls you to his office. You will have to complete this operation later.

**4** Click the Cancel button.

The dialog box clears, and you are now free to attend your meeting.

> **Tip**
>
> Whether you stop working or continue working on a presentation in a long session, you should periodically save your file to disk. Because you can lose your work in the event of a power failure, you should save a file every time you complete a slide—or more often if a particular slide is taking a long time to compose.

### Using the Open Dialog Box

Although you can open an existing presentation by clicking the Open button on the Standard toolbar, many users like the menu option. One reason is that the File drop-down menu also displays a list of the last four presentations you have opened. Selecting a file name from this list bypasses the Open dialog box and opens the presentation directly.

You can have several other reasons for using the Open dialog box. For example, you may have copied the presentation to another drive or directory and erased the original file. You may also have worked on more than four other presentations since preparing the presentation you now want to use. Or you may have forgotten the file name of the presentation and need the search facilities to locate the file.

**3**

## Opening an Existing Presentation from the File Menu

To open an existing presentation using the File menu, follow these steps:

**1** Choose **O**pen from the **F**ile menu.

The Open dialog box appears (see figure 3.2).

**Figure 3.2**
The Open dialog box.

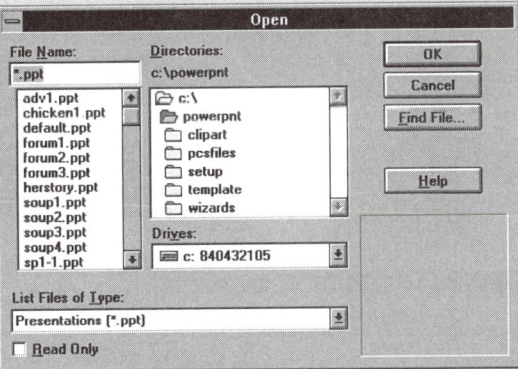

**2** Choose the drive from the Dri**v**es list box, if necessary.

**3** Choose the directory from the **D**irectories list box, if necessary.

A list of file names in the selected drive and directory appears. Although you know that the name of the file you want is CHICKEN1.PPT, you are curious about the **F**ind File button and decide to explore this option.

(continues)

**Opening an Existing Presentation from the File Menu (continued)**

④ Click the **F**ind File button.

The Search dialog box opens (see figure 3.3). The Saved **S**earches drop-down list box may be empty on your computer. This feature, which includes the maintenance buttons **S**ave Search As and **D**elete Search, enables you to record the search conditions for a file type and then to name the search for future reference and use.

**Figure 3.3**
The Search
dialog box.

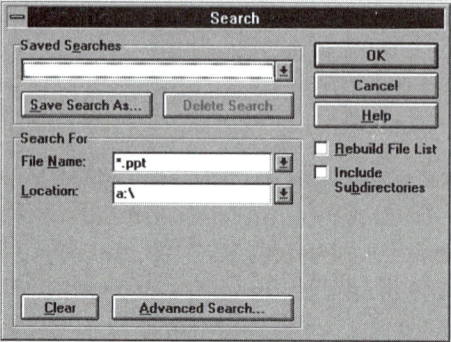

You use the File **N**ame drop-down list box to find or enter the name of the file you want and the **L**ocation drop-down list box to set the drive. The Include Su**b**directories option is particularly useful when you cannot recall the name of the subdirectory where you last saved the presentation. Once you have located the file in the subdirectory, you can select **R**ebuild File List to create a new list of file names that will appear in the File **N**ame drop-down list box.

You use the **A**dvanced Search button to find a presentation file that presumably is lost in (disk) space.

⑤ Click the **A**dvanced Search button.

The Advanced Search dialog box appears. This dialog has three tab selections; the **S**ummary tab selection is illustrated in figure 3.4.

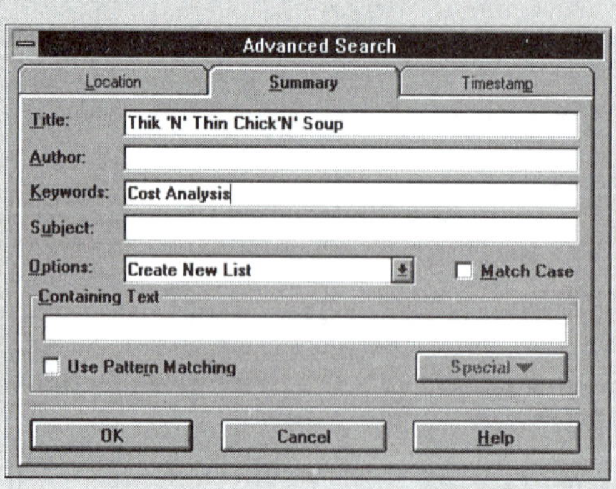

**Figure 3.4**
The Advanced
Search Summary
tabbed dialog
box.

The information required for this tab is almost the same as the information you provided when you first saved the file—with some differences. For example, if you don't remember all the keywords you originally used, you can enter only one (or more) of the keywords you do recall in the **K**eywords edit box. The **C**ontaining Text option enables you to enter a phrase, term, or special symbol that occurs in the presentation but not in the summary information.

The two other tab selections in this dialog box are **L**ocation, an option that is particularly useful when you are working on the same presentation with other users on a local area network; and the Timestam**p** tab selection, which is useful if you can recall when or about when you last worked on the presentation.

**6** Click the Cancel button to remove the Advanced Search dialog box.

**7** Click the Cancel button on the Search dialog box to remove it.

The Open dialog box remains displayed in the presentation window (refer to figure 3.2).

**8** Select CHICKEN1.PPT.

A preview of the presentation in the form of the title screen appears at the lower right of the Open dialog box.

**9** Click the OK button.

The presentation CHICKEN1 now appears in the presentation window.

When you use parts of one presentation as the basis for a new presentation, you must make a copy of the presentation if you want to save the unmodified original.

## Making a Copy of a Presentation

To make a copy of the current presentation, follow these steps:

**1** Choose Save **A**s from the **F**ile menu.

**2** Change the name of the current file in the File **N**ame edit box. In this case, change the name CHICKEN1.PPT to **STRUT1.PPT**.

**3** Select the drive and directory, if necessary.

**4** Click OK, and complete the Summary Info dialog box.

After the saving operation completes, the new name of the copy of the presentation appears in the presentation title bar.

# Objective 2: Delete or Add Slides

One way to create a new presentation is to add new slides to the slides retained from another presentation. In companies and organizations that require numerous presentations, a basic library file of slides is useful. These slides can contain standard information, such as a company or organization name and logo slide, an organization chart, maps showing regional offices or sales regions, product charts or lists, and updatable datasheets or charts.

When modifying an existing file, you can delete slides in any view by selecting the slide and choosing Delete Slide from the **E**dit menu. In the Outline view, you delete a slide by selecting the slide or slides to be deleted and then pressing either ⬅Backspace or Del.

You can add a new slide to a presentation in any view by clicking the New Slide button on the status bar or by choosing New **S**lide from the **I**nsert menu. In the preceding chapter, you learned that a new slide can also be added in the Outline view by selecting the current slide and pressing ↵Enter.

**Template**
A pattern for a slide or presentation.

**Outline Master**
A view in which an outline template can be created or modified.

**Slide Master**
A view in which a slide template can be created or modified.

**Placeholder**
A designated location on a slide into which an object can be inserted.

The two views that you have used thus far are Outline view and Slide view. Each of these views has a master view, which you can use to create or change a *template* design for a slide or presentation. A template is a pattern for a slide or presentation that contains information about the placement, style and type of text and graphics areas; special objects such as logos, boxes, or borders; and artistic text effects.

The master views for the Outline and Slide views are known, respectively, as the *Outline Master* and the *Slide Master*. You access the master views by holding down ⬆Shift when clicking a view button on the status bar. If you add a new slide from one of the master views, the new slide becomes the first slide in the presentation.

When you click one of the New Slide buttons, PowerPoint displays a New Slide dialog box, from which you can use an AutoLayout feature to specify a *placeholder*—or designated location on the new slide for titles, text, art, graphs, or charts.

## Deleting Slides

Because you will not require all the slides from the original presentation in the new presentation, you need to delete the unwanted slides. To delete those slides, follow these steps:

❶ Click the Outline view button to change the STRUT1 presentation to the Outline view.

❷ The number of slides in your version of this presentation will depend on the number of short projects you completed in Chapter 2. Beginning with slide 3, select all the slides down to but not including the slide called "Our Strengths."

③ Press Del.

You see a warning box stating that this action will delete a slide or notes page that contains graphics and outline text (see figure 3.5).

**Figure 3.5**
The PowerPoint warning box.

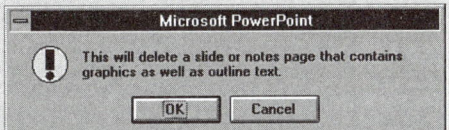

④ Click OK.

This deletion should leave a total of four slides in your presentation: the title slide, "Introducing," "Our Strengths," and "Recommendations." The Outline view is the most convenient way of deleting a group of slides at one time.

⑤ Click the Slide View button to change the presentation to the Slide view.

⑥ Select slide 2, "Introducing," by making it the active slide.

⑦ Choose Delete Slide from the **E**dit menu.

The slide is deleted, and you now have three slides in the presentation.

**Slide layout**

A slide design that contains placeholders for text and graphics objects.

In the preceding chapter, you learned that adding slides in the Outline view is convenient when you are adding a series of text-based slides. The advantage of adding slides in the Slide view is that you can specify certain AutoLayout designs that create a *slide layout*, or design, which inserts placeholders for text and graphics objects. In the next tutorial, you learn how to add slides to your presentation from Slide view.

## Adding Slides

To add slides and select an AutoLayout design in the Slide view, follow these steps:

① With the presentation STRUT1 in Slide view, make slide 1, the title slide, the active slide.

② Choose New **S**lide from the **I**nsert menu.

The New Slide dialog box appears (see figure 3.6). The Choose an **A**utoLayout box on the left side of the dialog box contains a series of graphics that depict a variety of slide layouts. Use the box's vertical scroll bar to scroll through the collection. A brief description of the currently selected graphic appears in the new slide name box at the lower right.

(continues)

## Adding Slides (continued)

**Figure 3.6**
The New Slide dialog box.

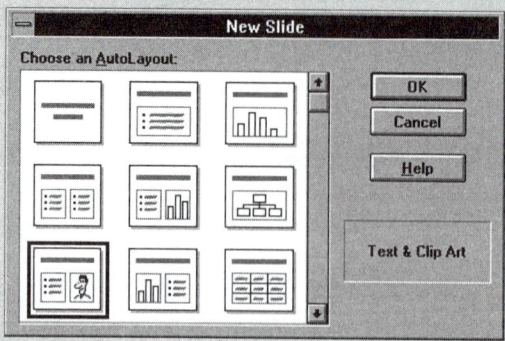

**③** Select the graphic that shows a title line above a text block on the left and a clip-art object on the right, and is described in the name box as `Text & Clip Art`.

**④** Click OK.

The presentation window now displays the new slide with each of the objects in the AutoLayout graphic now appearing as a *placeholder* (see figure 3.7).

**Figure 3.7**
The new slide with place-holders.

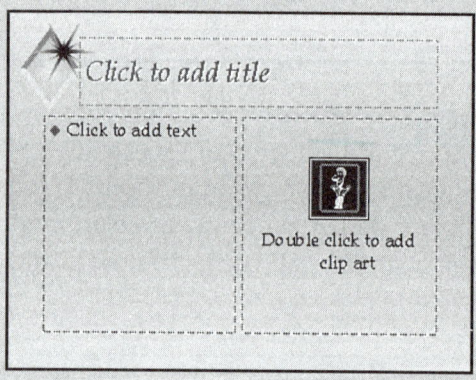

You now substitute your own text for the placeholders in order to create a slide with this design.

## Substituting Content for Placeholders

To insert content in a location marked by a placeholder, follow these steps:

**❶** Click the slide title placeholder.

A text entry area is highlighted.

**❷** Type the words **Start-up Strategy**.

**❸** Click the slide anywhere outside any placeholder.

The title of this slide now appears where the title placeholder was located.

**④** Click the text box placeholder.

**⑤** Type the following lines, pressing ⏎Enter after each but the last line.

**Mission Statement**

**Objectives**

**Organization**

**Market Strategy**

**Ad Campaign**

**Production**

**Timeline**

**Action Plan**

**⑥** Click the slide anywhere outside a placeholder or title area.

The bulleted lines are now added to the text.

The bulleted items in the text box of the current slide are also the titles of the slides that you will use to expand the start-up strategy. The clip-art placeholder will be replaced in a later tutorial.

## Adding the Series of Slides

To create the series of slides and expand the presentation, follow these steps:

**①** Click the Outline View button.

**②** Click the icon for slide 2, "Start-up Strategy," to select this slide.

**③** Click the Insert New Slide button on the Standard toolbar.

A new slide icon appears at the slide 3 position.

**④** Type the words **Mission Statement**, and press ⏎Enter.

A new slide appears at the slide 4 position. In the Outline view, you can create new slides at the title-line level by pressing ⏎Enter.

**⑤** Continue entering title lines and creating new slides, using the bulleted lines of slide 2, "Start-up Strategy," as the titles. Do not press ⏎Enter after entering the last title line. When you have finished, the presentation will contain 12 slides with the following titles:

1. Thik 'N' Thin Chik'N Soup

2. Start-up Strategy

3. Mission Statement

(continues)

## Adding the Series of Slides (continued)

4. Objectives

5. Organization

6. Market Strategy

7. Ad Campaign

8. Production

9. Timeline

10. Action Plan

11. Our Strengths

12. Recommendations

### Tip

If you press `↵Enter` after completing the last title line, you can easily reverse the mistake by choosing **U**ndo from the **E**dit menu.

## Adding a Subordinate Slide

Certain topics may require more than one slide. To add another slide to expand on the marketing strategy, follow these steps:

**1** In the Outline view, make slide 6, "Market Strategy," the active slide.

**2** Click New Slide on the status bar to insert a new slide 7.

**3** Type the title **Regional Distribution by Cases**.

**4** Highlight the title.

**5** Change the type size to 36.

# Objective 3: Choose the Layout

The method used to lay out a slide and groups of slides in a presentation is often a matter of convenience. Creating a new slide in the Slide view automatically introduces the AutoLayout dialog box for selecting preset design elements. This method is convenient when you are adding only a few slides. The Outline view is more convenient when you are building a complete presentation.

You can change the layout of existing slides in the Slide view by clicking the Layout button on the status bar or by choosing Slide Lay**o**ut from the F**o**rmat menu. Applying a new layout to an existing slide does not remove any existing text or graphics. Text and graphics boxes can be resized or rearranged to fit in the new layout.

## Applying a Layout to a Slide

To apply a layout to a slide, follow these steps:

**1** Click the Slide View button to change the presentation to the Slide view.

**2** Make slide 12, "Our Strengths," the current slide.

**3** Choose Slide Layout from the Format menu.

The Slide Layout dialog box appears with the current layout design selected. This dialog box is similar to the New Slide dialog box shown in figure 3.6.

**4** Using the list box vertical scroll bar, locate the slide layout named Text over Object, which shows a title line, a text box with bulleted lines, and an object box. Select this layout design.

A black border appears around the selection.

**5** Click **A**pply.

The new layout is applied to slide 12, which now appears with an object box at the bottom. The message beneath the object icon is `Double-click to add object`. Do not add an object at this time.

Unless you have created a blank slide, all slides created in the Outline view have a default layout based on the current template. You can also apply a layout by clicking the Layout button on the status bar. You learn how to apply a layout to a slide using the Layout button in the next tutorial.

## Applying a Layout to a Slide by Using the Layout Button

To use the Layout button to apply a new layout, follow these steps:

**1** Make slide 3, "Mission Statement," the active slide.

**2** Click the Layout button on the status bar. The Slide Layout dialog box appears.

**3** Select the layout design 2 Column Text.

**4** Click **A**pply.

Slide 3 is now displayed in a two-column text format.

**5** Select the left column, and type the following lines of text, pressing ⏎Enter after each line:

**Loyalty**

**Quality**

(continues)

**Applying a Layout to a Slide by Using the Layout Button (continued)**

**Need**

**Affordable**

**6** Select the right column, and type the following without pressing ⏎Enter:

**To build customer loyalty to a quality product that meets a need at an affordable price.**

# Objective 4: Add Graphs

In Chapter 2, you added a graph to a slide by selecting the Insert Graph button from the toolbar. You can also insert graphs and charts by applying the desired layout and then completing the information.

**Adding a Graph Layout to a Slide**

To add a graph to a slide by applying the appropriate layout, follow these steps:

**1** Make slide 7, "Regional Distribution by Cases," the active slide.

**2** Click the Layout button on the status bar.

The Slide Layout dialog box appears.

**3** Select the layout titled ~~Graph.~~ *Chart*

**4** Click the **A**pply button.

**5** Double-click the `Double-click to add graph` icon.

The datasheet appears.

**6** Use the following information to complete the datasheet:

|  | A | B | C | D |
|---|---|---|---|---|
|  | 1st Qtr | 2nd Qtr | 3rd Qtr | 4th Qtr |
| East | 4,400 | 12,000 | 21,000 | 21,000 |
| West |  | 1,400 | 6,000 | 12,000 |
| Mid-West |  | 1,400 | 3,200 | 6,000 |

When completed, the datasheet should look like the one in figure 3.8.

**Figure 3.8**
The completed
datasheet.

| | | A | B | C | D |
|---|---|---|---|---|---|
| | | 1st Qtr | 2nd Qtr | 3rd Qtr | 4th Qtr |
| 1 | East | 4,400 | 12,000 | 21,000 | 21,000 |
| 2 | West | | 1,400 | 6,000 | 12,000 |
| 3 | Mid-West | | 1,400 | 3,200 | 6,000 |
| 4 | | | | | |

STRUT1.PPT - Datasheet

**7** ~~Click outside the datasheet to close it.~~ *Click X to close data Sheet*

**8** ~~Click outside the~~ graph object to deselect it.

# Objective 5: Add Organization Charts

**3**

Organization charts are useful tools for illustrating the chain of responsibility in a company or division of a company. You can insert an organization chart by using the Insert Org Chart button on the Standard toolbar or by applying the appropriate layout design.

## Applying an Organization Chart Layout

To apply an organization chart layout, follow these steps:

**1** Make slide 5, "Organization," the active slide.

**2** Click the Layout button on the status bar.

The Slide Layout dialog box appears.

**3** Select the Org Chart icon in the Slide Layout dialog box (see figure 3.9).

**Figure 3.9**
The Slide Layout
dialog box with
the Org Chart
icon selected.

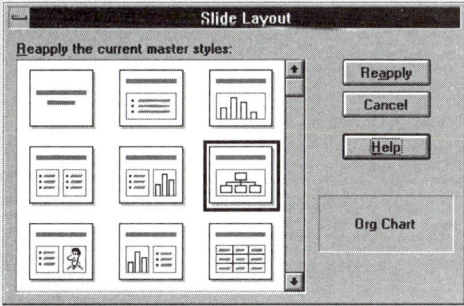

**4** Click **A**pply. The presentation window shows the organization chart window with the placeholders.

(continues)

## Applying an Organization Chart Layout (continued)

**5** Double-click the Org Chart icon.

The Microsoft Organization Chart window appears (see figure 3.10).

**Figure 3.10**
The Microsoft
Organization
Chart window.

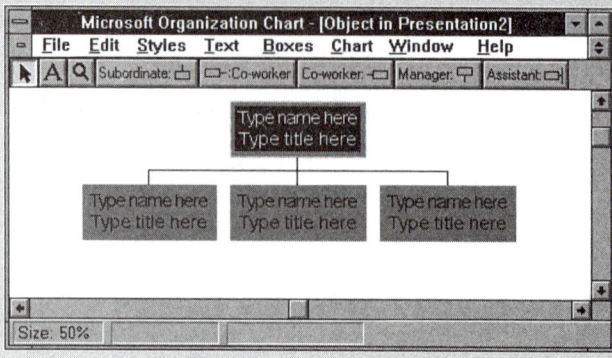

You can add colors and formatting to the organization chart to make it more appealing visually.

## Enhancing the Appearance of the Chart

To apply colors and formatting to the chart, follow these steps:

**1** Press Ctrl + A to select all elements in the chart.

**2** Choose **B**ackground Color from the **C**hart menu in the Microsoft Organization Chart window.

**3** Click the white color choice at the bottom of the Color list box.

**4** Choose Box Border [border Style] from the **B**oxes menu.

**5** Click the box immediately below the box that contains the word Hair line.

**6** Choose Box **C**olor from the **B**oxes menu.

**7** Click the white color choice at the bottom of the Color list box.

The displayed boxes turn black, and the text vanishes. Don't worry because this problem will be rectified in the next two steps.

**8** Choose C**o**lor from the **T**ext menu.

**9** Click the black color choice at the bottom of the column.

**10** Choose Line Col**o**r from the **B**oxes menu.

**11** Click the black color choice.

**12** Select Line **T**hickness from the **B**oxes menu.

**13** Click the 2 pt choice.

Next, you are going to work with the title of the chart and add your own text to the chart.

## Creating the Text of the Chart

To format the chart title and add your own text to the chart, follow these steps:

**1** Highlight the words `Chart Title`.

You may have to scroll the window to locate `Chart Title`.

**2** Choose Color from the Text menu.

**3** Click the black color choice.

**4** With the words `Chart Title` still highlighted, type the phrase:

**Thik 'N' Thin Chik'N Soup**

**5** Click the A button on the Org Chart toolbar below the menu bar.

**6** Click inside the top box.

**7** Select the words `Type name here`.

**8** Type the name **Mary Steel**.

**9** Select the words `Type title here`.

**10** Type the title **Project Manager**.

**11** Click the left-most subordinate box.

**12** Replace the name and title lines in that box with **Dennis Whitman** and **Plant Operations**, respectively.

**13** In the middle box, type your name and the title **Marketing Manager**.

**14** In the right box, type **Nancy Brown** and **Business Manager**, respectively, as the name and title.

Figure 3.11 shows the completed organization chart.

**Figure 3.11**
The completed organization chart.

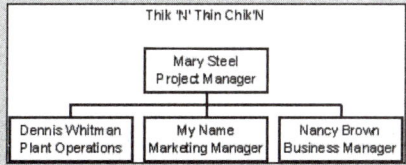

**15** Choose Update STRUTI.PPT from the File menu.

**16** Choose Exit and Return to STRUT1.PPT from the File menu.

The current slide is now updated with the new organization chart.

**17** Click the slide anywhere outside the text and graph boxes.

3

To Add to Org Chart
Click box, click what type to add
Click box to add type to. Type info in box

# Objective 6: Add Clip Art

Visual images add interest and attractiveness to presentations. They also clarify information and often add impact because of that clarity.

Visuals in PowerPoint are not limited to charts and graphs that you create yourself. Although you can create basic art with the drawing tools from the Drawing and Drawing+ toolbars, you can also import almost any computer image, including movies, pictures, and clip art.

Images imported into PowerPoint from other applications, such as painting and scanning programs, can be resized, moved, and sometimes recolored.

The PowerPoint ClipArt Gallery, a collection of more than 1,000 professionally designed illustrations, is distributed with the program. These illustrations include buildings, tools, people, animals, maps, and scenic backgrounds. You can also add your own art to the ClipArt Gallery.

## Adding Clip Art to a Presentation

To add clip art to a graph box on a slide, follow these steps:

❶ Make slide 2, "Start-up Strategy," the active slide in the Slide view.

❷ Double-click the icon in the placeholder box to add clip art to the slide.

The Microsoft ClipArt Gallery dialog box appears (see figure 3.12).

**Figure 3.12**
The Microsoft ClipArt Gallery dialog box.

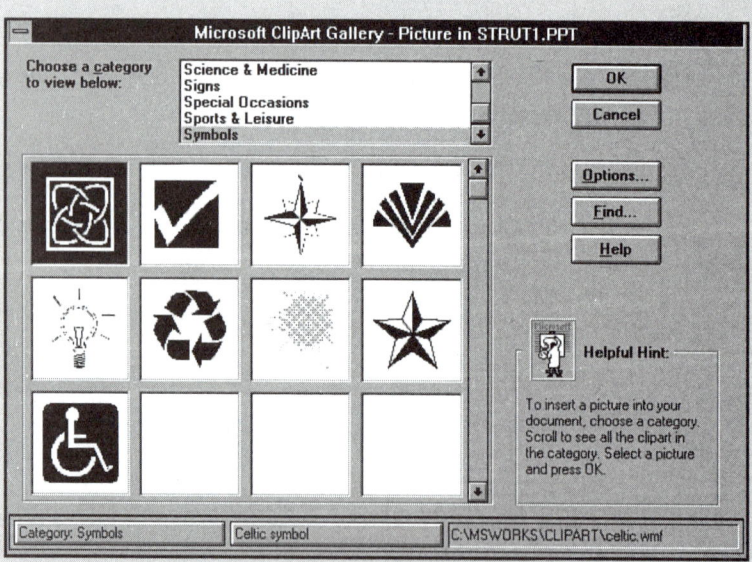

❸ Select Symbols in the Choose a **C**ategory to View Below list.

**Note:** *The Symbols category of clip art comes with PowerPoint. If your system does not have this category, select another available category from the ClipArt Gallery. Look for something like a check mark. The check mark is a symbol used by Mom's Home Cookin' Soup Company as part of its Check for Heart Health advertising.*

**4** Select the dark check mark in the small box (or a similar symbol).

**5** Click OK.

The clip-art symbol is now added to the slide.

When you apply a layout that includes a graphic object, you must choose the type of object you want to insert. This object can be an equation, clip art, a drawing created in another program, scanned art, digitized photographs, a chart or worksheet from Excel, another slide from this or another presentation program, a digitized movie, prerecorded sound, or a command button that initiates another presentation.

The Microsoft Insert Object dialog box provides a list of these choices, as well as options for using existing objects or creating new ones. In the next tutorial, you learn to add clip art to an object box.

**3**

## Adding Clip Art to an Object Box

To insert an object into an object box on a slide, follow these steps:

**1** In the Slide view, make slide 12, "Our Strengths," the active slide.

**2** Double-click the object box.

The Microsoft Insert Object dialog box appears (see figure 3.13).

**Figure 3.13**
The Insert
Object dialog
box.

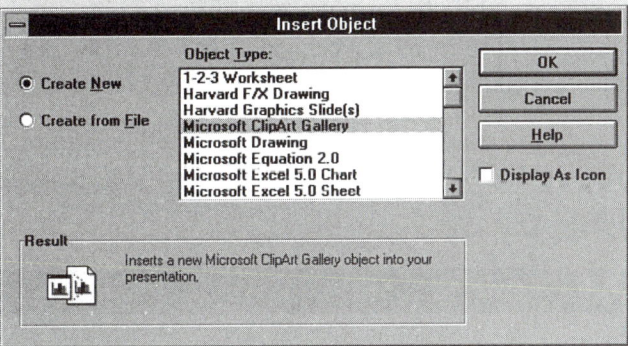

**3** Select Microsoft ClipArt Gallery from the Object Type list.

**4** Before completing the next step, use the vertical scroll bar to read the list of objects that can be inserted into a slide.

**5** Select the Create New option.

**6** Verify that Display As Icon is not selected.

**7** Click OK.

The Microsoft ClipArt Gallery dialog box appears (refer to figure 3.12).

**8** From the Symbols category, select the clip art that portrays a bowl of soup with bread, crackers, and a bottle of wine.

If you are curious about the wine, Mom, the founder of the company, fancied herself a bit of a gourmet.

**9** Click OK.

The selected art is inserted into the object location.

# Objective 7: Add Tables

Tables provide another way to display text and graphics. A Microsoft table resembles a datasheet in that the table can be divided into a grid of rows and columns with visible or invisible gridlines and borders. Although a datasheet has built-in operations for handling text and numbers, as well as predefined functions for performing arithmetic operations, a table is more user-structured, and both the format and the content can be modified directly on a slide.

Generally, you use tables to record information in rows and columns both to achieve consistency and to make the information easy to read and understand. The information can be in the form of lists, data, or numbers that require some arithmetic operations. The information recorded in columns is usually related to other items in the columns.

You can also use tables to format a layout on a slide. For example, if you require a two-column layout in which one column is narrow and other is wide, you can use a table. Setting up three columns or more on a slide is easy.

You can anchor a side heading next to a related paragraph. In this design, a word or phrase states the primary point, which is expanded in an adjacent paragraph.

## Using the Menu to Add a Table to a Slide

You insert a table into a slide either by using the Insert Microsoft Word Table button on the Standard toolbar or by choosing Microsoft **W**ord Table from the **I**nsert menu. To insert a table in a text box using the menu, follow these steps:

**1** In the Slide view, make slide 4, "Objectives," the active slide.

**2** Point the mouse pointer at the dotted line surrounding the text box, and click once to select the box.

The border is highlighted, and the sizing handles are visible.

**3** Choose Microsoft **W**ord Table from the **I**nsert menu.

The Insert Word Table dialog box appears (see figure 3.14).

**Figure 3.14**
The Insert Word
Table dialog
box.

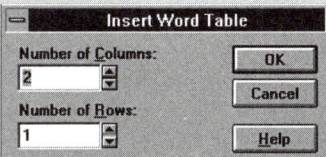

④ Set the Number of **C**olumns to 2 and the Number of **R**ows to 1.

⑤ Click OK.

The Table edit box appears (see figure 3.15). The edit box has a horizontal and a vertical ruler—both marked in inches. These markings do not correspond to screen sizes but to a printed slide size.

**Figure 3.15**
The Table edit
box.

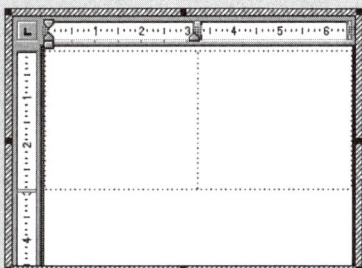

⑥ Position the mouse pointer on the dotted line that divides the two columns of the table.

The pointer changes to two parallel vertical lines with arrows pointing to the left and right.

⑦ Drag the dotted line to the left until the traveling ruler marker covers the number 3, and then release the mouse button.

The table is now divided into one narrow column and one wide column.

**Note:** *You select a column by positioning the mouse pointer in that column and clicking the left mouse button. Depending on the settings of your options, the ending paragraph marks (¶) may not be visible on your display.*

⑧ Enter the following data into the table columns as directed.

In column 1 of the table

    **a.** Type the words **Test Market**, and press ⏎Enter three times.

    **b.** Type the word **East**, and press ⏎Enter twice.

    **c.** Type the word **West**, and press ⏎Enter.

    **d.** Type the word **Mid-West**.

(continues)

**Using the Menu to Add a Table to a Slide (continued)**

In column 2 of the table, enter the following lines (including numbers), and press ⏎Enter after each line except for the last.

1. **Create product team**

2. **Pilot plant production**

3. **Begin advertising**

4. **Ship initial product**

5. **Expand marketing**

6. **Expand shipping**

7. **Review sales**

8. **Plant completion**

9. **Full-scale production**

When you have finished, the table should look like the one displayed in figure 3.16.

**Figure 3.16**
The completed table.

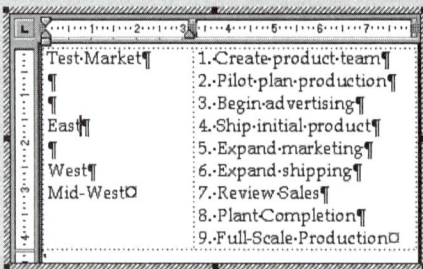

**9** Click anywhere outside the table area.

The Table edit box clears, and the slide contains the contents of the table (see figure 3.17).

**Figure 3.17**
The completed slide.

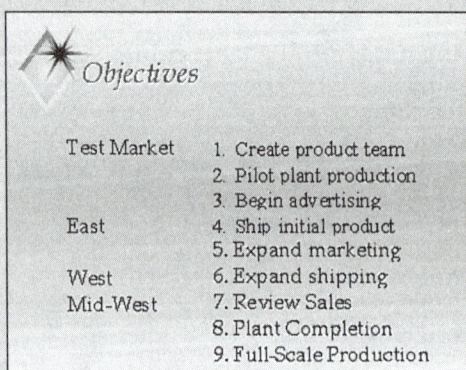

**10** Click anywhere outside the object box area.

A table can be inserted anywhere on a slide and can contain as many columns and rows as necessary. The size of a displayed table depends on what a single slide can accommodate. In the next tutorial, you learn how to insert a table using a toolbar button.

## Inserting a Table Using a Toolbar Button

To insert a table using a toolbar button, follow these steps:

**1** In the Slide view, make slide 9, "Production," the active slide.

**2** Select the text box by clicking the dotted line.

**3** With the box outline highlighted and the sizing handles visible, choose **C**lear from the **E**dit menu.

The text box object is deleted from the slide.

**4** Click the Insert Microsoft Word Table button on the Standard toolbar.

The Table Size menu appears (see figure 3.18). This menu is a visual representation of the rows and columns on a table. If you select the second box from the left on the top row, for example, you will create a table with two columns and one row, like the table you created in the tutorial, "Using the Menu to Add a Table to a Slide."

**Figure 3.18**
The drop-down
Table Size
menu.

Cancel

**5** Click the box in the lower right corner to create a table with four rows and five columns.

The table appears. Notice the type size and font on the Formatting toolbar. These default settings reflect the size that will print on a full-size slide.

**6** Select the entire table by placing the mouse pointer in the upper left cell, pressing the left mouse button, and dragging the highlight to the last cell on the lower right.

**7** Change the font to Times New Roman and the font size to 28.

**Note:** *Don't worry about the formatting in the text in step 8. You format in the next step.*

(continues)

## Inserting a Table Using a Toolbar Button (continued)

**8** Type the following data into the cells as shown (pressing `Tab` to move through the cells):

| Area | 1Q | 2Q | 3Q | 4Q |
|---|---|---|---|---|
| East | 4,400 | 12,000 | 21,000 | 21,000 |
| West | | 1,400 | 6,000 | 12,000 |
| Mid-West | | 1,400 | 3,200 | 6,000 |

**9** Select the entire first row, and click the Bold button on the Formatting toolbar.

**10** Select the four cells (1Q–4Q) on the top row beginning with cell 2, and click the Center button on the Formatting toolbar.

**11** Select all the cells that contain quantities (numbers with commas), and click the Right Align button on the Formatting toolbar.

**12** Click anywhere outside the table to remove the edit box.

**13** Click anywhere outside the object box to remove the sizing handles.

The table is now inserted into the slide.

There are, of course, many other ways to format information in a table. You might want to outline the table in a box and add shading. You might want to add gridlines so that each cell appears as a small box. You can select both of these options by choosing the **B**orders and Shading option from the F**o**rmat menu.

# Objective 8: Add Special Text Effects

You can enhance a slide in a variety of ways by adding special effects to the text. The simplest of these methods are the use of font and size selection and the addition of color. Changing the attributes of selected text, such as making portions boldface or italic or underline, is also effective. Special fonts, such as script and hollow fonts, are useful. Shadowing adds impact.

Be sure to use special fonts and effects wisely. Overuse of fancy fonts and enhancements such as shadowing can be distracting, thus lessening the impact of what you say.

In addition to adding special text effects from menu and toolbar options, you can create text art for special items. Text art is covered in a later chapter.

## Enhancing Text with Symbols and Color

To add a colored symbol to the slide, follow these steps:

**1** In the Slide view, make slide 8, "Ad Campaign," the active slide.

**2** Click the text box.

**3** Choose **B**ullet from the **Fo**rmat menu.

The Bullet dialog box appears (see figure 3.19).

**Figure 3.19**
The Bullet dialog
box.

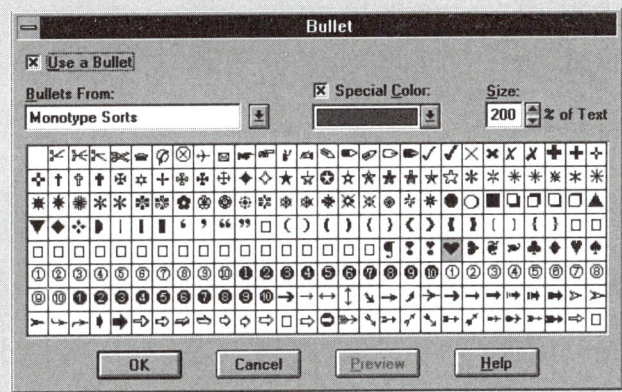

**4** Select the heart symbol.

**5** In the Special **C**olor drop-down list box, select red.

**6** In the **S**ize text box, set the size to 200.

Many other options can be selected from this dialog box. The **B**ullets From drop-down list box provides other symbol fonts. The **U**se a Bullet option can be deselected if no bullet is desired. The **P**review button shows how a particular selection will appear.

**7** Click OK.

The heart symbol appears on the slide.

The use of script for the company name on the title slide of the presentation makes this slide more attractive and increases its impact.

## Enhancing Text by Changing Fonts and Size

To use the toolbars to change the font and size to enhance text, follow these steps:

**1** Click the text next to the heart symbol, and type the text **Heart Check for Health**.

(continues)

## Enhancing Text by Changing Fonts and Size (continued)

**2** Highlight the text Heart Check for Health, and change the font to Brush Script MT (or another script if this font is not available).

**3** With the text still selected, change the font size to 60 points. If necessary, click the text box border to display the sizing handles.

**4** Click and drag the middle sizing handle on the bottom of the box upward to a position just below the text.

**5** Click anywhere outside the text box to remove the highlight.

**6** Click the Text tool button on the Drawing toolbar (the button with the letter A).

**7** Position the pointer in the middle of the slide and just below the right leg of the letter H in Heart, and click the left mouse button. (Refer to figure 3.20 to see how this slide will appear when the text is entered.)

A small text box appears with a blinking insertion point inside.

**8** Type the following lines (pressing ⏎Enter after the first two lines):

**The hearty taste of home-made soup…**

**Chock-Full of Chunky Broasted Chicken**

**and Selected, Garden-Fresh Vegetables**

**9** Select all three sentences, and click the Bold button on the Formatting toolbar.

**10** Click anywhere outside the text box to clear the highlight.

**11** Select the Text tool button, and position the pointer near the bottom of the slide on a line aligned approximately with the right edge of the heart symbol, and click.

**12** Type the phrase **Fat and Chloresterol Free**.

**Note:** *As in earlier chapters, type the text exactly as given here. You will correct spelling in another chapter.*

**13** Select the phrase, and change the font size to 32 points.

**14** With the phrase still selected, click the Bold button on the Formatting toolbar.

**15** Click anywhere outside any text box to remove the highlight.

Figure 3.20 shows the completed slide.

**Figure 3.20**
The completed slide.

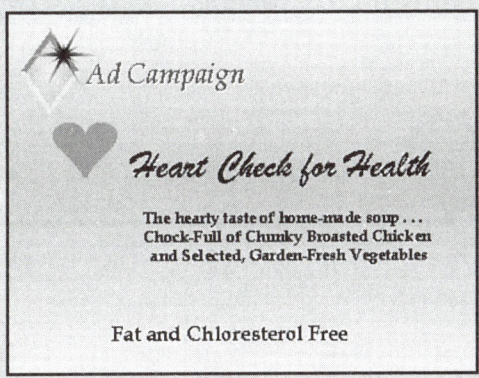

**16** Save the file as **STRUTI.PPT**.

You can also enhance text by adding a shadow. In the next tutorial, you learn how to add shadows to your work.

## Enhancing Text with Shadows

To add a shadow to selected text, follow these steps:

**1** In the Slide view, make slide 3, "Mission Statement," the active slide.

**2** Select the left column and the four words in that column.

**3** Change the font size to 32 points.

**4** Click the Bold button on the Formatting toolbar.

**5** Choose **Sh**adow from the **Fo**rmat menu.

The Shadow dialog box appears (see figure 3.21).

**Figure 3.21**
The Shadow dialog box.

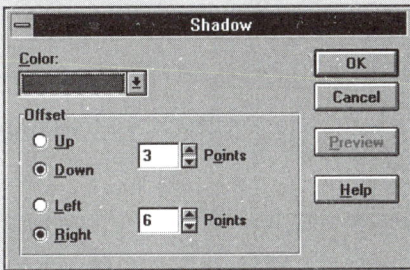

**6** From the **C**olor drop-down list box, select red.

**7** From the Offset options, select the **D**own button, and set the offset to 3 P**o**ints.

**8** Also from the Offset options, select the **R**ight button, and set the offset to 6 P**o**ints.

(continues)

**Enhancing Text with Shadows (continued)**

❾ Click OK.

❿ Click anywhere outside of the text box.

The four important points in the mission statement are now emphasized.

# Chapter Summary

In this chapter, you have learned how to open an existing presentation and prepare it for modifications. You also learned how to add new slides using both the menu and toolbar and how to select different layouts. This chapter also covers the techniques for adding graphs, organizational charts, clip art, and tables. Finally, you learned how to add special text effects to enhance and emphasize selected words and phrases.

You will finish the remaining uncompleted slides in this presentation in projects and later chapters.

# Checking Your Skills

### True/False Questions

For each of the following statements, circle *T* or *F* to indicate whether the statement is true or false.

T  F  **1.** You can access the Find File dialog box from both the **F**ile menu and the Open dialog box.

T  F  **2.** A new slide is always inserted preceding the active or current slide when you click New Slide on the status bar.

T  F  **3.** Applying a new layout to an existing slide does not remove any existing text or graphics.

T  F  **4.** PowerPoint slides can include visuals, such as movies, that are saved as computer images.

T  F  **5.** AutoLayout includes a layout in which the design consists of three parallel columns.

### Multiple-Choice Questions

In the blank provided, write the letter of the correct answer for each of the following questions.

____ **1.** You open an existing PowerPoint presentation by following the same procedures that are used in other Windows programs with the familiar _____.

    **a.** File Manager icon in the Program Manager window

    **b.** Open and Search dialog boxes

    **c.** Open and Search buttons on the Standard toolbar

    **d.** Tip of the Day dialog box appearing after you choose **O**pen from the **F**ile menu

____ **2.** The three tab selections **S**ummary, **L**ocation, and Timestam**p** are found in the _____.

    **a.** Summary Info dialog box

    **b.** Search dialog box

    **c.** Open dialog box

    **d.** Advanced Search dialog box

____ **3.** A placeholder is _____.

    **a.** a bookmark that designates a particular slide location

    **b.** a blank slide that can be completed at a later time

    **c.** a designated location on a slide for various objects

    **d.** used in the Outline view to store a graphic image

____ **4.** The object that displays in rows and columns and that can be modified directly on a slide in terms of both format and content is a _____.

    **a.** datasheet

    **b.** table

    **c.** chart

    **d.** graph

____ **5.** Points in a slide can be enhanced by a special character selected from a _____.

    **a.** Bullet dialog box

    **b.** Symbol dialog box

    **c.** Shadow dialog pox

    **d.** Font Size dialog box

**3**

### Fill-in-the-Blank Questions

In the blank provided, write the correct answer for each of the following questions.

1. In addition to opening a presentation using the PowerPoint dialog box, you can open a presentation by choosing **O**pen from the **F**ile menu or the Open button from the _____ toolbar.

2. You can add a new slide in any view by clicking the _____ button on the status bar or by choosing _____ from the **I**nsert menu.

3. _____ views are accessed by holding down the (⇧Shift) key when clicking a view button on the status bar.

4. Creating a new slide in the Slide view automatically introduces the _____ dialog box for selecting preset design elements; this dialog box is convenient for adding a few slides.

5. _____ charts are useful tools for illustrating the chain of responsibility in a company or division of a company.

# Applying Your Skills

## Review Exercises

### Exercise 1: Adding Text to a Slide
Your task is to add the following text to slide 6, "Marketing Strategy":

**Heart Check for Health Ad Campaign**

**Regional Roll-Out**

**Newspaper Coupons**

**Chuck the Chicken Contest**

Choose a font and size that will enhance the lines.

### Exercise 2: Adding Clip Art
Use the Insert ClipArt button from the Standard toolbar to add the Heart Check clip-art symbol to slide 6, "Marketing Strategy." Position the symbol so that it is pleasing in appearance.

### Exercise 3: Changing Bullets
The bullets on slide 2, "Start-up Strategy," could be changed to another character that would enhance the appeal of this slide. At least, that's what your boss says. Change the bullets on this slide to another symbol that you think your boss would like. **Hint:** The Heart Check for Health advertising and marketing campaign was his idea.

## Continuing Projects

### Project 1: Enhancing a Presentation for Sales

Your publishing company is releasing a new book entitled *The Rolling Stones' Favorite Senior Citizens' Discounts*. Create a presentation that will sell bookstores on reasons to stock the title. Use a layout, clip art, and tables, along with special text effects, to make the presentation appealing. Save as **BOOK1.PPT**.

### Project 2: Enhancing a Presentation to Create Impression

The assignment for Project 2 in Chapter 2 was to build a general presentation on one of three activities. Use the knowledge you have gained in this chapter to improve your presentation so that it leaves a favorable impression with the viewers. Crazy art, fancy letters, and silly charts are allowed, but only if they improve the presentation.

**3**

# CHAPTER 4

# Making Effective Presentations

The allusion to Mark Antony's delivering an extemporaneous eulogy aside, the most effective speeches are those that have been polished and refined, the content evaluated and reworked where necessary, and considerable effort and time devoted to practice. President Bill Clinton is said to work on the content and rehearsal of important speeches, like the State of the Union Address, to within moments of the actual delivery.

This chapter shows you how to develop notes pages to guide you through your presentation and how to organize your content to increase effectiveness. You learn how to rehearse the presentation for practice and timing, to add transitions between slides for a more polished effect, and to add hidden slides for backup information in case of questions from the audience. The chapter concludes by showing you how to present an effective slide show.

## Objectives

By the time you have finished this chapter, you will have learned to

1. Use Notes Pages for Talking Points

2. Use the Slide Sorter View

3. Rehearse for Practice and Timing

4. Add Transitions between Slides

5. Add Hidden Slides for Backup

6. Present a Slide Show

## Objective 1: Use Notes Pages for Talking Points

Whether one is a student giving a class presentation or a broadcaster on the evening news, practically every good speaker uses some form of notes. Although TelePrompTers have replaced cue cards on television programs, these machines still display notes that help make the broadcast more effective.

**Notes Pages view**
A view in which speaker's notes are attached to each slide.

In much the same way, PowerPoint includes a *Notes Pages view* that enables you to create the notes you will use for the talking points on your slides, thus improving your presentations. In this view, both the slides and the notes page are visible on-screen at the same time. This capability helps you maintain the focus of the point that you want to make. Although these notes are not displayed during a presentation, you can print copies for your own use.

## Preparing a Presentation for Adding Notes

When preparing your presentation, you can write your notes at the same time that you create a slide; however, some individuals prefer to write a draft or outline of the presentation first and then create both the slides and notes. In this section, you use the presentation you prepared in Chapter 3, STRUT1.

To prepare this presentation for adding notes, do the following:

❶ Open the file STRUT1.PPT, which you completed in Chapter 3.

This file should include the completed slide 6, "Marketing Strategy," which was the focus of the three review exercises at the end of the chapter.

❷ Save the file as **SOUP1.PPT**.

You will add notes to this presentation in the next tutorial.

In order to use Notes Pages view, you must have at least one slide in the presentation because the notes page is displayed with the current slide at the top and a notes section at the bottom.

## Adding Notes to a Slide

To add notes to a slide, do the following:

❶ In the Slide view, make slide 1, the title slide, the active slide.

❷ Click the Notes Pages View button on the status bar.

The presentation window now displays a page with the slide at the top and an area below for making notes (see figure 4.1).

**Figure 4.1**
The Notes Pages view of the title slide.

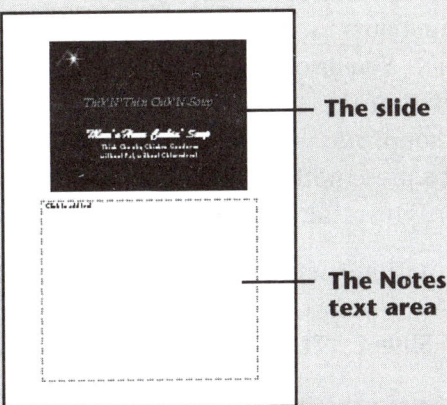

The slide

The Notes text area

**❸** Click the Zoom Control arrow, and change the percentage from 33 percent to 66 percent.

This percentage makes the text you type for your notes easier to read.

**❹** Click the Notes text box below the illustration of the slide. Type the following:

**Members of the board:**

**I and the other members of our team are rolling out one of the most exciting new products ever developed in Mom's kitchen: Thik 'N' Thin Chik'N Soup—a major breakthrough in no-fat, no cholesterol products.**

**Our start-up strategy is lean and mean. We have—no pun intended—cut the fat and cut to the chase. We're going after a new market, and we intend to own it.**

**We have the product. We have the customers. We have the means and methods to put the two together. And we have the Plan.**

**❺** Click anywhere outside the text box area, and save the presentation as **SOUP1.PPT**.

**Note:** *You should periodically save any presentation you are working on because any power interruption could cause you to lose all the work you have done since the last time you saved.*

**❻** Click the Next Slide button at the bottom of the vertical scroll bar to make the next slide active.

## Maintaining Tone and Theme

**Tone**

The voice of a presentation.

**Theme**

The specific and overall purpose of the presentation that is consistently supported by all the elements.

In the introductory statements for the title slide, you want to use action statements in the active voice. You also want to maintain that voice, or *tone,* throughout the presentation. These statements help establish your *theme*—you have a plan for selling soup, and you are confident that your plan is the best plan. In the context of a presentation, the theme is the basic purpose or specific goal of the presentation, the result that is to be accomplished.

All elements of a presentation should support or build on the essential theme. As you create and add notes to your slides, maintain a consistent tone and theme throughout your work. Slide 2, "Start-up Strategy," is the framework.

---

**Tip**

When you make a speech, first tell the audience what you are going to say, say it, and then tell them that you said it.

---

### Preparing Your Notes

To enter the text you will use during your presentation of slide 2, do the following:

**❶** Enter the following text on the notes pages for slide 2:

**We are covering a great deal of information today, from our mission and objectives, to the organization that drives our marketing strategy, to an innovative advertising campaign, to a tight production plan on a strict timeline that will produce maximum profits in the short-term and growth-oriented profits in the long-term. In short, this action plan focusses like a laser beam on the bottom line.**

**[NOTE TO SELF: POINT TO EACH UNDERLINED ITEM ON-SCREEN AS YOU HIT THAT POINT]**

**❷** Click anywhere outside the text box area.

You have just entered the notes for slide 2. In the next tutorial, you enter the notes you need for the rest of your presentation.

## Completing the Notes for Remaining Slides

Each slide will contain notes that you will use in your presentation. Add the following notes to the designated slides:

Slide 3, "Mission Statement"

**Market research shows that customers are loyal to products that taste good (quality), help fulfill some need such as weight loss or prevention of heart disease, and sell for a reasonable price.**

Slide 4, "Objectives"

**COVER EACH ITEM--NOTE THAT ITEMS 8 AND 9 ARE BASED ON ANTICIPATED REVENUES FROM SALES.**

Slide 5, "Organization"

**INTRODUCE MS. STEEL, WHO WILL DISCUSS QUALIFICATIONS OF TEAM MEMBERS AND WHY THEY WERE CHOSEN.**

Slide 6, "Market Strategy"

**!!!!!! GIVE BOSS CREDIT FOR COMING UP WITH HEART CHECK FOR HEALTH !!!!!!**

**Ad Agency: Bluster, Fudge, and Purjoin**

**Regional roll-out will target local television, soap-opera time (housewives) and evening news (families). Local newspapers and clip coupons during intro period. Press releases to newspapers, tv and radio.**

**With national roll-out, Chuck the Chicken will announce National Chuck the Fat contest. Boys and girls will try to track Chuck's diet and guess how much he weighs each week. Entry forms are on back of soup can labels. Winning entries are placed in chicken soup pot for sweepstakes drawing. Grand Prize: All expense-paid trip to Chuck the Chicken's Farmland Amusement Park for family. Other prizes.**

Slide 7, "Regional Distribution by Cases"

**Introduce Dennis Whitman to discuss.**

(continues)

**4**

**Completing the Notes for Remaining Slides (continued)**

Slide 8, "Ad Campaign"

**People are worried about their health. Our surveys show that people want to eat healthy. They are looking for foods they can eat without guilt. We are targeting that market.**

**And we're giving them something extra. Heart-healthy foods don't have to skimp on quality, taste, or ingredients.**

Slide 9, "Production"

**Dennis Whitman to discuss.**

Slide 12, "Our Strengths"

**Everyone here knows that we are the largest soup maker in the country and that we have an unblemished reputation for taste and quality. Recently, however, we have been beaten to the market by innovative products that required us to play catch up. We still haven't gained appreciable market share in Peanut Butter Cream--and Dad's Beer Dumpling Stew is still the biggest seller in the soups-men-take-to-work-in-their-thermos category.**

**But, here, we are seizing an opportunity that will propel our company back into the forefront--real chicken soup made with real chickens minus the fat and cholesterol. We have done the impossibles. We have taken out the nasties and left in the goodness. Tie that in with Mom's reputation, and we have a natural born winner.**

Slide 13, "Recommendations"

**Field all questions on budget to VP of Finance, M. T. Graves. He has latest figures.**

**Note:** *You will complete slides 10 and 11 in a later tutorial.*

# Objective 2: Use the Slide Sorter View

The Slide Sorter view displays in the presentation window a miniature of each slide (see figure 4.2). The number of slides that are visible on-screen at any one time depends on the percentage scale you are using for zoom control and the size of the window. This view resembles the view seen from a light table, a tool used in photography and printing composition to lay out rows of slides or negatives for viewing.

**Figure 4.2**
Slide view
showing 13 slides.

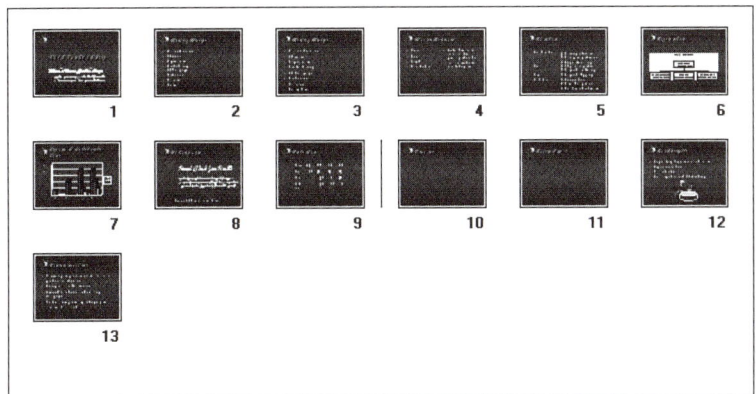

Slide Sorter view is particularly useful for rearranging slides, setting the timing and transitions between slides, adding or deleting slides, and envisioning the overall presentation.

## Changing to the Slide Sorter View

The Slide Sorter view is accessible either by selecting **Slide** Sorter from the **View** menu or by clicking the Slide Sorter View button. To change the presentation to the Slide view, do the following:

**❶** Click the Slide View button.

The presentation changes to the Slide Sorter view, and the Formatting toolbar is replaced by the Slide Sorter toolbar (see figure 4.3).

**Figure 4.3**
The Slide Sorter
toolbar.

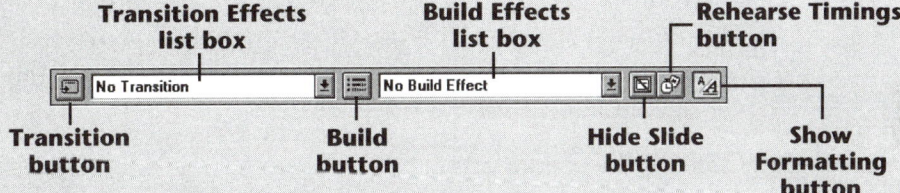

**❷** Click the Zoom Control button on the Standard toolbar, and set the presentation scale to 33 percent.

All the slides should now be visible on-screen. The selected slide is framed in a heavy border.

**❸** Click slide 9, "Production."

Slide 9 is now framed in a heavy border, indicating that it is the selected slide.

### Moving and Positioning Slides in a Presentation

You can rearrange slides in the Slide Sorter view by clicking and dragging a slide to a new position.

In this presentation, Dennis Whitman, the Plant Operations Manager, is responsible for addressing the issues in two of the slides, slide 7, "Regional Distribution by Cases," and slide 9, "Production." If these slides were together, Whitman could address both issues without interruption. In the next tutorial, you move these slides.

## Moving a Slide in Slide Sorter View

To move a slide in the presentation, do the following:

**1** In the Slide Sorter view, position the mouse pointer on slide 9; then press and hold down the left mouse button.

**2** With the mouse button still pressed, move the mouse slightly to the left.

The mouse pointer changes to a downward-pointing arrow with a small square attached. A vertical line marker appears between slides 8 and 9 with inward pointing arrows at each end of the line. The vertical line marker indicates where the slide will be positioned when the mouse button is released.

**3** Move the mouse pointer with the small square to the left, watching the vertical line marker. When the vertical line marker precedes slide 7 (between slides 6 and 7), release the left mouse button.

Slide 9 is now slide 7, and the original slide 7 is now slide 8.

**4** Click the Show Formatting button on the Slide Sorter toolbar.

The content of each slide is replaced by the basic formatting of the slides. This formatting, along with the current template, shows the top-level headings of the slides. You may find it easier to move slides in the Slide Sorter view because the display is often clearer.

**5** Click the Show Formatting button again to return the contents to the slides.

# Objective 3: Rehearse for Practice and Timing

You use both the Notes Pages and the Slide Sorter views in the preparation for an oral presentation. Now that you have the slides in the proper order, you can return to the Notes Pages view to print a copy of your notes. After you print your notes, you return to the Slide Sorter view so that you can see the entire presentation while you practice speaking and developing your timing.

Some comedians maintain that what makes a joke funny is often not the content but the delivery and the timing. Although Microsoft is not targeting comedians as primary PowerPoint users, PowerPoint does have a built-in feature that could improve many stand-up routines and presentations alike—automated timing.

You start automated timing by clicking the Rehearse Timings button on the Slide Sorter toolbar (the button with the clock and small slide). When you rehearse timing, the slides in the presentation are displayed in order, and you click the mouse button to move from slide to slide. When you finish, PowerPoint tells you how long your presentation took and prints the time for each slide presentation segment below that slide.

With PowerPoint, you can repeat your presentation as often as you like, changing and refining the timing to perfect your delivery.

## Printing Notes for an Oral Presentation

The first step in giving an oral presentation is to print the notes for each slide. To print the presentation notes, do the following:

**1** Click the Notes Pages View button, and make slide 1, the title slide, the active slide.

**2** Choose **P**rint from the **F**ile menu.

The Print dialog box appears.

**3** Select Notes Pages in the Print **W**hat list box and **A**ll in the Slide Ranges options box (see figure 4.4).

**Figure 4.4**
The Print dialog box with Notes Pages selected to print.

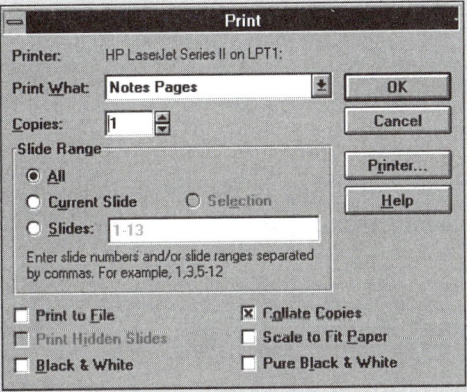

**4** Click OK.

A notes page for each slide is printed in sequence. Each page contains a small picture of the slide and the printed notes for that slide.

## Practicing Delivery and Timing

**Rehearsal**
A two-step process that entails learning the material and practicing delivery.

Any *rehearsal* consists of two steps: learning the material and practicing delivery. Although you may have written the notes for your presentation, writing notes and actually saying them out loud are two entirely different experiences.

The first step is to read your notes aloud until you can say each statement clearly and without hesitation. The second step is to practice your delivery. Initially, you don't need to worry about timing because PowerPoint keeps track of that information for you. After you complete a practice presentation, the time you used for each slide appears below the slide. Review the times to see how long you took with each slide. You may want to take more time with one slide and less time with another. You can use the timing as a guide to polish your delivery.

## Practicing Your Delivery

To become familiar with the notes and to practice delivery, do the following:

**1** Make the Slide Sorter view at 33 percent the active view.

**2** Read the notes for each slide, glancing from the printed notes page to the screen when appropriate.

**Note:** *When you come to the "Timeline" and "Action Plan" slides, simply state that both are in planning at this stage. When you come to slides that another person will be explaining, estimate the amount of time that person will need.*

**3** Repeat step 2 until you are familiar enough with the material to read it or say it aloud without hesitation.

**4** Once you are in front of your computer and prepared to begin your presentation, click the Rehearse Timings button on the Slide Sorter toolbar. Begin speaking when the title screen appears. Press ⏎Enter, or click the left mouse button to advance from slide to slide. Press Esc to terminate the timing at any point.

When you reach the end of the presentation, PowerPoint displays an information box listing the amount of time used in the presentation (see figure 4.5). Click **Y**es to post the times for each slide in the Slide Show view.

**Figure 4.5**
The PowerPoint information box for timing.

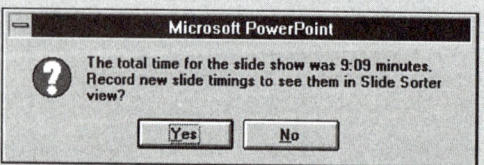

**5** Repeat the timed presentation if you feel that you need the practice.

You may want to change a time on a slide or set the slide back to manual that is, you may want to set the slide to change only when you are ready to continue. This feature is useful when you anticipate discussion or audience participation about a certain slide and feel that an automatic sequence to another slide might be distracting. In the next tutorial, you learn how to change the time to a new setting.

## Setting and Changing Times Manually

To change the time on a particular slide, do the following.

**1** Select slide 5, "Organization."

**2** Choose Transition from the Tools menu.

The Transition dialog box appears (see figure 4.6).

**Figure 4.6**
The Transition
dialog box.

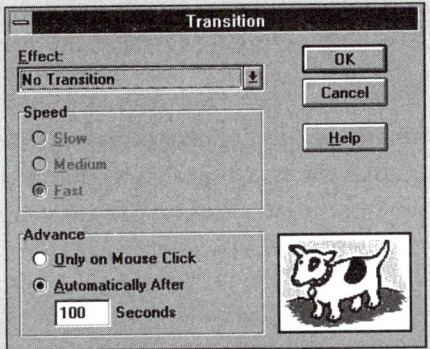

**3** In the Advance options box, change the time to 180 seconds.

**Note:** *You can also use this box to change the advance to manual.*

**4** Click OK.

The Slide Sorter view now displays the slide with the new time.

**Note:** *If the slide show does not run with timings on a computer you are using, you need to select **U**se Slide Timings in the Advance options box on the Slide Show dialog box. You access the Slide Show dialog box by choosing Slide Sho**w** from the **V**iew menu. This dialog box is covered in more detail under Objective 6.*

In an actual presentation, you may want to mix and match transition times. For example, you may want the title slide to remain on-screen while your audience settles in the for the presentation. In this case, set the advance to manual. In other cases, you may want to introduce a subject with one slide and then have an automatic transition to a supporting slide while you are speaking. Even when a time is set on a slide, however, you can interrupt that time and advance the slide manually by clicking the mouse.

# Objective 4: Add Transitions between Slides

When you have put a great deal of work into preparing your presentation, you probably have a mental image of what you want to cover with each point and what information you feel is important. Your task is to share what is in your head with your audience. If you do that job skillfully and convincingly enough, you will bring the audience around to your point of view.

Reread the opening statements you typed for the title slide. The first, or introductory, paragraph should establish what you are doing now—not what you plan to be doing or will be doing. This section uses verbs in the active voice, thus showcasing your actions and the product you are trying to sell.

The second paragraph tells your audience that you mean business and lets people know that you are serious about your presentation.

The third paragraph is the clincher. You have the audience's attention; now present your ideas forcefully. Show them your confidence; make them interested and eager to participate. Use short sentences, "nail" the points, and build anticipation. Make the audience want to see that next slide.

**Transition effects**
The visual way in which one slide replaces another.

Rather than have the next slide simply appear, you can use *transition effects*, such as fades and wipes that change the way one slide replaces another. These effects will add emphasize to your statements. You can add transitions either by choosing **T**ransition from the **T**ools menu or by clicking the Transition button on the Slide Sorter view toolbar.

## Adding Transitions to Your Presentation

To add transition effects to a slide, do the following:

**1** In the Slide Sorter view, select slide 2, "Start-up Strategy."

**2** Choose **T**ransition from the **T**ools menu.

The Transition dialog box appears (refer to figure 4.6).

**3** In the **E**ffect list box, select Box In as the transition effect you want.

**4** Click the **F**ast option button to set the time and preview the effect in the lower right corner of the dialog box.

You can click this button as often as you like. If you want to see some other effects, change the **E**ffect option, and preview various selections. When you finish viewing other options, return to the Box In selection.

**Note:** *The picture in the preview box is only an example.*

**5** Click OK.

A small transition icon appears below the selected slide to indicate that a transition has been set for this slide.

**6** Use the Transition button on the Slide Sorter toolbar to set a Blinds Vertical transition at **S**low speed for slide 8, "Regional Distribution by Cases."

# Objective 5: Add Hidden Slides for Backup

In creating your presentation, you may need to use hidden slides. For example, in this presentation, you have two slides for which the information is not yet available, so displaying these slides during a presentation would be awkward. You could delete these slides, but because they also remind you to obtain the information, you would rather keep them for now.

Another reason for hidden slides is that during a presentation, audience members often ask questions seeking elaboration or foundation for some point you are making. For example, if you are presenting a profit-and-loss statement, the statement itself may be sufficient for most of the members of the audience, but an accountant might want to see your supporting figures. With a prepared hidden slide, you could address those concerns immediately. On the other hand, if no one asks, you don't have to bore your audience with details.

You can hide a slide in any view by choosing **H**ide Slide from the **T**ools menu. If you want to hide multiple slides, you can use the Outline or Slide Sorter view. To hide one or more slides in the Slide Sorter view, select the slide(s), and click the Hide Slide button on the Slide Sorter toolbar.

**No-do bars**
Angled line across a simple picture indicating that the action depicted is not allowed.

When you hide a slide, the *no-do bar* appears over the slide number. This bar, familiar in traffic and warning signs as an angled line across a simple picture, indicates that an action is not allowed. (The no-smoking sign shows a cigarette crossed out by a no-do bar.)

**4**

## Hiding Slides in a Presentation

To hide a slide in the Slide Sorter view, do the following:

**1** In the Slide Sorter view, select slide 10, "Timeline."

**2** Choose **H**ide Slide from the **T**ools menu.

A no-do bar appears over the slide number.

**3** Select slide 11, "Action Plan."

**4** Click the Hide Slide button on the Slide Sorter toolbar. A no-do bar appears over that slide number.

# Objective 6: Present a Slide Show

You should never walk into a presentation without having practiced the presentation and without knowing as much as possible about the subject. Just as an attorney should never ask a witness on a stand a question to which the attorney does not already know the answer, you should never give a presentation in which you or one of your fellow presenters cannot address all the issues raised by that presentation.

Presentations should keep the audience's attention. Just as you added enhancements for the individual slides and transition effects between slides, you can also enhance the overall presentation in various ways. For example, you can have only a portion of a slide appear and build the contents line by line.

You can also annotate your slides during the presentation by using the penlike Freehand Annotation icon to underline words or draw on the slide. Clicking this icon changes the pointer into a pen that you can use to draw on the screen during a presentation. For example, you can put a check mark by a topic, underline a word, or circle a subject. The marks are temporary and disappear when you move to the next slide.

**LCD**

A type of computer screen that can be placed on top of a transparency projector in order to project computer-generated images on a screen.

If you have an *LCD* (Liquid Crystal Display) screen that is used with a transparency projector or a converter that enables you to plug your computer directly into a large television, you can run your slide show from your computer. LCD screens, which are positioned on top of a transparency projector and controlled by the computer, are particularly effective because the images are projected on to a large screen in front of an audience.

## Running a Presentation in a Continuous Loop

If you plan to run a marketing presentation in a continuous loop at a trade show, you will find this feature of PowerPoint particularly exciting. Another reason for running a presentation in a continuous loop is that it gives you an opportunity to observe what your audience will see and to catch any errors that may have crept in during the chaos of creation.

To run the presentation in a continuous loop, do the following:

**1** Choose Slide Sho**w** from the **V**iew menu.

The Slide Show dialog box appears (see figure 4.7).

**Figure 4.7**
The Slide Show dialog box.

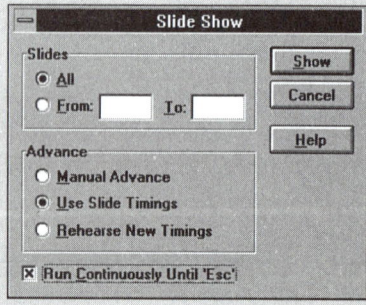

**2** Select **U**se Slide Timings in the Advance option box.

**3** Select Run **C**ontinuously until 'Esc'.

**4** Click **S**how.

**5** Press [Esc] when you have seen enough.

You may want to emphasize special points in a slide by having those points appear as you speak. You can build components of a slide by choosing **B**uild from the **T**ools menu, or by clicking the Build button on the Slide Sorter toolbar.

## Building a Slide for Effect

To build a slide during the presentation, do the following:

**1** In the Slide Sorter view, select slide 2, "Start-up Strategy."

**2** Click the Build button on the Slide Sorter toolbar.

The Build dialog box appears (see figure 4.8).

**Figure 4.8**
The Build dialog box.

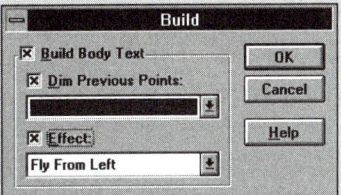

**3** If not selected, select **B**uild Body Text.

**4** Select **D**im Previous Points.

**5** Select the color yellow from the Color drop-down list box.

**6** Select **E**ffect.

**7** Select Fly From Left from the **E**ffects drop-down list box.

**8** Click OK.

The effect Fly From Left now appears in the Build Effects drop-down list box on the Slide Sorter toolbar.

**9** Run the slide show to see the results of your selections.

### Using the Freehand Annotation Tool

You access the Freehand Annotation tool by clicking the Freehand Annotation icon, the small microphone at the lower right of the screen, during a presentation. Any marks you make on the current slide using this tool are temporary and will disappear when you advance to another slide.

## Working with the Freehand Annotation Tool

To use the Freehand Annotation tool, do the following:

**1** Run the slide show.

**2** During the presentation, click the Freehand Annotation icon.

The mouse pointer changes into a pen.

**3** Underline a key word.

**4** Circle a key word.

**5** Click the Arrow icon.

**Note:** *Because this presentation contains hidden slides, a Hidden Slide icon also appears on the slide immediately preceding the hidden slide(s). This icon will be next to the Freehand Annotation icon. If you want to view a hidden slide, select the Hidden Slide icon.*

**6** Press [Esc] to end the presentation.

**7** Save your file to your floppy disk or correct directory as **SOUP1.PPT**

# Chapter Summary

In this chapter, you have learned how to construct and add notes that maintain the tone and theme of a presentation. You have also used the Notes Pages and Slide Sorter views to arrange the slide order for the most effective presentation. This chapter covers the importance of rehearsal and gives you tips on practicing the delivery and timing of your presentation. You have added transitions and used hidden slides. The chapter concludes with tutorials that show you how to build points on a slide and how to annotate a slide during a presentation.

# Checking Your Skills

### True/False Questions

For each of the following statements, circle *T* or *F* to indicate whether the statement is true or false.

T  F  **1.** The primary purpose for frequently saving a presentation file while you are working on it is to preserve a record so that you won't forget what you have done.

T  F  **2.** The mouse pointer appears as a vertical line marker in the Slide Sorter view and denotes the position of the currently selected slide.

T  F  **3.** You start automated timing by clicking the Rehearse Timings button on the Slide Sorter toolbar.

T  F  **4.** Any rehearsal consists of two steps: learning the material and displaying the slides.

T  F  **5.** Freehand Annotation has no permanent effect on a slide.

## Multiple-Choice Questions

In the blank provided, write the letter of the correct answer for each of the following questions.

___ **1.** In the Notes Pages view, _____.

    **a.** PowerPoint presents the suggested content for a presentation created with the AutoContent Wizard

    **b.** both the current slide and the notes page for that slide are displayed at the same time

    **c.** PowerPoint suggests the heading level for each of your talking points

    **d.** both the slide and the notes can be edited

___ **2.** The view that is particularly useful for rearranging slides, setting the timing and transitions between slides, adding or deleting slides, and envisioning the overall presentation is the _____.

    **a.** Slide view

    **b.** Outline view

    **c.** Slide Sorter view

    **d.** Notes Pages view

___ **3.** Both the Notes Pages and the Slide Sorter views are used to _____.

    **a.** insert clip-art images

    **b.** prepare for an oral presentation

    **c.** print outlines

    **d.** record the timing of a presentation

___ **4.** The sequence that best describes the preparation of an oral presentation is first to prepare the slides and then to write _____.

    **a.** and print notes, arrange slide order, and practice delivery and timing

    **b.** notes, arrange slide order, practice delivery and timing, and print notes

    **c.** notes, arrange slide order, print notes, and practice delivery and timing

    **d.** notes, arrange slide order and transitions, print notes, and practice delivery and timing

**4**

___ **5.** One reason for including hidden slides in a presentation is to _____.

    **a.** conceal information that you can use to get ahead

    **b.** include notes to yourself on things you might want to add later

    **c.** hide your mistakes

    **d.** have supporting documentation available in case a member of the audience asks for more information

## Fill-in-the-Blank Questions

In the blank provided, write the correct answer for each of the following questions.

**1.** In the Slide Sorter view, the number of slides that are visible on-screen at any one time depends on the percentage scale you are using and the size of the _____.

**2.** Some comedians maintain that often what makes a joke funny is not the content, but the delivery and the _____.

**3.** You can make certain points appear on-screen as you speak by using the _____ button on the Slide Sorter toolbar.

**4.** A(n) _____ screen is used with a transparency projector to display a presentation on a large screen.

**5.** A(n) _____ bar or line is used on a graphic to indicate that the action depicted by the graphic is not allowed.

# Applying Your Skills

## Review Exercises

### Exercise 1: Moving a Slide in a Prepared Presentation

Your boss has reviewed your presentation and recommends moving slide 12, "Our Strengths," to a position between slide 3, "Mission Statement," and slide 4, "Objectives." He feels that by listing the strengths of the company first, the presentation can build on that positive foundation. Move slide 12 to the position recommended by your boss, print a new set of notes pages, and make any changes in timing and transition that you feel would maintain the continuity of the presentation. Revise SOUP1.PPT, and save the presentation as **SOUP1A.PPT**.

### Exercise 2: Modifying a Prepared Presentation

You have just completed the first organizational meeting of your team, with Ms. Steel reviewing the presentation. Based on the team's agreement with your recommendations, an action plan is decided on and approved. Your task is to complete the "Action Plan" slide using effective text attributes and enhancements, move that slide to the end of the presentation, and make the necessary changes in timing to maintain the continuity of the presentation.

Here is the content for the Action Plan slide:

**Plan Approval**

**Lock in Test Sites**

**Start Pilot Production**

**Authorize Ad Campaign**

**Launch**

Here are the notes for the Action Plan slide:

**With immediate approval, we will target initial test sites, start production at our pilot plant, and authorize our advertising agency to begin the ad campaign. Product launch will occur in 60 days.**

### Exercise 3: Practicing Delivery and Timing

If delivery and timing are the key to a successful comedy act, a little practice can make you the life of the party. Take at least three of your favorite jokes, and create two slides for each one—a name slide that names the joke and a punch-line slide. Write out the joke on the corresponding notes page for each name slide, and print a copy. Practice your timing in the Slide Sorter view. Save your presentation.

---

**Tip**

The name slide will be displayed while you tell the joke. The punch-line slide should pop up when you reach the punch line.

---

## Continuing Projects

### Project 1: Adding Notes and Timing to a Business Presentation

Using the file BOOK1.PPT, which you created in Chapter 3 and the general knowledge that you gained from this chapter about giving an effective presentation, add transitions and notes to each slide. Then set up a timed presentation sequence. Save the presentation as **BOOK2.PPT**.

### Project 2: Adding Notes and Timing to a General Presentation

For the second long project in Chapter 3, you enhanced a general presentation. Now you can add notes, practice your delivery, and develop a timing scheme for the presentation. Save the presentation as **PROJECT1.PPT**.

# CHAPTER 5

# Planning and Building a Presentation

In many ways, PowerPoint makes planning and building an effective presentation easy. The AutoContent Wizard can create suggested presentations and content for a number of standard presentation types. In this chapter, you find out more about what a presentation is, and you learn how to use another PowerPoint feature—the many templates that are based on professional graphics designs. You also work with a Slide Master, which enables you to change certain slide elements on every slide in your presentation.

## Objectives

By the time you have finished this chapter, you will have learned to

1. Understand the Presentation Process

2. Use Templates

3. Work with a Slide Master

4. Work with Individual Slides and Change Their Appearance

## Objective 1: Understand the Presentation Process

"Hello, boss? I'm afraid I'm going to be late this morning. My dog swallowed the car keys. . . . What? Uh, yes, b-b-both sets."

Everyone has to explain something at sometime. Explanations can be as simple as an excuse, as eager as a salesman's pitch, as optimistic as an entrepreneur's business plan, as hopeful as an advertising campaign, as earnest as a resume, or as learned as a professor's lecture, but all have one thing in common. The best explanations are carefully planned.

Visual props—such as charts, graphs, and slides—add another dimension to an explanation, and their use in a presentation should be as carefully planned as the subject or content of the presentation.

**Overheads**

Black-and-white or color transparencies that are projected by a transparency projector.

PowerPoint has many built-in tools and features to help you design a presentation. The AutoContent Wizard offers a selection of starting points. PowerPoint also provides a wide variety of professionally designed templates for creating *overheads*, both in black and white and color; 35mm slides; and video screen displays. The Pick a Look Wizard provides access to different views of the same presentation. A Slide Master can be modified to change either a template or a presentation. Individual slides can be enhanced with special text effects, illustrations, and objects imported from other programs.

The creator of a presentation must pay close attention to both elements of the presentation—the content and the design—and the key to a successful and convincing presentation is careful planning. Although it is certainly possible to build a glitzy presentation full of color and attractive images that give the illusion of substance, ultimately your audience will perceive the lack of depth.

## Understanding Presentation Content

When developing a presentation, you should know as much about the content as possible because the audience will look on you as the expert. When planning the presentation, you must determine your objective because the audience expects you to provide the answers. When building a presentation, you must maintain the focus, because the audience expects you to be clear and convincing.

In earlier chapters, you learned some of the basics for creating a good presentation:

1. State the problem or project.

2. Present the salient points that support your premise.

3. Provide a solution or plan.

A variant of this structure is "Tell the audience what you are going to say, say it, and then tell the audience what you said."

If you examine any chapter in this book, for example, you will see that each chapter opens with a short statement about what the chapter contains and a list of objectives, followed by the substance in the middle, and ending with a short summary of what you should have learned. The substance is accurate and informative, and each chapter maintains focus by concentrating on a group of related activities. In addition, each chapter is professionally designed and laid out in a clear and attractive format.

If you keep these elements in mind when planning a presentation, you can build a strong, effective, and convincing presentation.

## Analyzing Presentation Plans

One way to learn about planning a presentation is to analyze an existing presentation. To analyze a presentation, do the following:

**1** Start PowerPoint, and load the file SOUP1.PPT.

**2** Make the Outline view the current view, and print a copy of the outline.

**3** Indicate the purpose of each slide by making a note next to each.

**4** In a short paragraph, describe the plan for this presentation.

Many people find it useful to draft an outline of a presentation before creating it in PowerPoint.

## Drafting a Presentation Plan

To draft a presentation outline, do the following:

**1** Some people believe that electronic textbooks are the wave of the future. Examine Chapter 4 in this book, and consider what would be involved in turning that chapter into a PowerPoint presentation. Would you reorganize the information in any way? What would each slide contain?

**2** Using your favorite word processing software, draft an outline of a proposed electronic presentation of Chapter 4.

**5**

# Objective 2: Use Templates

PowerPoint provides an extensive library of predesigned templates for black-and-white or color overheads or transparencies, 35mm slides, and video display screens—each of these groups containing templates specifically designed for that group.

**Template**
A pattern for a slide or presentation.

When you created your first presentation using the AutoContent Wizard, you were using a default template that contained information on colors, fonts and sizes, and object placement. A *template* is a pattern for a slide or presentation that contains information about the placement, style, and type of text and graphics areas, as well as special objects such as logos, boxes or borders, and artistic text effects. If you do not like the appearance of the default template, you can apply another template design. You can also create your own template if you like.

One of the benefits of using predesigned templates, however, is that each template was created by a professional graphics artist familiar with the use of text, color, and graphics in a presentation. In most cases, using a predesigned template frees you to concentrate on the content of the presentation instead of having to worry about the layout and design.

**Pick a Look Wizard**
A tool for changing the appearance of a presentation.

**Supplementary materials**
Additional materials provided by PowerPoint to assist in a presentation.

You can use the *Pick a Look Wizard* to select or change a template for a presentation. In addition, you can use this wizard to change or add the supplementary materials, such as speaker's notes and handouts, that you will use in your presentation. For example, you can use the Pick a Look Wizard to customize handouts that you give to the members of your audience.

You can also customize the *supplementary materials* by adding the name of your company or division, a message of some sort, page numbers, and the current date.

## Using the Pick a Look Wizard with an Existing Presentation

You can use the Pick a Look Wizard before building a presentation, or you can use it to apply a template to an existing presentation. To use the Pick a Look Wizard, do the following:

**1** Save the SOUP1 presentation as **SOUP2**, which will become the current presentation.

**2** In the Slide view, with slide 1, the title slide, the active slide, choose Pick a Look **W**izard from the **F**ormat menu.

The Pick a Look Wizard Step 1 of 9 dialog box appears (see figure 5.1).

**Figure 5.1**
The Pick a Look Wizard - Step 1 of 9 dialog box.

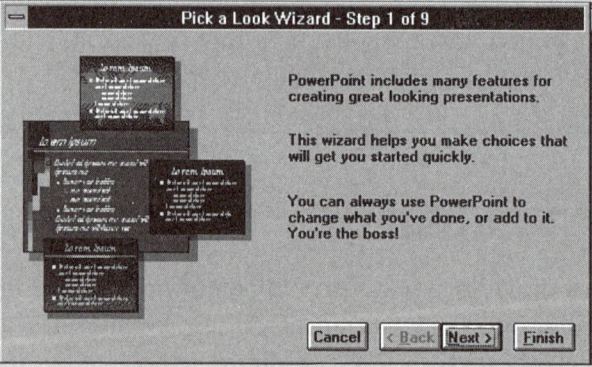

**3** Click the **N**ext button.

The Pick a Look Wizard Step 2 of 9 dialog box appears (see figure 5.2).

**Figure 5.2**
The Pick a Look Wizard - Step 2 of 9 dialog box.

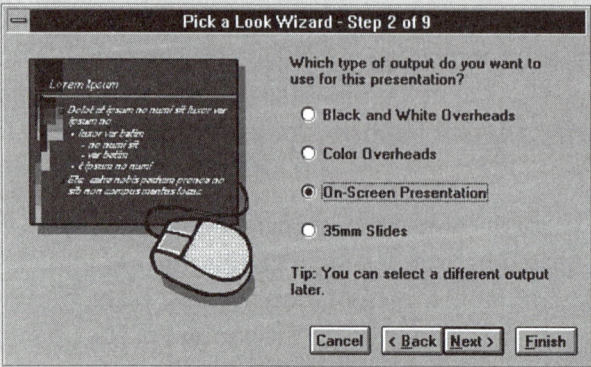

④ Select the On-Screen Presentation option.

⑤ Click the **N**ext button.

The Pick a Look Wizard Step 3 of 9 dialog box appears (see figure 5.3).

**Figure 5.3**
The Pick a Look
Wizard - Step 3
of 9 dialog box.

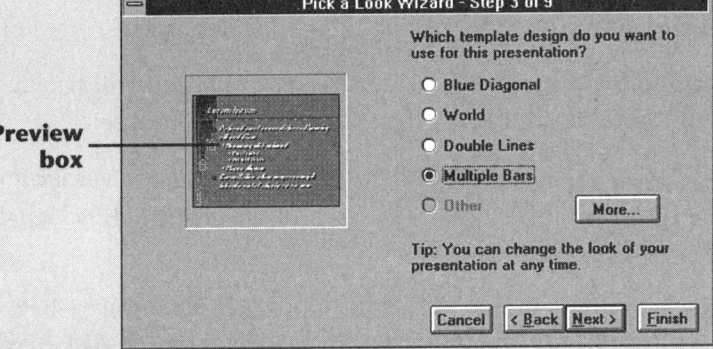

④ Select each in turn, and observe the change in the preview box.

Each selection is previewed as you make your selection. Notice that the Other selection is dimmed.

⑦ Click the More button.

The Presentation Template dialog box appears (see figure 5.4).

**Figure 5.4**
The Presentation
Template dialog
box.

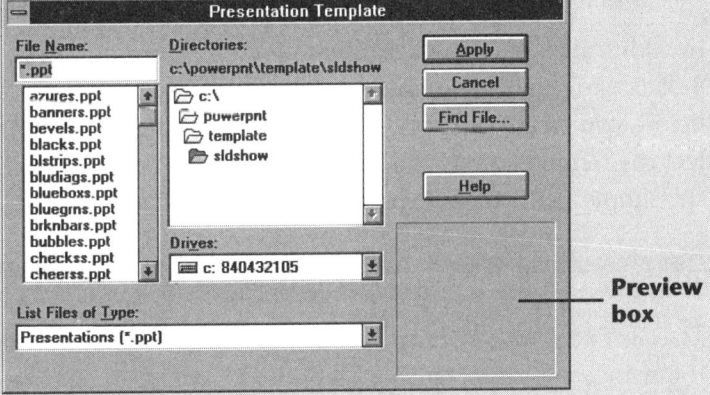

⑧ To view examples of each template design, start with AZURES.PPT, and click each desired file in turn.

⑨ Select the template SIDEBARS.PPT.

⑩ Click the **A**pply button.

(continues)

## Using the Pick a Look Wizard with an Existing Presentation (continued)

The Pick a Look Wizard Step 3 of 9 dialog box reappears. If you wanted, you could continue using the wizard's additional dialog boxes. Because you are only changing a template in this tutorial, these additional features will be examined in the next tutorial.

⓫ Click **F**inish to conclude the changing of the template.

Changing the template design for this presentation will take as long as several minutes, depending on the speed of your computer.

**Note:** *If a PowerPoint warning box appears saying that an element of the current presentation cannot be found, click OK. The application of the template will continue.*

⓬ The new template design and color scheme is on-screen. Click the Next Slide button, or run the presentation to view how the new design was applied to each slide in the presentation.

⓭ Save the presentation as **SOUP2.PPT**.

⓮ Close the presentation by choosing **C**lose from the **F**ile menu.

After planning a presentation, you generally have a good idea of how you want that presentation to appear. For example, if the presentation deals with travel plans to a tropical island, you probably would want to use either the travel template, which contains a plane in its basic design, or the island template. A plan for international financing of a global enterprise might use the world template.

In addition to selecting a template for a new presentation, you may want to make changes to that template. For this reason, selecting the template design before you create the presentation is usually a good idea. In addition, if you select the template first, you can use the Pick a Look Wizard to set the options for the supplements to your presentation.

## Choosing a Template for a New Presentation

To select a template design and set the options for a new presentation, do the following:

❶ Choose **N**ew from the **F**ile menu.

The New Presentation dialog box appears.

❷ Select the **P**ick a Look Wizard option.

❸ Click OK.

The Pick a Look Wizard Step 1 of 9 dialog box appears (refer to figure 5.1).

❹ Click the **N**ext button.

The Pick a Look Wizard Step 2 of 9 dialog box appears (refer to figure 5.2).

**5** Select the Color Overheads option, and click the **N**ext button.

The Pick a Look Wizard Step 3 of 9 dialog box appears (refer to figure 5.3).

**6** Click the More button, and select DIAMONDC.PPT as the template from the Presentation Template dialog box (refer to figure 5.4).

**7** Click **A**pply in this dialog box and the **N**ext button from the Pick a Look Wizard Step 3 of 9 dialog box.

The Pick a Look Wizard Step 4 of 9 dialog box appears (see figure 5.5).

**Figure 5.5**
The Pick a Look Wizard - Step 4 of 9 dialog box.

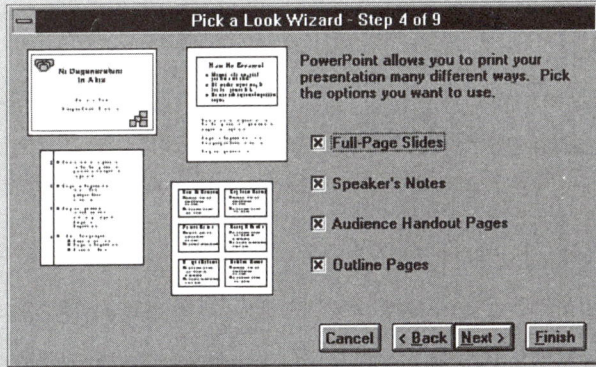

**8** Select all four options for printing the supplemental materials, and click the **N**ext button.

The Pick a Look Wizard Slide Options dialog box appears (see figure 5.6).

**Figure 5.6**
The Pick a Look Wizard - Slide Options dialog box.

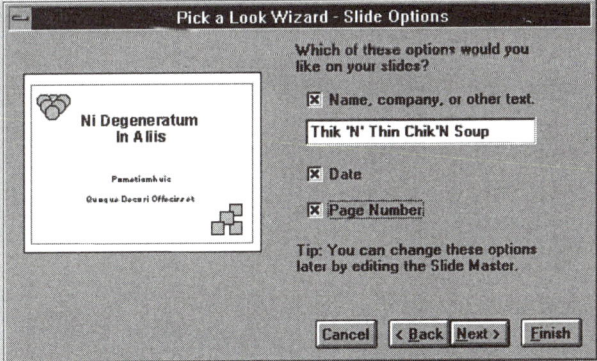

**9** Select the Name, Company, or Other Text option.

**10** In the edit box, type **Thik 'N' Thin Chik'N Soup.** (If necessary, delete any other text in the box.)

**11** Select the Date box.

**12** Select the Page Number box.

*(continues)*

**Choosing a Template for a New Presentation (continued)**

Selecting these options prints the text, date, and page number on each slide.

**13** Click the **N**ext button.

The Pick a Look Wizard Notes Options dialog box appears (see figure 5.7).

**Figure 5.7**
The Pick a Look Wizard - Notes Options dialog box.

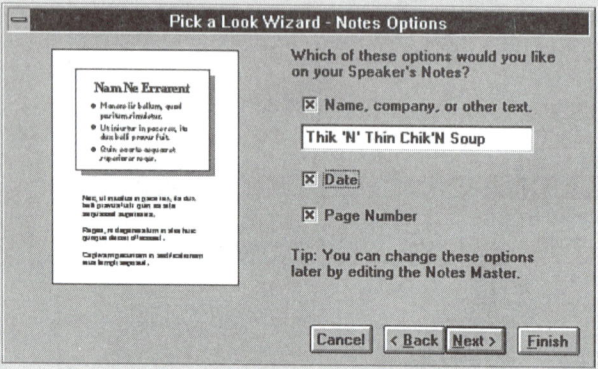

The text entered in the preceding dialog box was carried forward to this dialog box.

**14** Select the same options you selected in the preceding dialog box.

**15** Click the **N**ext box.

The Pick a Look Wizard Handout Options dialog box appears (see figure 5.8).

**Figure 5.8**
The Pick a Look Wizard - Handout Options dialog box.

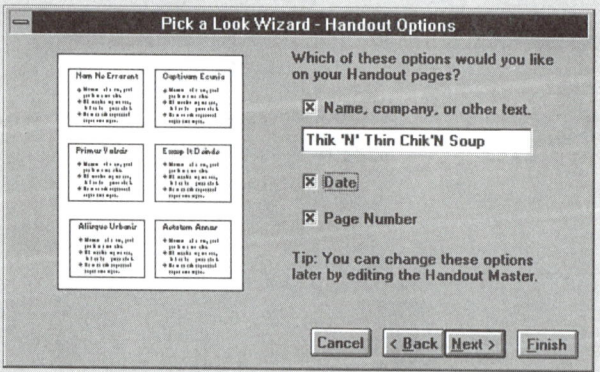

**16** Select all the options, and click the **N**ext button.

The Pick a Look Wizard Outline Options dialog box appears (see figure 5.9).

**Figure 5.9**

The Pick a Look Wizard - Outline Options dialog box.

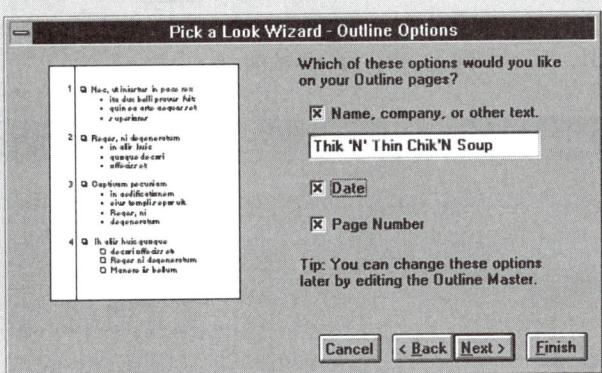

⑰ Select all the options, and click the **N**ext button.

The Pick a Look Wizard Step 9 of 9 dialog box appears. This information box marks the end of the Pick a Look Wizard dialog box series.

⑱ Click the **F**inish button.

⑲ When the title screen for this new presentation appears in the presentation window, move the title object box to the top of the slide. The title object will overlap the diamond in the upper left corner. Save the presentation as **ADV1.PPT**.

**5**

**Tip**

You can change the template for this file at any time by selecting the Pick a Look Wizard to choose and apply a new template. One drawback, however, is that the wizard does not remember any of the changes you may have made to this template; so you will have to set all the options again.

# Objective 3: Work with a Slide Master

**Master slide**

The slide that provides formatting of the basic slide elements for all slides in a presentation.

The key to a template design is the *master slide*, which is the slide in each template that controls the appearance of all slides in that presentation. By changing the design elements on a master slide, you change the template to a custom design and automatically apply that design to all the slides in the presentation.

If you save your new design before adding any slides, you can create your own template file for future presentations.

You can change the master slide for an existing or a new presentation. Changing the design of the master slide for an existing presentation changes the design for all slides in that presentation. Because this change can affect color schemes and other objects on the existing slides, it is usually best to customize the template design before building your presentation.

You access master slides by holding down ⬆Shift when clicking a view button on the status bar. If you add a new slide from one of the master slides, the new slide becomes the first slide in the presentation.

## Customizing a Master Slide Text Styles

When you customize a master slide, you can determine fonts and font sizes, add clip art such as a company logo, and even add text that will appear on every slide in the presentation.

To work with the Slide Master and customize the text styles in a master slide, do the following:

❶ With ADV1 as the current presentation, choose **M**aster from the **V**iew menu.

A submenu appears.

❷ Choose **S**lide Master from the submenu.

The master slide appears with placeholders indicating the existing elements that can be edited (see figure 5.10).

**Figure 5.10**
The master slide in the Slide Master view.

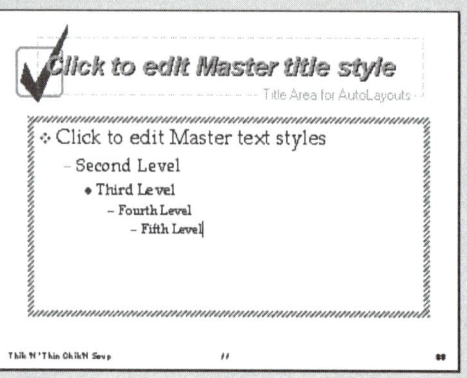

❸ Click the title placeholder box.

The border is highlighted, indicating that the title box has been selected.

❹ Position the mouse pointer immediately to the left of the `C` in `Click`, and highlight the words `Click to edit Master title style`.

❺ From the Font drop-down list box, select Arial.

❻ From the Font Size drop-down list box, select 40.

❼ Click the Bold button on the Formatting toolbar.

❽ Click the Text Shadow button on the Formatting toolbar.

❾ Click anywhere outside the title text box.

A new font, Arial, and size, 40 points, have been selected for the title line. The attributes applied to the title line are boldface and shadowed text. You can edit the text in the bottom placeholder text box in a similar way if you want.

**Permanent text**
Text on a master slide, that is reproduced on all slides in a presentation.

In the preceding tutorial, you made changes to the text in style, formatting, and attributes only. These styles will be applied to all the title lines of the slides in the presentation even though the actual text content will vary. You can, however, add to the master slide a *permanent text* block that will reproduce the same text on every slide.

## Adding Permanent Text to a Master Slide

To add a permanent text block to the master slide, do the following:

❶ Click the Text Tool button on the Drawing toolbar (the button with the letter *A*).

❷ Position the mouse pointer just above the T in the line `Thik 'N' Thin Chik'N Soup` in the lower left corner of the master slide, and click the left mouse button.

❸ Type the words **Mom's Home Cookin'**.

❹ Click anywhere outside the text box.

**5**

The company name is now part of the master slide. You can edit the text in this block and change the font, size, and formatting if desired. You can also add illustrations—including scanned photographs, clip art, and company logos—to the master slide.

## Adding Illustrations to a Master Slide

To add an illustration to the master slide, do the following:

❶ Position the mouse pointer on the diamond at the top of the master slide but outside the title text area, and click the left mouse button.

The diamond is actually contained within its own graphics box. When you click the diamond, the sizing handles for this box become visible (see figure 5.11).

(continues)

## Adding Illustrations to a Master Slide (continued)

**Figure 5.11**
The master slide with graphics box containing the diamond highlighted.

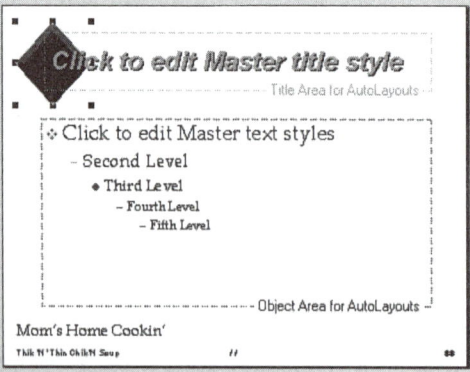

**2** Press ∂ .

This step removes the diamond design.

**3** Choose **C**lip Art from the **I**nsert menu.

The ClipArt Gallery dialog box appears.

**Note:** *If you had chosen **P**icture from the **I**nsert menu, an Insert Picture dialog box would have appeared, from which you could select a directory and a picture file with a PCX, TIF, BMP, or other extension compatible with PowerPoint.*

**4** Select the SYMBOLS clip-art file and the check mark clip art, and click OK.

The clip art appears in the center of the slide.

**5** Position the mouse pointer inside the graphics object box that contains the clip art. Press and hold the left mouse button, and drag the box to the upper left corner of the master slide, positioning the left border of the box so that it is aligned with the M in Mom's in the lower left corner (see figure 5.12). Change the size of the check mark if necessary.

**Figure 5.12**
The master slide with clip-art selection in position.

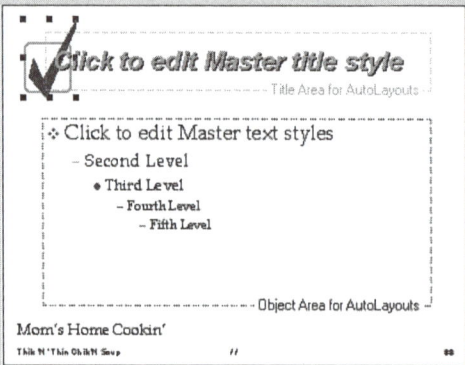

**6** Position the mouse pointer over the Drawing toolbar, and click the right mouse button.

The Toolbar menu appears.

**7** Select the Drawing+ toolbar.

The Drawing+ toolbar appears on-screen.

**8** Click the Send Backward button on the Drawing+ toolbar.

This step places the clip art in the background on the master slide.

Because the final design of the master slide will have the title line slightly over-lapping the clip art, the color of the title should be a contrasting color against the backdrop of the red check mark.

## Changing Text Colors on a Master Slide

To change the title line text color, do the following:

**1** Select the text line `Click to edit Master title style`.

**2** Click the Text Color button on the Formatting toolbar.

The Color drop-down list box appears (see figure 5.13).

**Figure 5.13**
The highlighted title text and Color list box.

**3** Select the color blue.

**4** With the title line still selected, click the Left Align button on the Format-ting toolbar.

**5** With the title line still selected, click the Bring Forward and Send Backward buttons on the Drawing+ toolbar, until the title line overlaps the clip art.

**6** Click anywhere outside the object box areas.

Objects on a slide can be grouped so that they maintain the same positions rela-tive to each other. You can then work with them as a group.

## Grouping Objects on the Master Slide

To group objects on the slide, do the following:

**1** Position the mouse pointer above and slightly to the left of the graphics object containing the clip art.

**2** Press and hold the left mouse button.

The mouse pointer changes to a cross.

**3** Drag the cross down and to the right to encompass both the clip art and the title line.

A black-dotted, rectangular lasso follows the cross.

**4** Release the mouse button.

**5** Choose **G**roup from the **D**raw menu.

You can also choose the Group button on the Drawing+ toolbar. Now the title line and the clip art move together.

**6** Save the file as **ADV1.PPT**.

**7** Click the Slide View button.

The changes made in the Slide Master will now be duplicated in all new slides added to the presentation.

You can duplicate the existing file format in a new file without copying the content.

## Duplicating an Existing File Format

To create a new presentation file with the format of the existing file (but not the same content), do the following:

**1** Make slide 1, the title slide of the file ADV1, the current slide.

**2** Choose **N**ew from the **F**ile menu.

The New Presentation dialog box appears.

**3** Select the **C**urrent Presentation Format bullet.

**4** Click OK.

The New Slide dialog box appears.

**5** Select the title slide.

**6** Click OK.

**7** Save the new file as **ADV2**.

You will use this file in a later tutorial.

**8** Close the file ADV2.PPT.

The file ADV1 should be the current presentation.

# Objective 4: Work with Individual Slides and Change Their Appearance

You can duplicate slides, insert new slides, and make changes in the layout, fonts, and colors on any individual slide. This capability enables you to control both the appearance of the individual elements of your presentation and its overall appearance. If you plan to make a series of slides with the same basic format but with individual enhancements, creating the format and individual enhancements before creating the presentation is usually the best method.

## Duplicating a Series of Slides

PowerPoint provides several quick ways to duplicate a slide. To duplicate a series of slides, do the following:

**1** With the file ADV1 as your current file, switch to the Slide Sorter view.

One slide is shown.

**2** With the title slide selected, choose **D**uplicate from the **E**dit menu.

A duplicate of slide 1, the title slide, appears as slide 2.

**3** With slide 2 selected, press Ctrl+D once.

The series now consists of five slides.

You can create text on one slide, copy it to another, and then change the colors.

## Changing Color on a Slide

To copy and change text colors on individual slides, do the following:

**1** In the Slide Sorter view, double-click slide 1, the title slide.

The screen changes to the Slide view.

**2** Click the title box, and type **Thik 'N' Thin Chik'N Soup 1**.

(continues)

5

## Changing Color on a Slide (continued)

**3** Highlight the title line, and click the Copy button on the Standard toolbar.

**4** Click the Next Slide button on the vertical scroll bar.

**5** Click the title box on slide 2.

**6** Click the Paste button on the Standard toolbar.

**7** Replace the 1 in the title line with the number **2**.

**8** Select the title line of slide 2, and click the Text Color button on the Formatting toolbar.

**9** Choose Other Color from the Text Color drop-down list box.

The Other Color dialog box appears (see figure 5.14).

**Figure 5.14**
The Other Color dialog box.

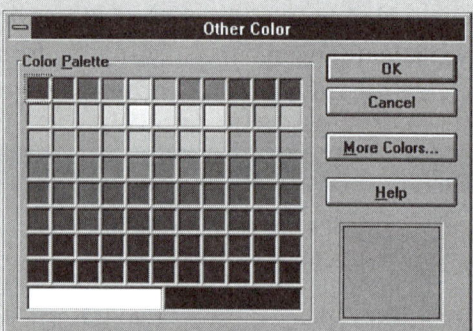

**10** Select the fourth box on the first row: yellow.

If these colors do not give the choice you want, you can click the **M**ore Colors button to see additional colors.

**11** Click OK.

**12** Click anywhere off the title box. The title line of slide 2 is now yellow.

In effect, you now have two title slides: numbers 1 and 2. The use of different colors for the title lines is designed to alert the audience that the second slide is different from the first.

Although the master slide sets the colors for slides added by using the New Slide button on the horizontal toolbar, you can change the colors.

## Changing Backgrounds on a New Slide

To change the colors on a new slide, do the following:

**1** With ADV1 the current file, click the **N**ext Slide button, and make slide 3 the active slide.

**2** Click the New Slide button on the status bar.

**3** The New Slide dialog box appears (see figure 5.15).

**Figure 5.15**
The New Slide dialog box.

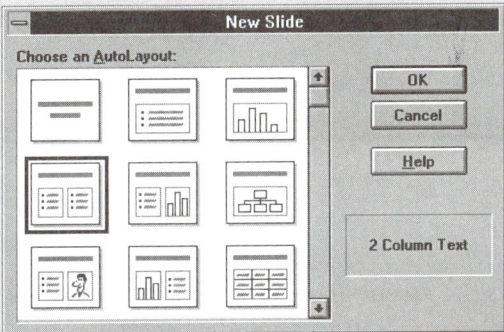

**4** Select the 2 Column Text slide, and click OK.

**5** With the new slide the active slide, select the left-column text box.

**6** Click the Fill Color button on the Drawing+ toolbar.

The Fill Color list box appears (see figure 5.16).

**Figure 5.16**
The two-column slide with the Fill Color list box.

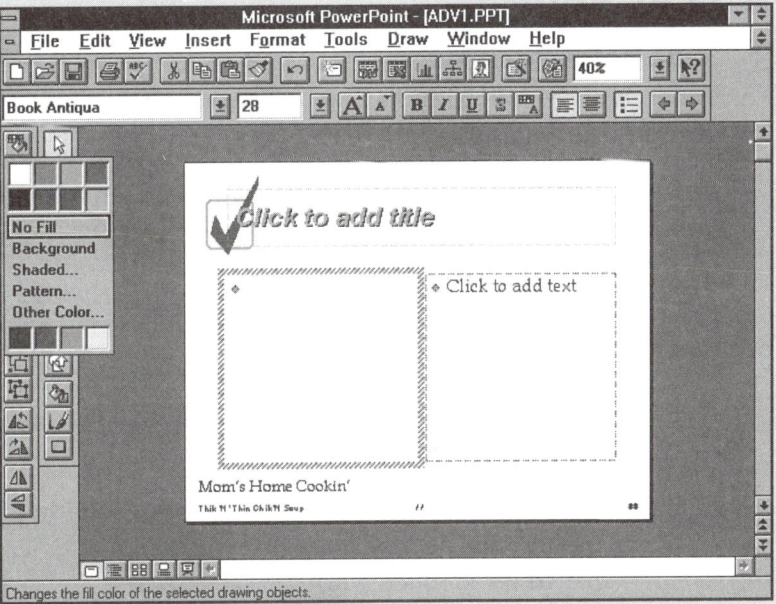

(continues)

**Changing Backgrounds on a New Slide (continued)**

**7** Select the Other Color option.

The Other Color dialog box appears.

**8** Select the yellow box on the first row, and click OK.

**9** Select the right-column text box.

**10** Click the Fill Color button again, and select the color blue.

The background of the first column is now yellow, the second, blue.

**11** Save and close the file as **ADV1.PPT**.

# Chapter Summary

This chapter covers the essential elements of a presentation, stressing that careful planning is important to effective and convincing presentations. The chapter shows how to use any of the many predesigned templates provided by PowerPoint and how to use the Slide Master to modify the master slide in a presentation so that elements attached to the master slide are repeated throughout the presentation. You also learned how to duplicate slides and how to change certain elements of both duplicated and new slides.

# Checking Your Skills

### True/False Questions

For each of the following statements, circle *T* or *F* to indicate whether the statement is true or false.

T  F  **1.** One way to learn about planning a presentation is to analyze an existing presentation.

T  F  **2.** In most cases, a predesigned template frees you to concentrate on the content of the presentation without having to worry about the structure and design.

T  F  **3.** The Pick a Look Wizard enables you to select and print supplements for a presentation.

T  F  **4.** Customizing the template design before building your presentation is usually best because changing the design after a presentation is completed is too much work.

T  F  **5.** The fastest way to duplicate a slide is to click the New Slide button on the horizontal toolbar in the Slide view.

## Multiple-Choice Questions

In the blank provided, write the letter of the correct answer for each of the following questions.

___ **1.** The creator of a presentation must pay close attention to both elements of a presentation. These elements are _____.

    **a.** the content and the design

    **b.** the content and the template

    **c.** the content and the visuals

    **d.** the problem and the solution

___ **2.** One category of predesigned templates not provided by PowerPoint is _____.

    **a.** color overheads

    **b.** 35mm slides

    **c.** color on-screen presentations

    **d.** color story boards

___ **3.** When you created your first presentation using the AutoContent Wizard, you were using a default template that contained information on colors, fonts and sizes, and _____.

    **a.** object placement

    **b.** creating an outline

    **c.** the company logo

    **d.** the number of slides in the presentation

___ **4.** By changing the design elements on a master slide, you change the template to a custom design and automatically apply that design to all _____.

    **a.** the text slides in the presentation

    **b.** the slides in the presentation

    **c.** future presentations built in the current session

    **d.** title slides in currently active multiple presentations

___ **5.** Objects placed in the background on a slide are _____.

    **a.** transparent

    **b.** not visible on-screen

    **c.** displayed behind objects placed in the foreground

    **d.** displayed in front of objects placed in the foreground

5

### Fill-in-the-Blank Questions

In the blank provided, write the correct answer for each of the following questions.

1. The best explanations or presentations are those that are carefully _____.

2. You can change the _____ for a presentation design at any time by selecting the Pick a Look Wizard.

3. The key to a template design is the _____ slide.

4. One way to duplicate a slide is first to select the slide to be duplicated and then to press Ctrl + _____.

5. You can copy just the _____ of a presentation file and not the content to a new file if you like the template design.

# Applying Your Skills

## Review Exercises

### Exercise 1: Analyzing a Presentation for Structure

Load and print an outline of the file CHICKEN1. Analyze the outline, and evaluate the slides for the role each slide plays in the presentation.

### Exercise 2: Changing the Look of a Business Presentation

With the file CHICKEN1 as the active file and using the Pick a Look Wizard, select a new template design for this presentation. Save the file as **CHICKEN2**. Be prepared to justify your selection.

### Exercise 3: Adding New Art to an Existing Presentation

Create a new presentation, **CHICKEN3**, by copying just the format of CHICKEN2 to the new file. Modify the master slide by adding the check-mark clip-art symbol. Make sure that the art object is in the background and the title line is in the foreground.

## Continuing Projects

### Project 1: Planning a Presentation

Your company is awarding an all-expense paid trip to London for the lucky customer who writes the winning last line of a company jingle. The trip is for a family of four. It includes air fare from any city in America to Philadelphia, first-class seats from Philadelphia to London's Heathrow Airport, hotel accommodations, and return fares. All taxis and tips to and from the White House Hotel are prepaid.

Here is the London itinerary:

Day 1: Arrive in London at 6 a.m., register at hotel, noon luncheon, bus tour of London, dinner.

Day 2: Visit Buckingham Palace, Hyde Park, lunch, Tower of London, dinner, night tour of London.

Day 3: Morning shopping tour, afternoon free, dinner, theatre.

Day 4: Day trip to Shakespeare's home, evening free.

Day 5: Return to America.

Here is the jingle:

I have baked many a cake,

From white to brown to yellow,

But the very best cake I ever did bake,

_____.

Planning is one of the most important elements in creating a presentation. Your task is to use your favorite word processing program to write a rough draft for a presentation that will be used to promote the contest. Your company is considering distributing the presentation to cooking classes given in continuing education courses. Your draft should focus on the purpose of the presentation and contain all the elements of an effective presentation. Save the file as **PROJECT1.PPT**.

**Exercise 2: Using an Existing Presentation as the Basis for a New Presentation**
Your company has decided to go ahead with the presentation on the London prize. Load PROJECT1.PPT, and save it as **JINGLE1.PPT**. Make appropriate changes to the master slide that will give this presentation its own unique character. Use the Outline view to create an outline based on your rough draft completed in the first long project.

**5**

# CHAPTER 6

# Converting Existing Information into a Presentation

One of the benefits of using PowerPoint is the program's capability to import material from other programs, such as word processors, databases, spreadsheets, and graphics programs. Many businesses and other groups require materials from various applications. For example, business and educational materials are often created in several different programs. A business plan could require a word processor to write the documentation, a spreadsheet program to calculate the financial statements, and a database to store customer and product names. A psychology report might require a word processor to produce the surveys and documentation, a database to record and tabulate the results of a survey, and a statistical program to generate meaningful statistics. PowerPoint enables you to import the data rather than retype it.

**Import**
To bring a document or selection created in one computer program into another computer program.

PowerPoint has the capability to *import* information created in a variety of other programs. As a result, you can bring in files created in other programs and adapt these files for use in PowerPoint. For example, you can take an outline written in a word processing program and use that outline to create a new presentation, or you can incorporate the outline into an existing presentation. You are not restricted to Microsoft products. You can also use such programs as AmiPro, Lotus 1-2-3, WordPerfect, and Harvard Graphics for source material.

This chapter uses information from two Microsoft products, Word 6 for Windows and Excel 5, as well as information created in other programs to build presentations. You learn how to use existing information in your presentations and how to update a presentation automatically when the source information changes.

In this chapter, you build a presentation based on the history of Mom's Home Cookin' Soup Company. The creation of this presentation is made much easier because of PowerPoint's capability to use information that was created in other programs.

# Objectives

By the time you have finished this chapter, you will have learned to

1. Turn a Word Document into a Presentation

2. Insert Word Outlines into Presentations

3. Copy Text from Word into PowerPoint

4. Copy from Excel

5. Add Worksheets from Excel

6. Use Automatic Links to Excel Data

7. Move Slides between Presentations

# Objective 1: Turn a Word Document into a Presentation

**RTF**
A method used by many word processing programs to format text documents that retain certain minimal attributes.

Outlines formatted in Word 6 for Windows can be imported and used to generate an entire presentation or segments of a presentation. PowerPoint can also use outlines created in Word for DOS or any other word processing programs capable of having files saved either in *RTF* (Rich Text Format) or in *ASCII* (an acronym for American Standard Code for Information Interchange). RTF is a method of saving a file so that it retains certain minimal formatting attributes, and ASCII is a plain-text format that can be used to create outlines.

**ASCII**
A seven-bit standard code that produces an electronic file consisting primarily of alphanumeric characters.

With Word 6 for Windows, a presentation can travel in both directions. A PowerPoint feature known as Report It can export a presentation outline to Word, which you can start from within PowerPoint. You can then use Word's powerful editing features to edit the document. When you finish editing, you can return to PowerPoint and import the edited file.

## Writing an Outline in Word 6 for Windows

**Note:** *If you don't have or use Word 6 for Windows, write the outline in your favorite word processor, and save the file in RTF format if available. If RTF is not available, write the outline using tabs to mark the outline levels, and save your work in an ASCII (plain or text) format.*

To write an outline in Word 6 for Windows, do the following:

**❶** Start Word for Windows; then open the file MOMSAGA.DOC.

**Note:** *A copy of this file is available on the instructor's resource disk for this book.*

In the following outline, section headings are leftmost, with each indent representing a sublevel. If you are using Word's Outline view (see figure

6.1) to construct the outline, select the heading style from the Style drop-down list box on the Formatting toolbar. Do not use any numbering.

**Figure 6.1**
The Outline view in Microsoft Word 6 for Windows.

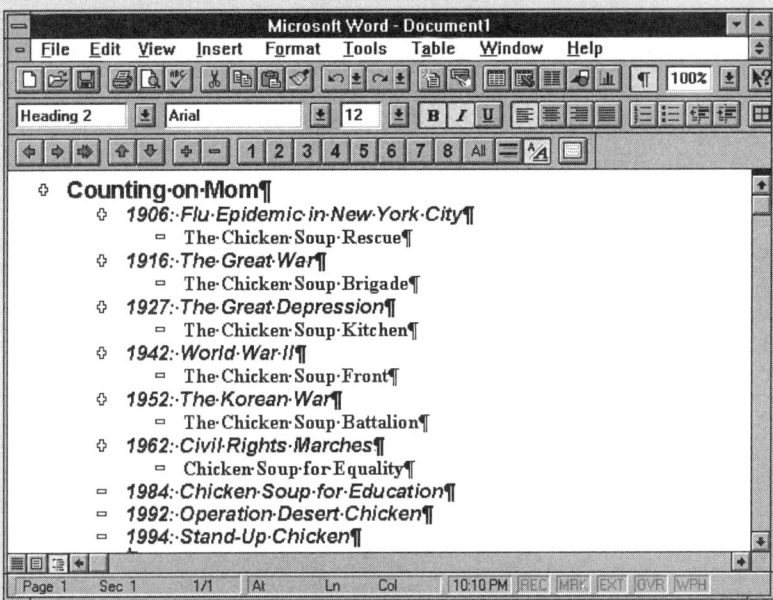

**2** Create an outline by typing the following information:

**Counting on Mom**

**1906: Flu Epidemic in New York City**

    **The Chicken Soup Rescue**

**1916: The Great War**

    **The Chicken Soup Brigade**

**1927: The Great Depression**

    **The Chicken Soup Kitchens**

**1942: World War II**

    **The Chicken Soup Front**

**1952: The Korean War**

    **The Chicken Soup Battalion**

**1962: Civil Rights Marches**

    **Chicken Soup for Equality**

**1984: Chicken Soup for Education**

**1992: Operation Desert Chicken**

(continues)

**1994: Stand-Up Chicken**

   **A Real American Heroine**

The 20th Century dawned in America, full of promise, with portents of economic and intellectual advances unparalleled in human history. In New York City, a young maiden was getting married. The year was 1900. Her name was Rebecca Weissman.

Her personal tragedy: Her first-born child died in childbirth. She could never have another child.

But Rebecca was the stuff of destiny. Unable to have any more children of her own, she was to become America's mother, known affectionately throughout the land simply as "Mom."

1906: Flu Epidemic in New York City

The Epidemic

   Thousands of children were sick with fever

   Mothers were too ill to cook

   Families were starving

The Chicken Soup Rescue

   Rebecca travels to Long Island on a mission of mercy

   She begs Long Island chicken farmers for help

   Thousands of chickens were donated

   Healthy volunteers cooked gallons of chicken soup

   Still others carried chicken soup to the sick

1916: The Great War

   Nary a Chicken Over There

   Our boys were in the trenches

   Farms and hamlets devastated by war

   No chicken soup in Gay Paree

The Chicken Soup Brigade

   President Wilson authorizes tanker conversion

   Ship load of soup arrives at front

   Red Cross sets up chicken soup distribution

**Classic Picture:**

**Doughboy eating cup of steaming chicken soup**

**1929: The Great Depression**

**Stock Market Crashes**

**Thousands lose jobs**

**No work, no food**

**Thousands starving**

**The Chicken Soup Kitchens**

**Rebecca journeys to Georgia on a mission of mercy**

**She begs Georgia farmers for help**

**Thousands of chickens donated**

**Volunteers set up chicken soup lines in cities**

**1942: World War II**

**The Chicken Soup Front**

**Mom converts plants to war effort**

**Women replace men in factories**

**Produces thousands of tins of chicken soup for GIs**

**Organizes chicken soup bond rallies**

**Announces powdered chicken soup**

**Classic Picture:**

**GI Joe eating steaming chicken soup from helmet**

**1952: The Korean War**

**The Chicken Soup Battalion**

**Mom announces Chicken Soup C-Rations**

**Chicken soup stalls Chinese invasion**

**Allies award Mom Medal of Valor**

**Classic Picture:**

**Jarhead drinking steaming chicken soup from shell casing**

(continues)

6

**1962: Civil Rights Marches**

Chicken Soup for Equality

Mom meets Dr. King

Mom organizes school bus kitchens

Chicken soup cooked on marches

President Johnson gives Mom Freedom Medal

**1967: An Era Passes**

Mom goes public

Mom passes reins to younger generation

Mom retires to Miami Beach

Thousands attend Mom's funeral

**1984: Chicken Soup for Education**

Free chicken soup for poor children

Chicken soup scholarships announced

Chicken soup panacea research funded

Chuck the Chicken Hatched

**1992: Operation Desert Chicken**

Chicken Soup Coolers Unveiled

Chuck the Chicken Dons Desert Camouflage

Chuck the Chicken goes to war

Classic Picture:

Chuck the Chicken jogs with President Bush

**1994: Stand-Up Chicken**

Chuck the Chicken, the Movie

Chuck the Chicken Day Care Centers Open

Thik 'N' Thin Chik'N Soup Announced

Chuck the Chicken Releases Exercise Video

**3** If you are typing this material, make sure that you save the file as **MOMSAGA.DOC.** (If you are using another word processor, save the file as **MOMSAGA.TXT.**) Close MOMSAGA.

**4** If you have not already started PowerPoint, do so now.

**5** If PowerPoint is running, select **N**ew from the **F**ile menu. If you are starting PowerPoint at this time, go to step 6.

The New Presentation dialog box appears on-screen.

**6** Select **T**emplate from the New Presentation dialog box, and click OK.

The Presentation Template dialog box appears (see figure 6.2).

**Figure 6.2**
The Presentation Template dialog box.

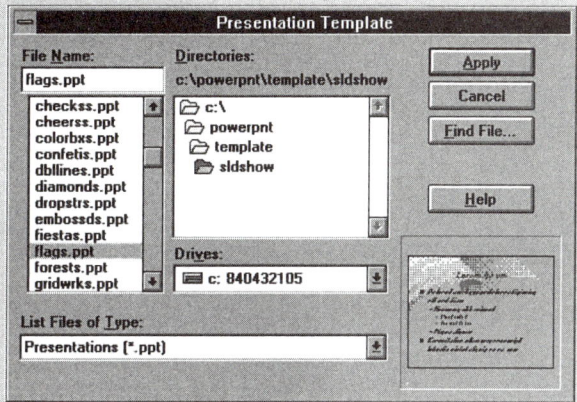

**7** Select FLAGS.PPT from the template directory SLDSHOW.

**8** Click the **A**pply button.

The New Slide dialog box appears (see figure 6.3). At this point, you would normally select the title slide icon to begin a new presentation, but because you are designing a presentation comprised of title lines and bulleted information, you should select the Bulleted List slide layout.

**Figure 6.3**
The New Slide dialog box.

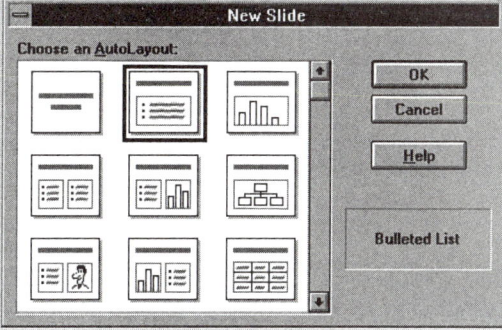

**9** Select the Bulleted List layout, and click OK.

**10** Save the presentation as **HERSTORY.PPT**.

**11** From the **I**nsert menu, choose the Slides from Out**l**ine option (see figure 6.4).

(continues)

**Writing an Outline in Word 6 for Windows (continued)**

**Figure 6.4**
The Insert menu in PowerPoint.

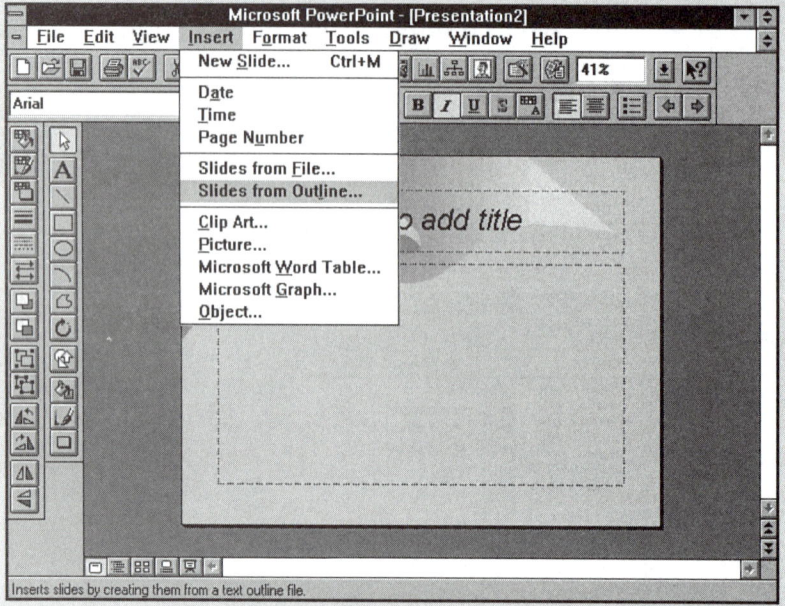

The Insert Outline dialog box appears (see figure 6.5).

**Figure 6.5**
The Insert Outline dialog box.

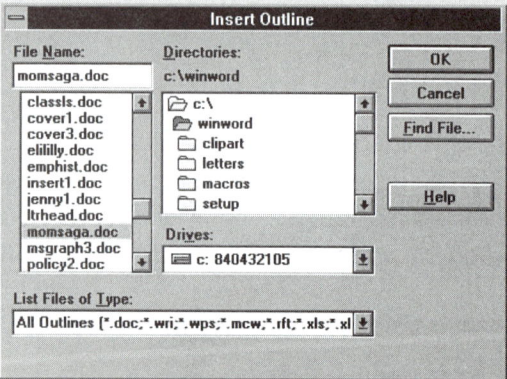

With this dialog box on-screen, notice the List Files of **T**ype drop-down list box. The extensions DOC, MCW, XLS, WRI, and so on, show the wide variety of application programs you can use when writing outlines for PowerPoint.

⓬ Select the outline file MOMSAGA.DOC from the directory or disk where you saved the file.

⓭ Click OK.

It may take a few moments for PowerPoint to import the outline file. PowerPoint displays a Reading Outline message box and a percentage indicator while this process is taking place.

When the Reading Outline message box disappears, the active slide is still slide 1. Outlines are always imported after the current slide.

**⑭** In the Slide view, click the Next Slide button on the vertical scroll bar to review the slides that have been generated from the outline.

You will notice that the text for some of the slides overflows from the text box area on the slides. In the next section, you learn how to use the editing features of PowerPoint to fit the information on the slides.

# Objective 2: Insert Word Outlines into Presentations

Although the MOMSAGA outline was created specifically for building a presentation, sometimes you may want to use an existing outline as the basis for a new presentation. For example, you may have prepared a Word 6 for Windows report that includes titles, subtitles, and short explanations in addition to the text of the report; and you may decide to use this work as the basis for a presentation.

You use Word's Outline view to attach heading styles and promote and demote components. The collapse feature enables you to create the outline that you will import into PowerPoint.

After you import the text, you can use the Slide or Outline view in PowerPoint to edit the content, move portions to new slides, or reduce or increase font sizes so that the content fits attractively on the slides. In addition, you can use the PowerPoint Report It button to launch Word automatically and export the outline to Word for additional editing.

When you want to add to a presentation by importing an outline that you still have to create, you can launch Word, write the outline, and then import the outline into an existing presentation.

This process, however, does have limitations. For example, if you add any text to a slide using the Text Tool button, this text does not appear in Word, nor does the second column of a two-column slide. If you add any notes to the slides, you can access these notes in Word.

## Editing a Presentation Based on an Outline

When you import an outline into PowerPoint, you often have to edit components of the outline to make each slide effective and attractive. Remember that the purpose of a slide is to emphasize a point, not necessarily to contain the entire argument. Additionally, a slide must have a certain visual appeal; too much information or too many words in a point can make a slide appear cluttered and hard to understand.

(continues)

## Editing a Presentation Based on an Outline (continued)

To edit the presentation created from an outline, do the following:

**1** Switch to the Outline view.

**2** Highlight the words `Counting on Mom` on slide 2.

**3** Click the Copy button on the Standard toolbar.

**4** Position the pointer to the right of the icon for slide 1, and click the left mouse button.

**5** Click the Paste button on the Standard toolbar.

The words `Counting on Mom` appear as the title of this slide.

**6** Type **1** after the title line on slide 1 so that it reads `Counting on Mom 1`.

**7** Type **2** after the title line on slide 2.

**8** On slide 2, select all the text from `1906: Flu Epidemic in New York City` through `The Chicken Soup Front` (down to but not including `1952: The Korean War`).

**9** Click the Cut button on the Standard toolbar.

**10** Position the pointer just after the 1 in the text `Counting on Mom 1`, and click the left mouse button.

**11** Click the Paste button on the Standard toolbar.

You have now divided the former content of slide 2 into two slides.

If you recall, the information from the MOMSAGA outline caused some of the text on the slides to overflow from the text box area. This overflow can take away from a slide's visual appeal. In the next tutorial, you learn how to eliminate text overflow.

## Editing Slides to Eliminate Text Overflow

To edit the text of a slide, do the following:

**1** Double-click the slide 1 icon.

The Slide view appears, and slide 1 is the active slide. No text overflow appears on this slide.

**2** Click the Next Slide button.

Slide 2 now contains all its text.

**3** Click the Next Slide button.

Slide 3, "A Real American Heroine," has overflowing text.

**4** In the bottom text box, select all the text, and press `Del`.

The `Click to add text` bulleted line appears.

**5** Type the following lines, and press `↵Enter` after each line:

**New York City, 1900**

**Rebecca Goldberg marries Sam Weissman.**

**A child dies ...**

**But Rebecca embodied destiny's courage.**

**America's Mother:**

**Mom**

**6** Click anywhere in the second line, which begins with `Rebecca`.

**7** With the insertion point in the second line, click the Demote button on the Formatting toolbar.

**8** With the insertion point in the fourth line, beginning with `But Rebecca`, click the Demote button on the Formatting toolbar.

**9** Demote the last line `Mom`.

The essential points covered by this slide are now clear and concise. The speaker will elaborate on these points during the presentation.

**10** Save the file as **HERSTORY.PPT** to preserve your work to this point.

**11** Using the Outline view, edit slides 4 through 7 so that they read as follows:

**1906: Flu Epidemic in New York City**

   **The Epidemic**

   **Thousands of children were sick with fever.**

   **Mothers ill; families were starving.**

   **The Chicken Soup Rescue**

   **Rebecca asks Long Island chicken farmers to donate thousands of chickens.**

   **Volunteers cooked and carried chicken soup to the sick.**

(continues)

**6**

**1916: The Great War**

**Nary a Chicken Over There**

**Our boys were in the trenches**

**Farms and hamlets devastated by war**

**The Chicken Soup Brigade**

**President Wilson authorizes tanker.**

**Ship load of soup arrives at front.**

**Classic Picture:**

**Doughboy eating cup of steaming chicken soup**

**1929: The Great Depression**

**Stock Market Crashes**

**Thousands lose jobs**

**No work, no food; thousands starving**

**The Chicken Soup Kitchens**

**Rebecca begs Georgia farmers for help**

**Thousands of chickens donated**

**Volunteers set up chicken soup lines in cities; thousands were fed.**

**1942: World War II**

**The Chicken Soup Front**

**Women workers produce thousands of tins of chicken soup for GIs**

**Mom organizes chicken soup bond rallies**

**Announces powdered chicken soup**

**Classic Picture:**

**GI Joe eating steaming chicken soup from helmet**

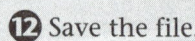 Save the file.

There are a number of ways you can leave PowerPoint and create an outline of slides you want to add to an existing presentation. You can simply exit the program and start your word processor; you can use the standard **S**witch To command, available from the application control menu; or you can use the Report It feature in PowerPoint.

## Creating and Importing an Outline into an Existing Presentation

To use Report It and create an outline in Word 6 for Windows, do the following:

**1** In the Outline view, make slide 1 the current slide.

**2** Click the Report It button on the Standard toolbar.

Word for Windows 6 starts, and the current outline from PowerPoint is displayed as an RTF file. You can edit this file if you like and save it to be imported again into your presentation.

**3** Save the RTF file to your floppy disk or personal directory.

**4** Close the file.

**5** Start a new document, and enter the following outline:

**Taking the Market by Soup**

    **1969: $100 Million in Sales**

    **1970: Mom's Buys Iron Pot Bean Soup, Inc.**

    **1972: $150 Million in Sales**

    **1973: Mom's Takes Over Southern Soups**

    **1975: Mom's Purchases Seabisq Chowders**

**Building the Best**

    **1976: $200 Million in Sales**

    **1978: Mexican Plant Opens**

    **1980: Chinese Plant Opens**

    **1981: $250 Million in Sales**

    **1982: $300 Million in Sales**

**The Soup Wars**

    **1985: The Beer Soup Battles**

    **1986: Mom's Fends Off Dad's Take-Over Attempt**

    **1987: Chuck the Chicken Becomes Ad Spokeschicken**

    **1989: $400 Million in Sales**

**6**

(continues)

## Creating and Importing an Outline into an Existing Presentation (continued)

**6** Save the file as **HISTORY.DOC**, close the file, and open a new document. Enter the following memo:

**To: Ms. Anna M. Singleton**

> **MHC Legal Department**

**From:** *Your Name*

**Re: Proprietary Information**

**I am writing a presentation based on the history of MHC for the chicken soup division. This is in connection with the announcement and release of our new flavor, Thik 'N' Thin Chik' Soup, which is both fat and cholesterol free.**

**I would like to include a slide in that presentation that highlights this product and underscores both its unique position in the market and its staggering potential for millions of diet- and health-conscious Americans.**

**Here is what I propose to say:**

**Thik 'N' Thin Chik'N Soup**

**The #1 Choice for Health**

|  | Thik 'N' Thin | Regular |
|---|---|---|
| **Calories** | 90 | 160 |
| **Protein (Grams)** | 2 | 2 |
| **Carbohydrate** | 8 | 10 |
| **Fat (Grams)** | 0 | 6 |
| **Cholesterol** | 0 | 24 mg/serving |
| **Salt** | 815 mg | 815 mg |

**Would you evaluate this data in light of our legal and proprietary requirements and determine if I can release this information at this time? Because I have to give this presentation next Friday, I will need your report as soon as possible.**

**Thank you.**

**7** Save the file as **LAWMEMO.DOC**; then choose E**x**it from the **F**ile menu.

Word for Windows closes, and you return to PowerPoint. You actually accomplished two tasks while you were working in Word: you completed a short outline, and you wrote a short memo.

**8** In the current presentation, make slide 10, "1967: An Era Passes," the current slide.

⑨ From the **I**nsert menu, choose Slides from Out**l**ine.

⑩ Select the HISTORY.DOC file from the Insert Outline dialog box, and click OK.

After the message box that shows PowerPoint importing the outline disappears, the new slides appear in the presentation.

⑪ Switch slide 13 and slide 14 because slide 13, "The Soup Wars," would be better positioned after the current slide 14, "Chicken Soup for Education."

⑫ Save the file as **HERSTORY.PPT**.

# Objective 3: Copy Text from Word into PowerPoint

In addition to importing an outline created in Word for Windows into PowerPoint, you can also move blocks of text directly into your presentation. Although you are learning techniques that apply to Word, they also apply to other Windows applications.

## Dragging Text from Word into PowerPoint

As you refine a presentation, you may want to move text for a variety of reasons. By moving text from other applications, you can avoid retyping material, make room for additional material, and reorganize material to emphasize a particular point.

To copy selected text from a Word for Windows file and paste it into a slide in HERSTORY.PPT in PowerPoint, do the following:

❶ In the Outline view, make slide 16, "1994: Stand-Up Chicken," the current slide.

❷ Click the New Slide button on the horizontal toolbar.

A new slide, number 17, appears.

❸ In the title line, type the following title:

**Our Gift to America**

❹ Switch to the Slide view.

Slide 17 is the current slide.

❺ Click the application control menu box in the upper left corner of the PowerPoint application window.

The application control menu appears.

**6**

(continues)

## Dragging Text from Word into PowerPoint (continued)

**6** Choose Switch To from the application control menu.

The Task List dialog box appears (see figure 6.6).

The Task List dialog box appears (see figure 6.6).

**Figure 6.6**
The Task List dialog box.

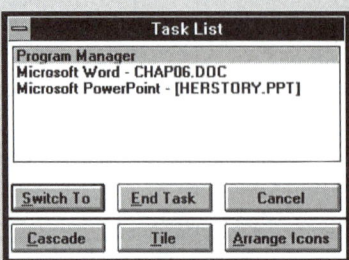

```
                        Task List
  Program Manager
  Microsoft Word - CHAP06.DOC
  Microsoft PowerPoint - [HERSTORY.PPT]



    Switch To      End Task       Cancel

    Cascade         Tile       Arrange Icons
```

**7** If Word for Windows is already open, select this application, and click the Switch To button. If Word is not open, select the Program Manager, and click the Switch To button; then open Word from the Program Manager.

**Note:** *If Word is not open, you can use the Report It shortcut you learned earlier. Don't forget that the current presentation outline will appear in the document window. If you use this shortcut and you want a document copy of the outline, go ahead and save it. Otherwise, continue with the following steps.*

**8** In Word for Windows, open the LAWMEMO.DOC file. Select all the following text, and click the Copy button on the Standard toolbar:

```
Thik 'N' Thin Chik'N Soup

The #1 Choice for Health


                    Thik 'N' Thin     Regular

Calories            90                160

Protein (Grams)     2                 2

Carbohydrate        8                 10

Fat (Grams)         0                 6

Cholesterol         0                 24 mg/serving

Salt                815 mg            815 mg
```

**9** Either close Word for Windows, or use the Switch To feature to return to PowerPoint.

**10** In PowerPoint, click the bottom text box to select the box; then click the Paste button on the Standard toolbar.

The nutritional information is now inserted and overflows the text box.

**11** Select the first three lines of the text, and click the Bullet On/Off button on the Formatting toolbar.

⑫ Select the first line, and click the Bold button on the Formatting toolbar.

⑬ Select the second line, and click the Italic button on the Formatting toolbar.

This step removes the italic attribute in this case.

⑭ With the second line still selected, click the Center Align button on the Formatting toolbar.

⑮ Select the third line, and click the Underline button on the Formatting toolbar.

⑯ Select all the remaining bulleted lines, and choose Line Spacing from the Format menu.

The Line Spacing dialog box appears (see figure 6.7).

**Figure 6.7**
The Line
Spacing dialog
box.

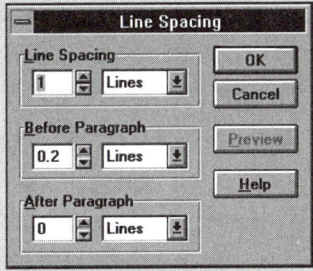

⑰ Set Before Paragraph and After Paragraph to 0; then click OK.

⑱ Remove the text /serving, from the end of the Cholesterol line; then insert tabs or spaces to align the numbers or columns.

When you have completed the formatting, the slide should look very much like figure 6.8.

**Figure 6.8**
The slide with
data aligned.

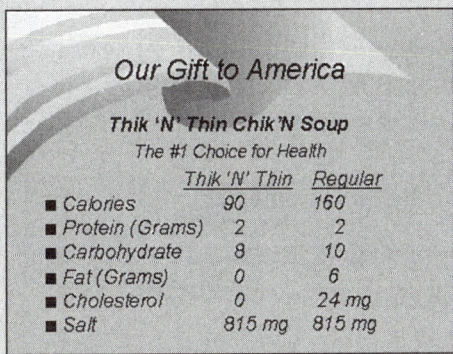

**6**

⑲ Save but do not close the file.

# Objective 4: Copy from Excel

PowerPoint can import worksheets created in spreadsheet programs such as Excel or Lotus 1-2-3. Using PowerPoint, you can also access Excel 5 directly with the Insert Microsoft Excel Worksheet button on the toolbar. This button enables you to create worksheets while you create your presentations. This button is convenient for working with small worksheets that don't require a great deal of editing, but you should generally switch to the Excel program in its own window for any substantial work.

## Preparing an Excel Worksheet as a Source Document

In this tutorial, you are using an Excel workbook that is created directly in Excel. Depending on what your instructor wants, you can create the file yourself, or it is available on the instructor's resource disk as GROWTH.XLS.

If you start with the source file, open the file in Excel, review the worksheets, and save the sheet titled Correlation as the active sheet.

To create the Excel workbook required in this tutorial, do the following:

**1** Using the application control menu, switch to the Program Manager, and start Excel.

**2** On Sheet1 of the new workbook, type the following:

In cell C3, type **Mom's Home Cookin' Soup Company**.

In cell D5, type **Variety**.

In cell E5, type **Flavor**.

In cell F5, type **Quality**.

In cell E7, type **1905-1995**.

In cell D9, type **America's Soup**.

**3** Select cell C3. Change the font to Brush Script MT and the font size to 14, and click the Bold button on the Formatting toolbar.

**4** Select cells C3 through G3.

**5** Choose Cells from the Format menu.

The Format Cells dialog box appears (see figure 6.9).

**Figure 6.9**
The Format Cells
dialog box in
Excel 5.0.

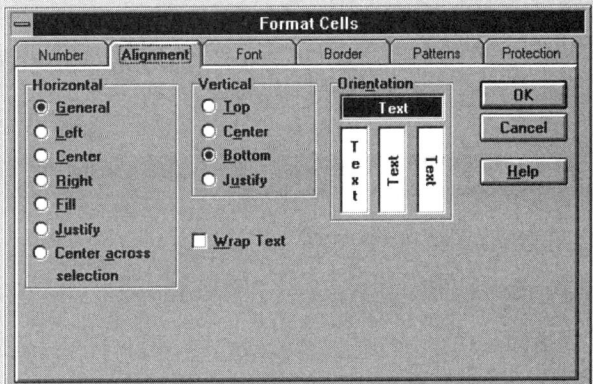

**6** Click the Alignment tab.

**7** In the Horizontal option box, click the Center **Across** Selection option.

**8** Click OK.

**9** Select cells D9 through F9, and repeat steps 5 through 8.

**10** Select cells D5 through F5, and click the Center button on the Formatting toolbar.

**11** Select cell E7, and click the Bold button on the Formatting toolbar.

**12** Using the right mouse button, click the Sheet1 tab.

**13** Rename the sheet **Title**.

**14** Click the Sheet2 tab, and rename the sheet **Correlation**.

**15** Complete the Correlation worksheet using the following data:

Variety and Revenue - An Analysis
Revenue in Thousands

|      | Varieties | Revenue | Major Product Introduction |
|------|-----------|---------|----------------------------|
| 1925 | 4         | 78.2    | Mom's Own Chicken Dumplings |
| 1935 | 7         | 101.4   | Chicken and Rice |
| 1945 | 10        | 789     | Chicken Stew |
| 1955 | 22        | 4,237   | Mom's Hot Lunch Chicken Noodle |
| 1965 | 31        | 34,871  | Mom's Chunky Chicken and Rice |
| 1975 | 88        | 182,326 | Fiesta Chicken |
| 1985 | 101       | 340,926 | Chicken Burger and Cheese |
| 1995 | 202       | 512,456 | Thik 'N' Thin Chik'N Soup |

**16** Save the workbook as **GROWTH.XLS**.

Copying data from one program to another is easier if you arrange the application windows so that a portion of each is visible. Then you have only to click the appropriate window to make it active. Otherwise, you must switch between programs by using the application control menus.

## Copying Data from an Excel Worksheet

To copy data from Excel to PowerPoint, do the following:

**1** Arrange your Excel and PowerPoint windows so that both are accessible.

**Note:** *Adjust the right or left border of the PowerPoint application window so that you have about 1/4 inch between the border and the edge of the viewing screen. Switch to Excel, and raise the bottom border of the application window about 1/4 inch from the bottom of the viewing screen.*

*When Excel is active, you can click the visible portion of the PowerPoint window at the bottom of the screen to switch to that application. When PowerPoint is active, you can click the visible portion of Excel at the edge of the screen to make Excel active.*

*You can also press* Alt+Tab↹ *repeatedly to cycle through the various applications windows. This method is faster than using the menus but slower than using the mouse.*

**2** Make slide 16 in the current PowerPoint presentation, HERSTORY.PPT, the active slide.

**3** Click the New Slide button, and select the blank slide format.

**4** Repeat steps 2 and 3 to insert a second blank slide.

The two blank slides should occupy positions 17 and 18. Select slide 17.

**5** Switch to Excel; make GROWTH.XLS the active file, and Title the active worksheet.

**6** Select cells C3 through G9 (see figure 6.10).

**Figure 6.10**
The selected
cells in Excel 5.0.

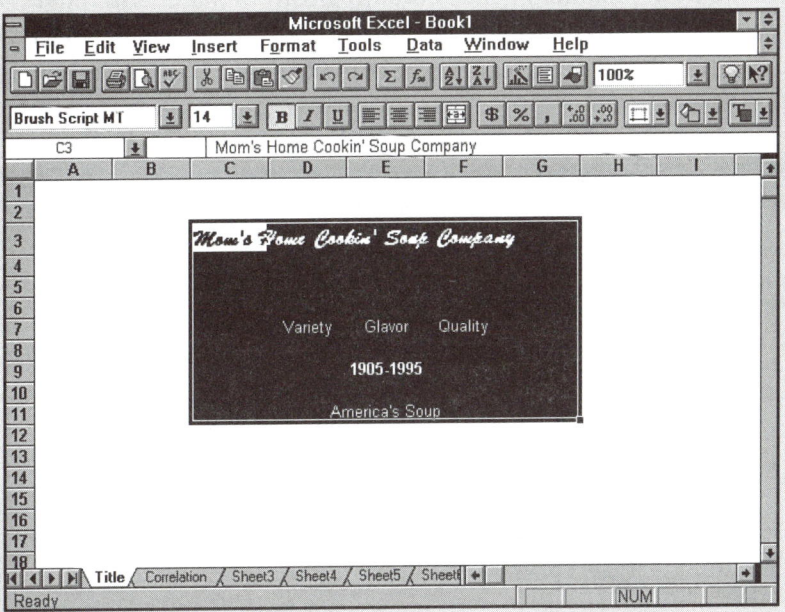

**7** Click the Copy button on the Standard toolbar.

**8** Switch to PowerPoint; make slide 17 the active slide.

**9** Choose Paste **S**pecial from the **E**dit menu.

The Paste Special dialog box appears (see figure 6.11).

**Figure 6.11**
The Paste
Special dialog
box.

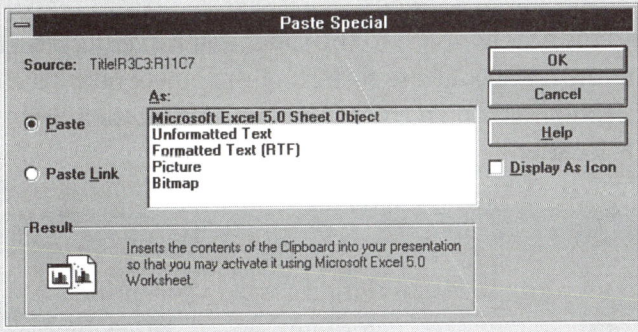

**10** Select Microsoft Excel 5.0 Sheet Object.

**11** Click OK.

**12** The copied data appears on the slide.

**13** Close Excel.

**6**

The copied image may contain gridlines. Frequently, data or worksheets copied or imported into PowerPoint have gridlines and sizes that are inappropriate. Fortunately, you can easily correct these situations as you learn in the next two tutorials.

## Improving Spreadsheet Image Sizes in Slides

To adjust the size of the spreadsheet object, do the following:

**1** Select the object.

The sizing handles become visible.

**2** Choose Scal**e** from the **D**raw menu.

The Scale dialog box appears (see figure 6.12).

**Figure 6.12**
The Scale dialog box.

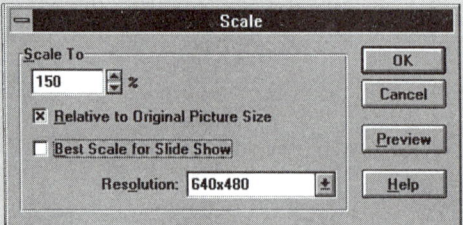

**3** Select **B**est Scale for Slide Show, and click OK.

The object is now adjusted to the slide. You can adjust the image further by dragging the handles at the corners of the object box. To change the position, you click and hold down the left mouse button; then move the dotted line box to a new location.

## Removing Gridlines

You can use Excel to remove gridlines on a spreadsheet object copied into PowerPoint. To remove the gridlines, do the following:

**1** Double-click the worksheet object.

The PowerPoint menus and toolbars are replaced by the Excel menus and toolbars; the worksheet object appears in an editing window.

**2** Choose **O**ptions from the **T**ools menu.

The Options dialog box appears (refer to figure 6.13).

**Figure 6.13**
The Options
dialog box.

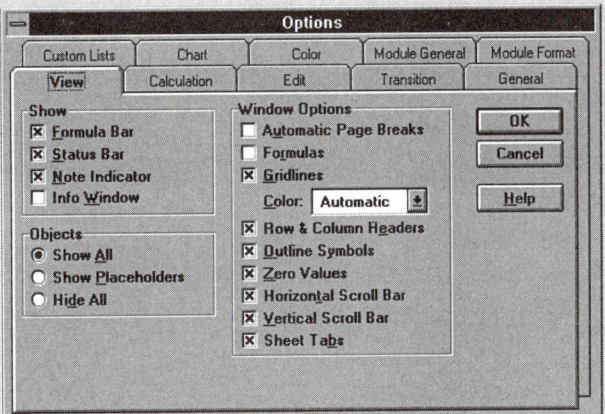

③ Click the View tab.

④ Deselect **G**ridlines (which may already be deselected).

⑤ Click OK.

⑥ Click anywhere off the worksheet object.

The gridlines disappear.

The text and data from worksheets may be difficult to read on some slide backgrounds. If you think that the text is difficult to read because of the colors, changing the font color is usually better than changing the background color because changing the background affects the appearance of every object on the slide.

**6**

## Changing Slide Backgrounds to Make Data More Readable

To change the background of a slide, do the following:

① Choose Slide Back**g**round from the F**o**rmat menu.

The Slide Background dialog box appears (see figure 6.14).

*(continues)*

## Changing Slide Backgrounds to Make Data More Readable

**Figure 6.14**
The Slide Background dialog box.

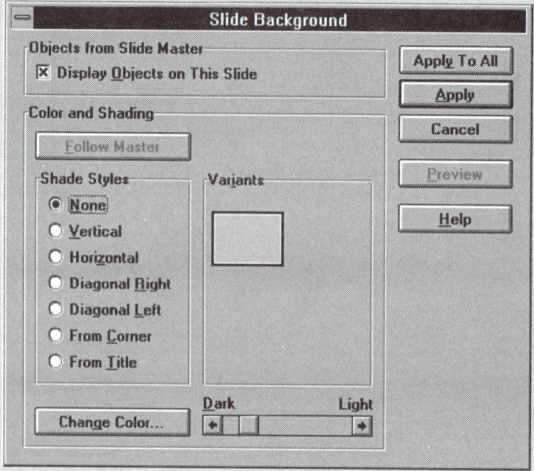

❷ Click the Change Color button.

The color drop-down menu appears.

❸ Select white, and click OK.

❹ Select the **A**pply button on the Slide Background dialog box.

**Note:** *The Apply To All button will change the background of all the slides to white.*

❺ Make slide 18 the active slide, and change its background color to white.

# Objective 5: Add Worksheets from Excel

PowerPoint can build and insert a worksheet or chart directory from a spreadsheet file. With Excel 5.0 workbooks that contain multiple worksheets, PowerPoint creates a spreadsheet object based on the worksheet that contains data and was active when the file was last saved.

**Link**

The connection between a source document and a picture of the source that appears on a slide.

You can set up a *link*, or connection, between PowerPoint and other applications, that enables you to update objects without having to exit PowerPoint. A link is a connection between a source document and the slide. Updates to the source document are immediately reflected on the slide. Linked objects are not actually stored in a presentation. By linking and displaying the worksheet on a slide, you can edit the worksheet directly from PowerPoint; you simply double-click the spreadsheet object. Excel starts with the object as the active worksheet.

## Adding a Worksheet to a Slide

To create and place a worksheet object from an existing spreadsheet file, do the following:

**1** Make slide 18 the active slide.

**2** Select **O**bject from the **I**nsert menu.

The Insert Object dialog box appears with the Object **T**ype list box open and a list of file types.

**3** Select Microsoft Excel 5.0 Sheet (or other spreadsheet file if you created the GROWTH file in another program), and click OK (see figure 6.15).

**Figure 6.15**
The Insert Object dialog box.

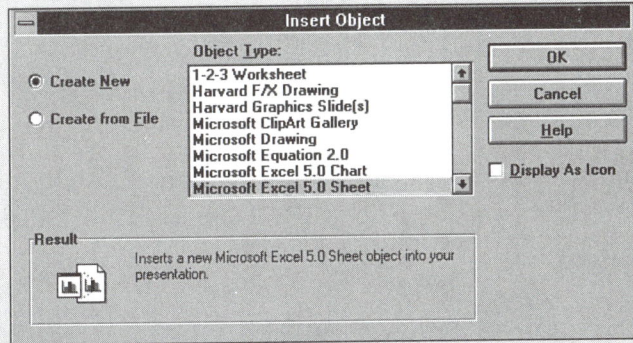

**4** Select the Create from **F**ile option.

The dialog box changes slightly (see figure 6.16).

**Figure 6.16**
The changed Insert Object dialog box.

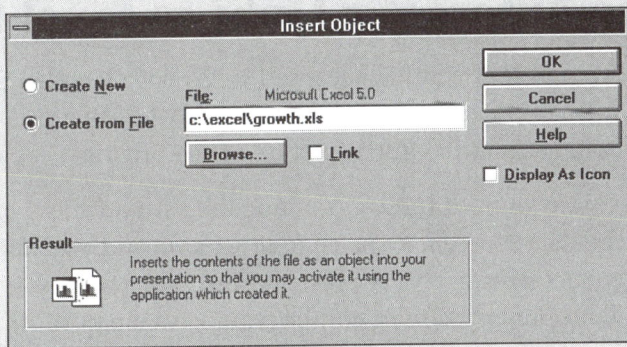

**5** Click the Create from **F**ile option and then the **B**rowse button.

The Browse dialog box appears (see figure.6.17)

(continues)

6

**Adding a Worksheet to a Slide (continued)**

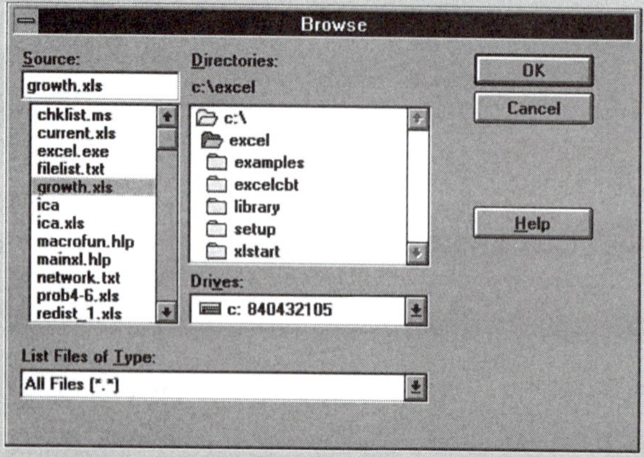

**Figure 6.17**
The Browse
dialog box.

6 Select GROWTH.XLS, and click OK.

7 When the Insert Object dialog box returns, select the **L**ink option.

A picture of the worksheet is inserted into the slide and linked to the source file so that changes to the file will also appear in the presentation.

8 Click OK.

The worksheet object appears on the slide.

9 Use the techniques you learned under Objective 4 to size the worksheet.

# Objective 6: Use Automatic Links to Excel Data

The techniques that you have learned so far have resulted in the placement of objects with automatic links to the original data—that is, any changes in the original will be reflected in the picture of the original that appears on the slide.

You may want or need these automatic links for a variety of reasons. For instance, the data source may be changing daily, and you need the latest figures before you actually give your presentation. You may also be building different parts of your presentation in conjunction with a report. As you update the information in your report, you also want to update the information in your presentation.

All updating, however, is limited to your particular computer system. Although the linked object appears in your PowerPoint presentation, the original program actually contains all the instructions for displaying that object. It is as if you are seeing on a miniature computer screen an object that has its own tiny version of the other program running inside.

If you distribute your program to another computer, however, the linked objects will not be available to the new viewer. For example, if you have linked objects from Excel in your program, the remote viewer cannot view these objects, even if that viewer has a copy of Excel and the worksheets. The instructions for displaying that object are contained in your computer with your version of Excel.

**Embedded objects**
Objects that are a permanent part of the presentation.

Fortunately, you can convert linked objects into *embedded objects*, which means that you can break the link after your final update and lock a permanent image into your slide. Linked objects can be converted to embedded objects, but once converted, embedded objects can no longer be updated automatically. Of course, the only way the viewer (or you) can update that object in the future is to edit the object manually.

You can import many types of visuals into PowerPoint as linked objects. The application that creates the object, however, must support linking and embedding. The types of objects include charts from Excel, movies from Media Player for Windows, tables from Microsoft Word, and organizational charts from Microsoft Organization Chart.

You can update a linked object in either of two ways. You can choose automatic updating, which occurs each time you open a presentation, or you can update the object manually.

## Updating a Link Manually

To update a link manually, do the following:

**1** From the **E**dit menu, choose Lin**k**s.

The Links dialog box appears (see figure 6.18).

**Figure 6.18**
The Links dialog box.

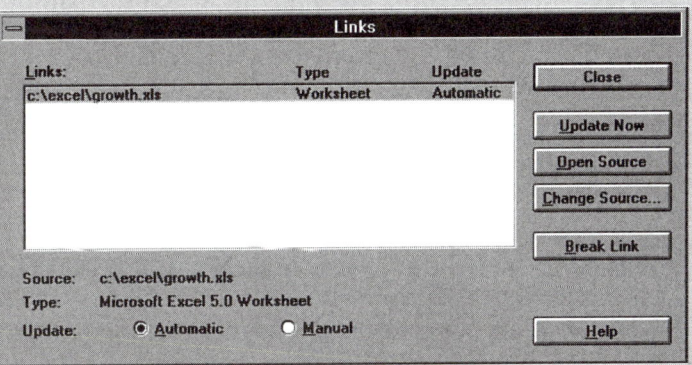

**2** Select the Link you want to update from the **L**inks list box.

**3** Click the **U**pdate Now button.

You can also change the way a link works. For example, you may want to break a link at some point to freeze the data shown on the slide so that you can show the status of the data at some specific time. You can continue to update the data in the original program, but with the link broken, the object in the presentation remains the same as it was when you broke the link.

6

## Changing the Way a Link Works

To change the way a link works, do the following:

**1** From the **E**dit menu, choose Lin**k**s, if neccessary.

**2** Select the link you want to change from the **L**inks list box in the Links dialog box.

**3** To update a link automatically, select the **A**utomatic option button (the default).

**4** To break a link, click the **B**reak Link button. PowerPoint displays a warning box. Read the message, and click OK.

**5** Close the Links dialog box.

**6** Save but do not close HERSTORY.PPT.

After a link is broken, the embedded object can no longer be updated by data from the original file. However, a picture of the object as it appeared after its last update remains in the presentation.

If you move the original document to which an object is linked to another directory or disk, the original loses track of the document. Technically, a moved source is not a broken link, but a link in which the path is no longer viable.

To reestablish a link if the original document is moved, in the Links dialog box, click the **C**hange Source button. You can now enter the new location of the document to be linked in a Directory dialog box. To edit a linked object in the application that created the object, click the **O**pen Source button.

# Objective 7: Move Slides between Presentations

You can also move and copy slides from one presentation to another. If you create a large number of presentations, you may want to build a slide library, which is simply a presentation file containing slides that you need in a number of presentations.

Title screens are useful library slides for a company. Title slides often include the name of the company and its logo. Other useful library slides are organizational charts, schedules, credit slides listing the names of the editors and contributors, and product lists. If you have a large number of standard slides, you can give the presentations descriptive names. For example, you could name a library presentation file containing product models and descriptions PRODUCTS.PPT.

When you copy a slide from one presentation to another, the copied slide is changed to match the attributes of the master slide in the receiving presentation.

## Moving and Copying Slides

To move and copy slides in a presentation or from one presentation to another, do the following:

1. Make HERSTORY.PPT the active presentation, and change to the Slide Sorter view.

2. Select slide 18, which contains the title object from Excel.

3. Move this slide to the front of the presentation so that it becomes slide 1.

4. Save but don't close the HERSTORY.PPT presentation.

5. Open the SOUP2.PPT presentation in the Slide Sorter view.

6. Select slide 1, the title slide.

7. Click the Copy button on the Standard toolbar.

8. Close the SOUP2.PPT presentation.

   The HERSTORY.PPT presentation is now in the presentation window.

9. Move the insertion point to the right of the last slide and click the left mouse button.

10. Click the Paste button on the Standard toolbar.

    The slide that was copied from the SOUP2.PPT presentation is now inserted as the last slide in the current presentation, HERSTORY.PPT. Its attributes have been automatically changed to match those of the master slide in this presentation.

11. Save and close the HERSTORY.PPT file.

**6**

# Chapter Summary

This chapter shows you how to use information created in other applications to help build a presentation in PowerPoint. You wrote an outline in a word processor and used it to create a presentation. You also learned how to insert an outline into an existing presentation to create new slides. You copied text and data from other applications and pasted that information into slides. You also imported linked objects from a spreadsheet program, and you learned how to change or break the links. Finally, you learned how to move and copy slides from one presentation to another.

# Checking Your Skills

## True/False Questions

For each of the following statements, circle *T* or *F* to indicate whether the statement is true or false.

T  F  **1.** The extensions DOC, MCW, XLS, WRI, and so on, show the wide variety of applications programs that you can use to write outlines for PowerPoint.

T  F  **2.** One reason for using Microsoft Word for Windows is that it is the only word processing program that you can use to copy and paste information to and from PowerPoint.

T  F  **3.** In PowerPoint, you can remove headers and gridlines appearing on spreadsheets that are copied from Excel by using the Excel menu.

T  F  **4.** In order to update a link automatically, you must select the **A**utomatic option button in the Links dialog box; otherwise, the default is a manual update.

T  F  **5.** When you copy a slide from one presentation to another, the copied slide is changed to matched the attributes of the master slide in the receiving presentation.

## Multiple-Choice Questions

In the blank provided, write the letter of the correct answer for each of the following questions.

___ **1.** RTF refers to _____.

    **a.** Regular Template Format

    **b.** Rich Text Format

    **c.** Rich Template Format

    **d.** Regular Text Format

___ **2.** When you demote a text line on a slide, you _____.

    **a.** make that line less important

    **b.** reduce the line one outline level

    **c.** reduce the line one slide level

    **d.** reduce the line to tears

___ **3.** One item that you cannot export to Word 6 for Windows using the PowerPoint Report It feature is _____.

    **a.** outline levels

    **b.** notes from notes pages

    **c.** any text from two-column slides

    **d.** level 3 headings

___ **4.** ASCII is an acronym for _____.

    **a.** American Standard Code for Information Interchange

    **b.** American Simple Code for Information Interchange

    **c.** American Standard Code for Interchange of Information

    **d.** American Standard Code for Intellectual Information

___ **5.** It is usually easier to switch from one application to another in Windows by _____.

    **a.** overlapping application windows so that a portion of each is always visible on-screen

    **b.** using the application control menu boxes and the Switch To feature

    **c.** selecting the window you want from each application's Window choice on the main menu bar

    **d.** arranging document windows so that a side or bottom portion is always visible on-screen

## Fill-in-the-Blank Questions

In the blank provided, write the correct answer for each of the following questions.

**1.** ASCII files also are known as plain or _____ files.

**2.** One reason to _____ data from another program is to avoid re-typing the information.

**3.** PowerPoint can access Excel 5 directly for creating _____ while creating presentations by using the Insert Microsoft Excel Worksheet button on the toolbar.

**4.** PowerPoint can build and insert a worksheet or chart directly from a spreadsheet _____.

**5.** Once a link is broken, a _____ of the embedded object remains in the presentation file.

# Applying Your Skills

## Review Exercises

### Exercise 1: Editing and Formatting a Presentation Built from an Outline

The HERSTORY presentation could greatly benefit from text formatting. For example, the dates on slides 1 and 2 would stand out more if they were in boldface or had shadows added. Go through the slides for this presentation, and add various enhancements and attributes to selected portions of the text to make these slides more visually appealing. Save the file as **MOMSTALE.PPT**.

### Exercise 2: Using an Outline to Create a Presentation

Your instructor thinks that you have done so well with this chapter that you are the perfect choice to create a presentation to accompany his lecture on this chapter to students next semester. Using the headings in this chapter, with the objectives being the primary headings and the tutorials being the second-level headings, write an outline in your favorite word processor; then use that outline to generate the basic presentation. Be sure to select an appropriate template design.

### Exercise 3: Adding Linked Objects to a Presentation

Your professor likes the presentation you created to go with his lecture on Chapter 6 but would like to see the actual linked objects on the slides that discuss these issues. Add the data from Excel to the two slides that require this information by inserting linked objects.

## Continuing Projects

### Project 1: Creating a Television Commercial

The advertising agency for Mom's Home Cookin' Soup Company wants to create a television commercial that tells the consumer how Mom's took the fat and cholesterol out of Thik 'N' Thin Chik'N Soup.

Here is a copy of a new story that appeared in the *Wail Street Journal*:

Reinventing the Chicken

Mom's Announces Heart-Healthy

No Fat, Cholesterol-Free Chicken Soup

What do a peanut farm in Georgia, a tropical bay in New Zealand, and a beauty salon have in common? The answer may surprise you. Each of these played a significant role in a major scientific and culinary break-through: Mom's Home Cookin's no fat, no cholesterol chicken.

In a process so revolutionary that there are more than 32 patents pending, Mom's culinary wizards have produced a chicken product rich in quality and taste and completely free of fat and cholesterol.

"This is a major boon to millions of weight-conscious Americans who are concerned about the health and appetites of themselves and their families," said Mrs. Sara Ann Feinberg, president and CEO of Mom's Home Cookin' Soup Company.

It is also a major boon to Mom's stock, which rose 7 points on the New York Stock Exchange on news of the product. By contrast, the stock of Mom's largest competitor, Dad's Homebrew, dropped four points even though Dad's is rumored to be developing its own fat-free, cholesterol-free chicken.

While Mom's is keeping a number of the steps involved in extracting the fat and cholesterol from chicken proprietary, the basic process has generated much excitement in the beef and pork industries for its potential in these products.

"Mom's process starts with peanut oil in which oxygen atoms in long-chain hydrocarbons are replaced with sulfur atoms in order to create an oil that is unstable at high temperatures," says Mom's chief chemist, Dr. Bill Overhill, who says he got the idea while waiting for his wife to get a permanent in a beauty parlor.

"The only way you can get hair follicles to accept a permanent is by substituting sulfur atoms in the hair protein," Dr. Overhill said. "This relaxes the hair so that it will accept a curl. Later, you remove the sulfur atoms and the hair is now both curly and stable."

To test his idea, Dr. Overhill placed white chicken breast meat in pressurized tanks filled with the converted peanut oil, which dissolved and replaced all the natural animal fat in the chicken. "Next, we broke down the protein with additional sulfurization and then bathed the chicken in high-pressure steam," Dr. Overhill said.

"The hot-steam breaks down the unstable oil and leaves the chicken completely free of oil, fat, and cholesterol." To plump out the chicken meat and restore the taste and texture, the chicken was next placed in a bath of chicken-flavored, synthetic fat derived from a species of seaweed found off the coast of New Zealand.

"The result was a tasty, healthful chicken meat," said Dr. Overhill.

Despite this obvious bias, Dr. Overhill may be right. According to the company, preliminary taste trials of a new soup based on the processed chicken have all been positive.

**6**

Here is a confidential product development memo from Mom's kitchen labs:

Process for Removing Fat and Cholesterol from Chicken

1. Start with boneless chicken breasts.

2. Wash in hot water to remove surface fat and residual particulates. 3 minutes.

3. Pressurize in sulphogenated peanut oil: 60 psi @ 65° C for 5 minutes.

4. Drain.

5. ****Rinse with alkalization reagent: 5 minutes

6. Introduce pressurized steam: 60 psi @ 145° C for 180 seconds.

7. ****Introduce pressurized carbon dioxide: 60 psi @ 24° C for 180 seconds.

8. Marinate in Z145-223A for five hours @ 25° C.

The items with asterisks next to them in the memo are proprietary and must not be revealed. The marinade, Z145-223A, is a chicken-bouillon-flavored synthetic fat made from a seaweed extract.

Your task is to use Microsoft Word to write an outline of a commercial that shows the pertinent steps in creating this marvel of a chicken product, and then use that outline to generate a presentation. Use the ADV2 file for your PowerPoint presentation.

Assume that Mom's Kitchen Lab technicians have further refined the process and have changed the following processing times: Step 3, pressurizing in peanut oil, was found to be more efficient if increased from 5 minutes to 7.5 minutes. Step 9, marinating in the seaweed extract, could then be reduced to 3 hours, 25 minutes.

Make the required changes in the Excel worksheet, and then use PowerPoint's Link dialog box to update the ADV2 presentation.

### Project 2: Linking Data

Create a spreadsheet in Excel that illustrates the processing steps and times required to produce no-fat, no-cholesterol chicken. Insert the chart into the appropriate slide in the ADV2 presentation you created in Project 1. Assume that changes are being made daily to the Excel worksheet as the kitchen labs perfect the process.

# CHAPTER 7

# Embellishing a Presentation with Text Effects

In PowerPoint, you can turn words into art by either of two subprograms; one comes with Microsoft Word and Microsoft Publisher, and the other is provided with PowerPoint. Both are accessed through PowerPoint. In this chapter, you use these subprograms to turn letters and words into *objects d' art*—or at least interesting objects. In addition to exploring WordArt text effects, this chapter also covers other aspects of text management, including changing styles, colors, and alignment; finding and replacing; and using the Microsoft Spelling Checker.

## Objectives

By the time you have finished this chapter, you will have learned to

1. Create Text Objects

2. Manipulate Text Objects

3. Change Text Style and Color

4. Select and Align Text and Group Objects

5. Find and Replace Text

6. Use the Spelling Checker

## Objective 1: Create Text Objects

WordArt is fun. With WordArt you can create the obvious special effects with words. Special text effects can add emphasis to a word and visual interest to a slide. You can also create less obvious special effects that are limited only by your imagination. To add emphasis to a sentence, you can create a combination of normal words and enhanced words. Figure 7.1 shows some examples of WordArt text. You can combine any of these words with regular text.

**Figure 7.1**
Examples of
WordArt text.

**WordArt**
Subprograms used
to create special
effects with text.

If you are familiar with Microsoft Word for Windows or Microsoft Publisher, you may have used *WordArt* to create special text effects for brochures, newsletters, or advertising materials. WordArt uses a set of special fonts for creating text effects. WordArt has its own dialog box with various options for creative wordart.

WordArt 2 is distributed with PowerPoint 4.0 and uses the TrueType fonts that are installed with the application. WordArt 2 also has its own dialog box but uses PowerPoint menus and formatting tools. WordArt 2 has different special effects from WordArt 1.

**Text object**
A term used to
describe text in a
text box. This text is
actually a graphic
object.

Although WordArt is created with text fonts and is sometimes referred to as a *text object*, a WordArt creation is actually a graphic object.

## Preparing to Add WordArt to a Presentation

At any time, you can add WordArt to the current slide in an active presentation. When you complete this tutorial, the slide on your screen should look like that in figure 7.2.

**Figure 7.2**
The title slide with text lines.

To prepare the presentation for adding WordArt, do the following:

**1** Start PowerPoint, and load the file ADV1.PPT.

**2** Click the text box `Click to add subtitles` to select the border.

The sizing handles appear.

**3** Press `Del` to remove the text object.

**4** Click the Text button on the Drawing toolbar.

**5** Position the mouse pointer below the left border of the check mark box and in the horizontal middle of the slide, and click the left mouse button.

**6** Select 32 points from the Font Size list box on the Formatting toolbar.

**7** In the text box, type **Fat-Free for the Thin in You**.

**8** Click and drag the text box to the right, positioning the box in the horizontal middle of the slide with the left border below the `h` in the word `Thin` that appears in the title line.

**Note:** *Refer to figure 7.2 to see the exact positioning.*

**9** Click the Text button on the Drawing toolbar, and position the mouse pointer below the left border of the check mark box and midway between the title line and the Fat-Free line.

**10** Select 32 points from the Font size list box.

**11** In the new text box, type **Thick Healthy Hunks of Chicken**.

(continues)

7

**Preparing to Add WordArt to a Presentation (continued)**

**⑫** Click and drag the text box to the right so that the right border aligns with the right edge of the Fat-Free line.

**⑬** Using the techniques described in this tutorial, type the line **Cholesterol-Free for Your Heart** aligned flush-right with the Fat-Free line and midway between that line and the tag line `Mom's Home Cookin'`.

Text and objects like WordArt can be manipulated as single units. By creating individual text boxes for these lines, you are preparing a layout in which you can manipulate individual and combined elements. These techniques are covered later in this chapter.

**Note:** *If you do not have WordArt 1 on your system, skip the following tutorial, and go to the tutorial "Creating a Text Object with WordArt 2."*

**Creating a Text Object with WordArt 1**

To create a text object with WordArt 1, do the following:

**❶** Choose **O**bject from the **I**nsert menu.

The Insert Object dialog box appears (see figure 7.3).

**Figure 7.3**
The Insert Object dialog box.

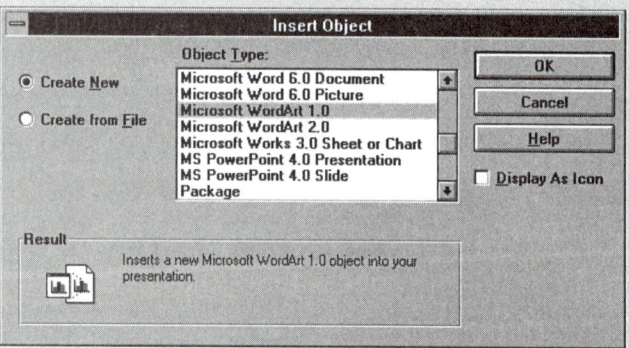

**❷** Choose Microsoft WordArt 1.0 from the Object **T**ype list box.

The Microsoft WordArt dialog box appears with the line `Your Text Here` already highlighted in the text box (see figure 7.4). Do not click the mouse or position the insertion point.

**Figure 7.4**

The Microsoft
WordArt dialog
box.

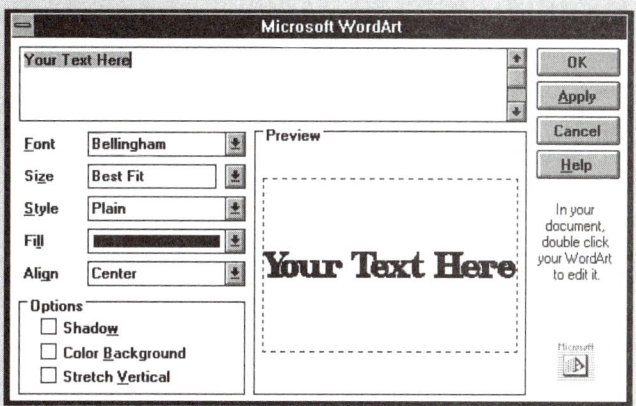

**3** Type the word **Thick**.

The word Thick appears in the text box, replacing the line Your Text Here.

**Note:** *If you clicked the mouse or positioned the insertion point before typing your text, highlight* Your Text Here, *and then type* **Thick**.

**4** Click the down arrow on the **F**ont drop-down list box.

The font selection list appears.

**5** Using your up- and down-arrow keys, move the selection from font to font, and view the changes to the word Thick in the Preview box.

**Note:** *When viewing previews, always use the arrow keys. If you click a selection, that selection is chosen, and the drop-down list box closes.*

**6** Select the font named Walla Walla by clicking this selection.

**7** From the Fi**l**l drop-down list box, scroll down to and select the dark blue color.

**8** Leaving all other options with the default settings, click the **A**pply button.

**9** Click the OK button.

The text object from WordArt now appears in a large graphic box over the current slide.

**10** Position the mouse pointer over the lower right corner of the graphic box.

The pointer changes to a diagonal double-headed arrow.

**11** Click and drag the corner of the graphic box inward, shrinking the box to about half the size of a regular postage stamp.

**12** Click and drag the graphic box to a position just to the left of the word Thick in the first text line (see figure 7.5).

(continues)

7

## Creating a Text Object with WordArt 1 (continued)

**Figure 7.5**
Positioning a
graphic object
from WordArt
on a slide.

🔟 Click the text box containing the first line and position the insertion point just to the left of the ⊤ in the word Thick.

🔟 Press Del repeatedly to delete the word Thick and move the word Healthy to the left border of the text box.

Now that you have successfully created a text object, you can dress up this line still more

## Adding Another Text Object to Your Slide

To add another text object to this line, follow these steps:

❶ Move the insertion point to the left of the word Hunks, and press Del repeatedly to delete the word.

❷ With the word *Hunks* deleted, press [ Spacebar ] repeatedly to insert enough spaces to align the n at the end of the line with the u that ends the second line.

❸ Choose **O**bject from the **I**nsert menu and WordArt 1 from the Insert Object dialog box (refer to figure 7.3).

❹ When the Microsoft WordArt dialog box appears, type the word **Hunks** in the text box.

❺ Choose the font Sequim in the **F**ont drop-down list box.

❻ Click the down-arrow on the **S**tyle drop-down list box.

Using the arrow keys, scroll through the selections to view the various styling attributes.

❼ Select Arch Up from the **S**tyle drop-down list box.

❽ Select the color dark red from the Fi**l**l drop-down list box.

❾ Select Shado**w** in the Options box.

**10** Click the **A**pply button.

**11** Click the OK button.

A large, curved `Hunks` appears in a graphic box over the current slide in the presentation window.

**12** Using the lower right sizing handle, shrink the graphic box to about the size of a postage stamp.

**13** Click and drag the graphic box to a position between the word `Healthy` and the words of `Chicken` in the first line.

**14** Using the right and left sizing handles, adjust the size of the box so that it fills the space attractively (see figure 7.6).

**Figure 7.6**
A WordArt
graphic object
in a text line.

If you skipped the preceding two tutorials because you do not have WordArt 1 on your system, complete steps 1 through 15 of the following tutorial to learn how to use WordArt 2. Then return to the preceding tutorials to learn how to apply the special text effects in that tutorial using WordArt 2.

## Creating a Text Object with WordArt 2

To create a text object with WordArt 2, do the following:

**1** Click the third line that begins with the compound word `Cholesterol-Free` to select that area of the slide.

WordArt allows the approximate placement of a graphic object as you apply the special text.

**2** Choose **O**bject from the **I**nsert menu.

**3** Choose WordArt 2 from the Insert Object dialog box.

The WordArt 2 application window opens (see figure 7.7). This window contains a text box for typing your text and two command buttons: **I**nsert Symbol and **U**pdate Display.

(continues)

7

## Creating a Text Object with WordArt 2 (continued)

**Figure 7.7**
The WordArt 2 application screen.

Notice that the PowerPoint application window is still present, and that the current slide is overlaid with a graphic box that contains the words Your Text Here. This graphic box shows the approximate location where the graphic object created in WordArt 2 will be placed on the current slide.

In addition, the regular PowerPoint menu and toolbars have been replaced with the WordArt 2 menu and toolbar. The WordArt 2 toolbar is similar to the Formatting toolbar in PowerPoint but contains buttons specific to the WordArt 2 application.

❹ In the WordArt 2 application window text box, enter the compound word **Cholesterol-Free**.

❺ Click the down-arrow button on the Font drop-down list box (the middle list box on the WordArt 2 toolbar.)

The list of TrueType fonts loaded on your system appears in the list box. You can use the arrow keys to move the selection and view the various fonts. (You will notice that the application of these fonts to your text is a bit slower than with WordArt 1.)

❻ Select the font Arial Rounded MT, or if this font is not available on your system, use Century Gothic.

❼ Click the down-arrow button on the Style drop-down list box, which shows the default style—Plain Text.

The Style drop-down list box appears and displays a collection of shapes (see figure 7.8). Each shape designates how the text will be shaped. In the upper left corner is a straight line, which represents the Plain Text default shape. The arch shape in the box immediately below the Plain Text shape arches the text. The bold circle shape two columns to the right and one row down turns the text into a boldface circle.

**Figure 7.8**
The Style drop-down list box.

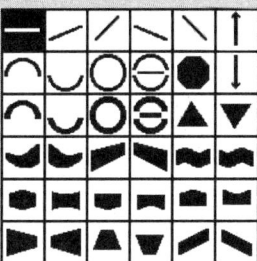

**8** Select the curve up shape, which is in the first column, fourth row.

The text is molded into this shape.

**9** Click anywhere outside the WordArt 2 application window.

When the window clears, the new graphic object overlays the current slide.

**10** Use a corner sizing handle to reduce proportionately the size of the graphic object to about the size of a postage stamp.

**11** Click the middle sizing handle on the right side of the graphic object, and increase the length horizontally to about twice the length of a postage stamp.

**12** Select the text box that contains the third line beginning with the words `Cholesterol-Free`, and delete the words `Cholesterol-Free`.

**13** Move the text box to the right if necessary.

This position is not the text box's final position. You merely want to get it out of the way in order to position the Cholesterol-Free graphic object.

**14** Move the Cholesterol-Free graphic object to a position near the left edge of the slide and just above the `Mom's Home Cookin'` label (refer to figure 7.9 for the correct position).

**15** Position the text box containing the words `for Your Heart` to the right of the Cholesterol-Free graphic object.

**16** If you don't have WordArt 1, return to the preceding tutorials, "Creating a Text Object with WordArt 1," and "Adding Another Text Object to Your Slide." Use WordArt 2 to make the changes described there.

When you have finished, your slide should look like figure 7.9.

(continues)

7

**Creating a Text Object with WordArt 2 (continued)**

**Figure 7.9**
Positioning a
WordArt 2
graphic object
on a slide.

# Objective 2: Manipulate Text Objects

When you are creating graphic and text objects on a slide, you generally have a certain image in your mind, particularly if you are creating the design yourself. However, the way objects actually appear on a slide does not always match that mental image.

Design elements that may seem appropriate in the design stage may not work in the presentation stage. And even when designs work as expected, the design may simply provide the basis for improvements that will result in a more effective presentation.

PowerPoint provides many ways to manipulate text and text objects. For example, to edit any of the text objects you created in Objective 1, you have only to select and double-click the object. The application that created that object starts automatically, and you can proceed to edit the object as desired.

You also can add colors, shading, and other effects to both the text and the text objects to make the slide visually appealing.

**Editing a WordArt 1 Object**

The word Hunks in the first line is too chunky to be clear. In fact, it looks rather like a blob. To edit this object, do the following:

**❶** Select the Slide Show button.

Slide 1 enlarges. Note that the word Hunks is chunky in this view.

**❷** Press Esc to stop the show.

**❸** Double-click the Hunks graphic object.

WordArt 1 starts with the Hunks object selected.

**Note:** *If you are working in WordArt 2, follow the instructions in the following tutorial to change this object.*

**4** From the **F**onts drop-down list box, choose the font Vashon.

The text is still a little bunched, but this font has possibilities.

**5** Deselect Shado**w** in the Options box.

The Preview image is now sharp and clear.

**6** Click **A**pply to apply the change and OK to exit.

The new font minus the shadow is now clear.

Double-clicking a WordArt 2 image also makes it available for immediate editing. In this mode, however, the text object appears on the slide in its current location. This position often makes it easier to review the changes as they are made.

## Editing a WordArt 2 Object

To edit a WordArt 2 image, do the following:

**1** Double-click the Cholesterol-Free graphic object.

The WordArt 2 application window opens, the PowerPoint menu and the Formatting toolbar change, and the graphic object appears in its current location on the slide.

**2** Click the Shading button on the Formatting toolbar.

Shading is the third button from the right, and its icon is a small box with diagonal lines to indicate shading. The Shading dialog box appears (see figure 7.10).

**Figure 7.10**
The Shading dialog box.

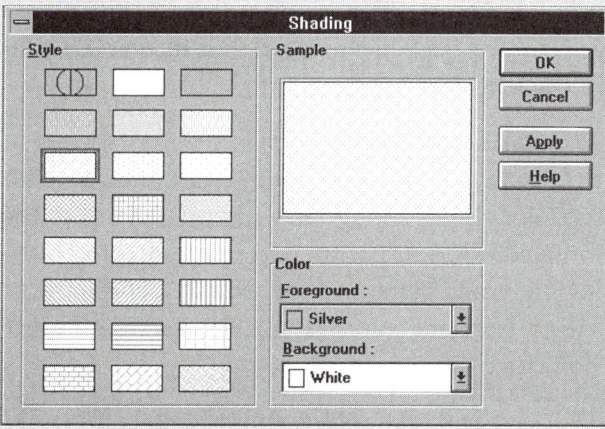

7

(continues)

**Editing a WordArt 2 Object (continued)**

**❸** In the Color box, click the **F**oreground drop-down list box.

**❹** Choose the color Lime.

**❺** Click A**p**ply and OK.

**❻** Click anywhere on the screen outside of the WordArt 2 application window.

PowerPoint returns with the Cholesterol-Free graphic object now in lime green.

# Objective 3: Change Text Style and Color

As you manipulate WordArt objects and apply different effects, shading, and color, the regular text that appears on the slide may be overshadowed by the colorful and interesting text objects. In fact, the real challenge may not be what to add with WordArt but how to handle the surrounding text.

Professionals follow some general principles for text design, but these principles are not rules. Sometimes the most effective presentation designs are those that go against accepted conventions.

**Balance**

A general matching of like elements on a slide so that elements do not overwhelm each other.

Generally speaking, you should strive for *balance*—a term used to describe the more-or-less matching of different elements. For example, neither the text object nor the text should overwhelm or overshadow the other. If too much emphasis is placed on the text object, the actual text, which contains the meat of the slide, may be lost. Conversely, tiny or inappropriate graphic objects next to boldface confrontational text may be ludicrous. Always consider the size of the text or objects you are combining on a slide.

Balance also concerns the placement of text and text objects. Too many large text objects next to each other rob attention. A slide filled with large type may be readable from the back of the room, but its message may be no more meaningful than the letters on an eye chart.

**Harmony**

The complementary relationship of various elements on a slide; the use of elements appropriate to the theme or content of the presentation.

In addition to balance, strive for *harmony*. Colors should complement each other, not clash. In general, all elements should work together to convey a point or message. Color choice should be appropriate both to the content and to the presentation medium. Soft pastels and subtle shading may be nice on a wedding presentation but could generate pink slips in a corporate boardroom considering a down-sizing plan. Dark colors do not project well from slides but can be clear on transparencies.

Type fonts for text and text objects should also complement each other. The use of script to explain the block-lettered points for fighting crime on the streets would most certainly detract from the seriousness of the message. A Medieval Gothic font used in a presentation extolling the virtues of a Caribbean retreat would be appropriate only if the destination were Devil's Island.

## Changing Text Containing a Text Object

The text that surrounds the word Hunks appears drab and ordinary. To dress up this text, do the following:

**1** Click the word Healthy to select this text object.

**2** Starting with the letter H in Healthy, select all the words, Healthy...of Chicken, in the text box.

The Hunks graphic object is partially obscured. Don't worry, it is not involved.

**3** Change the font to Impact and the font size to 36 points.

**4** Position the insertion point before the words of Chicken.

**5** Press the [Spacebar] repeatedly to insert enough spaces to move these words to the right, aligning the n in Chicken with the u in the last word of the second line.

**6** Adjust the size of the Hunks graphics box by using the left and right sizing handles. Locate this graphic object so that it looks natural in the line.

The use of color on the first line of text that contains a text object may overwhelm the text object. Then again, it might not. This is one case where you may want to experiment with the use of color. If color helps, keep it. If color overwhelms the text objects, use basic black.

The third line, however, cries out for color. With a lime-green text object that has the appearance of good news, the black text line that follows is depressing.

## Adding Style and Color to Text

To change the style and add color to a text line, do the following:

**1** Highlight the phrase for Your Heart in its own text box.

**2** Change the font to Impact and the font size to 48 points.

You want to balance the type size of the text line with the text object that precedes it.

**3** With the phrase still highlighted, click the Text Color button on the Formatting toolbar.

The Color list box appears.

**4** Click the Other Color option.

The Other Colors list box appears.

*(continues)*

7

**5** Click the color red.

**6** Click OK.

The new style, size, and color are now applied to the text.

**7** Select the text box, and click the Bring Forward button on the Drawing+ toolbar.

**8** Select the Cholesterol-Free graphic box, and click the Send Backward button on the Drawing+ toolbar.

In order to balance these two elements and achieve a pleasing visual flow to the line, the text box and graphic box will have to overlap slightly, thus blocking out a portion of the content. By putting one box in the foreground and the other in the background, you make any overlap transparent.

**9** Adjust the placement of the text box so that the words `for Your Heart` appear to flow naturally out of the words `Cholesterol-Free` (see figure 7.11).

**Figure 7.11**
The natural flow of text when combined with WordArt.

**10** Save the presentation as **ADV1.PPT**.

# Objective 4: Select and Align Text and Group Objects

**Alignment**
The positioning of text on a slide, such as centered, right, left, and justified; affects the entire paragraph.

*Alignment* generally refers to the way text is positioned on a slide. Although other attributes, such as style, color, and shading, can be used on a single letter, word, or phrase, alignment applies to an entire paragraph. A paragraph can consist of one or more lines in a text box.

Although the Formatting toolbar provides buttons for centering and left-aligning text, the menu provides choices for right-aligned and justified text. On slides that use larger font sizes for ease of viewing, justified text may look awkward because generally fewer words can be spaced evenly in a line, and you may have very large spaces between words.

Graphics professionals often use the word *alignment* to apply to the grouping of all the elements in a design. For example, captions are aligned with illustrations, blocks of text are aligned in columns, and the tops and bottoms of facing pages—as in a book—are aligned for a generally pleasing appearance.

**Group**
A collection of objects on a slide that can be treated as a single object.

In PowerPoint, the alignment of text and graphic objects is handled by combining elements in a *group*. After the elements are grouped, the group of elements can be treated as a single unit that can be moved and repositioned. The internal positions of the grouped elements—and their positions relative to each other—remain unchanged.

## Aligning Text on a Slide

You may have many reasons to align text on a slide, but the most common reason is to present the material in a clear and appealing manner. There are also several ways to align text on a slide. To create an alignment pattern and to align text, do the following:

**1** Make slide 2 of the ADV1 presentation the active slide.

**2** Click the text box to add subtitle text, and type **A Hardy, Heart-Healthy Soup**.

**3** Highlight the text you just typed.

**4** Click the Center button on the Formatting toolbar.

**5** With the text still highlighted, click the Text Color button on the Formatting toolbar, and select the color red.

**6** Click the Increase Font Size button on the Formatting toolbar once.

**7** Position the insertion point at the end of the text line, and press .

**8** Click the Bullet On/Off button.

**9** Choose **B**ullet from the F**o**rmat menu.

The Bullet dialog box appears (see figure 7.12).

**Figure 7.12**
The Bullet dialog box.

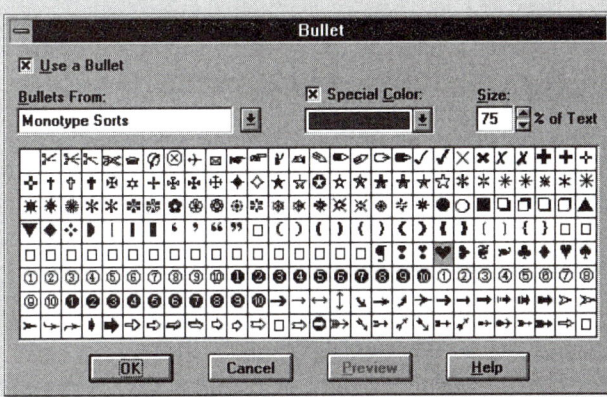

(continues)

## Aligning Text on a Slide (continued)

**10** Select the heart-shaped symbol (refer to figure 7.12).

**11** In the **S**ize list box, set the size to 150%.

**12** In the Special **C**olor list box, select the color red, and click OK.

**13** Change the font selection to Book Antiqua, and set the font size to 32 points.

**14** Click the Text Color button on the Formatting toolbar, and change the text color to blue.

**15** Type the following lines, pressing ⏎Enter after each but the last:

**Real Chicken**

**Garden-Fresh Vegetables**

**No Fat**

**No Cholesterol**

The result should appear similar to the slide illustration in figure 7.13. Notice that centering each line makes the overall appearance confusing. Because the lines are different lengths, the alignment pattern appears to be random.

**Figure 7.13**
Bulleted items on a slide in a centered alignment pattern.

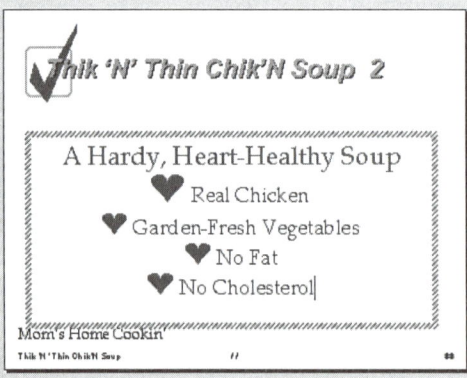

**16** Position the insertion point in the line Real Chicken, and click the Left Alignment button in the Formatting toolbar.

**17** Position the insertion point in the line No Cholesterol.

**18** Choose **A**lignment from the F**o**rmat menu.

The Alignment submenu appears.

**19** Choose **R**ight from the Alignment submenu.

The heart-shaped bullets now descend in a slanting line from left to right. Although the line lengths are still random, the slanting bullets give the appearance of an alignment pattern.

## Creating and Aligning a Graphic Object

When you create a graphic object, you generally want to align that object with the other elements on the slide. This type of alignment is not text alignment but design alignment. To create and align a graphic object, do the following:

**1** Choose **O**bject from the **I**nsert menu.

**2** Select WordArt 2 as the Object **T**ype from the Insert Object dialog box, and click OK (refer to figure 7.3).

The WordArt 2 application window appears (refer to figure 7.7).

**3** From the Font drop-down list box on the Formatting toolbar, select the font Book Antiqua.

**4** Type **Heart-Check for Health** in the Enter Your Text Here dialog box.

**5** Click the **I**nsert Symbol button.

The Symbol dialog box appears.

**6** Select the trademark symbol TM, and click OK.

**7** From the Style drop-down list box on the Formatting toolbar, select the thin circle shape.

The text is reshaped into a circle.

**8** Click the Shading button on the Formatting toolbar.

The Shading dialog box appears.

**9** From the **F**oreground drop-down list box, select the color navy.

**10** In the **S**tyle option box, click the dark style box in the upper right corner.

**11** Click A**p**ply and OK to close the dialog box.

**12** Click anywhere outside the WordArt 2 application window.

The graphic object overlays the current slide.

**13** Click and drag the sizing handle at the lower right corner inward and reduce the graphic box to about 50 percent larger than a conventional postage stamp.

**14** Position the graphic object just above the tag line Mom's Home Cookin', as shown in figure 7.14.

(continues)

7

**Creating and Aligning a Graphic Object (continued)**

**Figure 7.14**
Multiple
selected
elements and
sizing handles.

After you have designed and created text and graphic elements, you frequently want to keep related items together in a group.

**Grouping Elements in a Block**

To group a text and graphic element, do the following:

❶ Click one of the bulleted lines.

The gray text box outline appears.

❷ Position the mouse pointer on the outline, and click the left mouse button. The sizing handles appear.

❸ Hold down ⬆Shift, and click inside the circle of the graphic object.

The graphic object sizing handles appear as well (refer to figure 7.14).

❹ Choose **G**roup from the **D**raw menu.

New sizing handles appear, indicating the single group. You can now size, move, and position this group as a single unit.

You may want to move a group to provide a more pleasing appearance to your slide or to provide space for entering additional elements.

**Moving a Group to Make Room for Additional Elements**

To move a group, do the following:

❶ With the group sizing handles visible, click and hold down the left mouse button.

The group border appears.

❷ Drag the group slightly lower on the slide. Release the left mouse button.

You can now use the area above the group for additional elements.

**3** Click the Text Tool button on the Drawing toolbar.

**4** Position the mouse pointer beneath the left border of the check-marked box, and type **Announcing . . . .**

**5** Select the word `Announcing. . .`, and change the font size to 48.

One way to edit elements in a group is to choose **U**ngroup from **D**raw menu, edit the element, and then choose **R**egroup from the **D**raw menu. Another way is to edit the element directly.

## Editing Grouped Elements

To edit a text element in a group, do the following:

**1** Select the subtitle line, `A Hardy, Heart-Healthy Soup`.

**2** Click the Italic button on the Formatting toolbar.

The slide should now look similar to figure 7.15.

**Figure 7.15**
Grouped elements with a new element and a new style added to slide.

You can group many different elements on a slide, including graphic objects that are part of text objects.

## Grouping Multiple Elements

To group multiple elements, do the following:

**1** Make slide 1 the active slide.

**2** Click the Hunks graphic object.

**3** Hold down ⇧Shift, and click the word `Chicken`.

**4** Continue holding down ⇧Shift, and click the Thick graphic object.

(continues)

7

**Grouping Multiple Elements (continued)**

⑤ Choose **G**roup from the **D**raw menu.

⑥ Create a new group composed of the Cholesterol-Free graphic object and the For Your Heart text object.

⑦ Save and close the file **ADV1.PPT**.

# Objective 5: Find and Replace Text

The techniques used to find and replace text in PowerPoint are similar to those used in other Microsoft applications. The **F**ind option enables you to search quickly through a presentation to locate a specific word or phrase. The Find/ Replace option enables you make global changes to the presentations.

When you use Find/Replace, the replacement text follows the same format as the text being replaced.

**Finding Text in a Presentation**

The trademark attorneys have determined that you may have a problem with the word *hearty*, as in *hearty taste*, in your presentations—even though you thought it was a cute play on words. Another company may have used it first. The attorneys want to know whether you actually used the word. To locate this word in a presentation, do the following:

❶ Load SOUP2.PPT as the active presentation, and save it as **SOUP3.PPT**.

❷ In Slide Sorter view, choose **F**ind from the **E**dit menu.

The Find dialog box appears (see figure 7.16).

**Figure 7.16**
The Find dialog box.

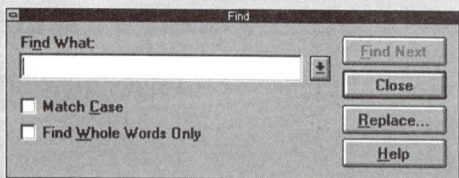

❸ Type the word **hearty** in the Fi**n**d What text box.

❹ Click the **F**ind All button.

The procedure locates one instance of the word on slide 9.

❺ Close the Find dialog box if necessary.

Sure enough, the attorneys come back and say that you can't use the word.

## Finding and Replacing Text

To use the Find and Replace option to replace the word, do the following:

**1** Make slide 1 the active slide in Slide Sorter view.

**2** Choose **R**eplace from the **E**dit menu.

The Replace dialog box appears (see figure 7.17).

**Figure 7.17**
The Replace
dialog box.

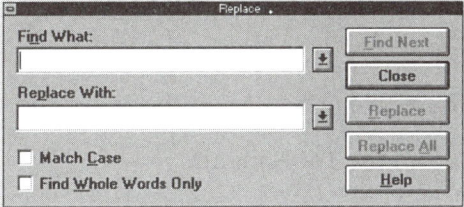

**3** Type **hearty** in the Fi**n**d What text box.

If you have just completed the preceding tutorial, the word hearty is already displayed in the Fi**n**d What text box. Normally, you would not be this lucky.

**4** In the Re**p**lace With text box, type **hardy**.

**5** Click the Replace **A**ll button.

**Note:** *If you want to verify that all occurrences of the word* hearty *were replaced by the word* hardy, *after using Replace **A**ll, you can click the **F**ind Next button. If you want to verify each change as it is made, you can click the **F**ind Next button and the **R**eplace button for each change.*

**6** Click the Close button.

**7** Save the presentation **SOUP3.PPT**.

7

# Objective 6: Use the Spelling Checker

**Spelling
Checker**
A subprogram that
checks the spelling
of titles and text
used on slides.

Aside from presenting irrelevant or inaccurate information, nothing harms a presentation more than spelling errors—especially in front of an audience. Errors in spelling convey an impression of sloppy, hasty work. At the very least, it is hard to be authoritative and convincing when you are embarrassed by mistakes.

PowerPoint uses the same Spelling Checker that is used by Microsoft Word, Publisher, and Excel and is similar to those used by other Windows-based word processing programs. Of major significance is the program's capability to add words or names to a custom dictionary.

The Spelling Checker locates and displays not just spelling errors, but any words that do not conform to words in the Spelling Checker's dictionary—names of people, trade names, and jargon, for example. You access the Spelling Checker from the Tools menu and with the Spelling button on the Standard toolbar.

### Using the Spelling Checker

To see how the Spelling Checker works and to correct any spelling errors, follow these general steps:

1. Make slide 1 of the active presentation the active slide.

2. Choose **S**pelling from the T**o**ols menu.

   The Spelling Checker starts, and the Spelling dialog box appears on the screen (see figure 7.18).

**Figure 7.18**
The Spelling
dialog box.

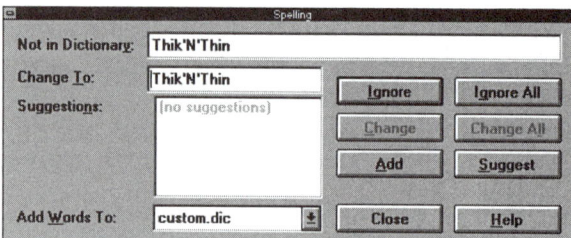

The first incorrect or unrecognized word appears in the Not in Dictionary text box. This box lists the current word(s) under scrutiny.

If the spelling dictionary contains similar words, the Spelling Checker lists these words in the Suggestions list box.

The Change **T**o box normally contains the word that the Spelling Checker is recommending. If there are no suggestions, the box shows what you originally wrote.

The **I**gnore button tells the Spelling Checker to ignore the current word and proceed to find the next word to check.

The I**g**nore All button stores the current selection in a temporary supplemental dictionary. The Spelling Checker will ignore all occurrences of this word during the current spelling check.

The Change A**l**l button changes to the correct spelling any occurrence of the displayed "misspelling" anywhere in the presentation.

The Spelling Checker also locates words by spaces, that is, when there is a space before and after a collection of letters, that collection is viewed as word.

3. Continue spell checking until the Spelling Checker returns to the first slide.

If you tell PowerPoint to accept a word it doesn't recognize, a warning box appears (see figure 7.19).

**Figure 7.19**
A PowerPoint warning box with spelling questioned.

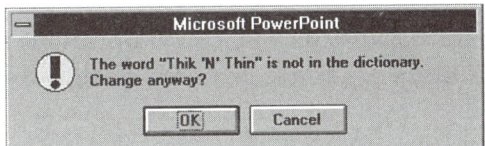

4. Click OK to accept the new word.

5. Click Close in the Spelling dialog box to leave the Spelling Checker.

6. Save the file as **SOUP3.PPT**.

# Chapter Summary

This chapter is about text—text as words and text as art. In this chapter, you have learned how to use WordArt 1 and WordArt 2 and noted the differences between them. The creative use of lettering and the placement of wordart on a slide is discussed, as is the importance of balance and harmony in combining color, text, and graphic objects. You learned how to group various elements on a slide so that the grouped elements are treated as a single unit. You also learned how to find and replace text elements and how to use the Spelling Checker to find errors.

# Checking Your Skills

### True/False Questions

For each of the following statements, circle *T* or *F* to indicate whether the statement is true or false.

T  F  **1.** WordArt 1, sometimes known as WordArt, is distributed with its own set of fonts.

T  F  **2.** One reason to put objects in the background on a slide is so that they will be transparent when overlapping another object.

T  F  **3.** The term *alignment* means one thing when referring to text and another when referring to layout and design.

T  F  **4.** To make global changes to a presentation, you use the **F**ind option on the **E**dit menu.

T  F  **5.** In addition to spelling errors, the Spelling Checker also finds unknown words and unusual terms.

7

## Multiple-Choice Questions

In the blank provided, write the letter of the correct answer for each of the following questions.

___ **1.** When you are viewing the application of various fonts to text in the Preview box of the Microsoft WordArt dialog box, it is usually best to _____.

    **a.** click the selection to see the result

    **b.** use a font that best fits the word

    **c.** use the arrow keys to scroll through the font list

    **d.** click the Apply button to see how the word actually appears in context

___ **2.** When two elements of a slide, such as a text line and a graphic object, are matched for maximum effectiveness, these elements are said to be _____.

    **a.** in rapport

    **b.** in balance

    **c.** in harmony

    **d.** inappropriate

___ **3.** Double-clicking an existing WordArt 2 object on a slide _____.

    **a.** makes it available for deletion

    **b.** selects it for grouping with other elements

    **c.** makes it available for editing

    **d.** starts the WordArt 1 application

___ **4.** Alignment can apply _____.

    **a.** only to a single text box

    **b.** only when you are using the Text tool

    **c.** only to a single paragraph

    **d.** to all the text elements on a slide

___ **5.** If you suspect that you have made the same spelling error throughout a presentation, you probably should _____.

    **a.** use the Find and Replace options from the File menu

    **b.** use the Change button in the Spelling Checker

    **c.** use the Change All button in the Spelling Checker

    **d.** review all the slides one by one

### Fill-in-the-Blank Questions

In the blank provided, write the correct answer for each of the following questions.

1. WordArt 2 uses _____ fonts.

2. Although WordArt is created with text fonts and is sometimes referred to as a *text object*, WordArt is actually a _____ object.

3. _____ is one of the major factors to consider in the placement of text and text objects on a slide so that neither overwhelms the other.

4. Elements on a slide that complement each other are said to be in _____.

5. _____ elements can be moved as a single unit.

# Applying Your Skills

## Review Exercises

### Exercise 1: Using WordArt to Enhance a Presentation

The opening slide of the presentation ADV1 contains the line *Fat-Free for the Thin in You*. The two words *Fat* and *Thin* can be enhanced with special text effects such as using fat or rounded letters for *Fat* and thin or tall letters for *Thin*. Use the version of WordArt you prefer to enhance these words and position them in the sentence. Save the file as **ADV1A.PPT**.

### Exercise 2: Add Color to Text and Text Objects

Load the file ADV1A.PPT and save as **ADV2.PPT**. Add appropriate colors to the text and text objects for line 2, the line to which you added the WordArt effects. Be sure to use colors that complement not only the line elements but the elements in lines 1 and 3 as well. Keep in mind that garish or loud colors may distract from your presentation, but complementary colors may emphasize a particular point.

### Exercise 3: Grouping, Editing, and Balancing Slide Elements

Load the file ADV2.PPT, and save it as **ADV3.PPT**. Group the elements of line 2. Edit line 2 to read *Fat-Free for the Thin You Love*. Ungroup if you need to reposition any elements, and then regroup. Realign the groups of all three lines to balance the slide.

## Continuing Projects

### Project 1: Using WordArt to Improve a Presentation

The project ADV2.PPT is a bit dull. Liven up the presentation by using one of the WordArt subprograms to dress up the slides. Remember that you want to engender a feeling of excitement in your audience. You are selling both yourself and the product. Make the presentation work for you by using colors and effects that say something positive about your idea. Save your work as **ADV2A.PPT**.

7

**Project 2: Building Power Presentations**

The presentation HERSTORY.PPT, which provides the background history on the company, is very important to the board of directors. They are planning to use it at the next stockholders' meeting. Dress up the presentation using WordArt, but be judicious. You want the presentation to be exciting but not glitzy. After completing your changes, use the Spelling Checker to correct any errors in spelling.

# CHAPTER 8

# Illustrating a Presentation

One way to make a presentation exciting is to add drawings and illustrations. This chapter explains how to use the PowerPoint drawing tools to illustrate presentations with a variety of basic shapes and free-form illustrations known as drawing objects. Like other objects used in PowerPoint, drawing objects can be sized, placed in precise locations, and enhanced with complementing colors.

## Objectives

By the time you have finished this chapter, you will have learned to

1. Use Drawing Tools

2. Use AutoShapes

3. Use the FreeForm Tool

4. Edit Lines and Shapes

5. Enhance Objects

6. Use Guides, Grids, and Rulers

7. Understand PowerPoint's Color Capabilities

## Objective 1: Use Drawing Tools

**Drawing object**
An illustration created with PowerPoint drawing tools.

You do not have to be a professional artist to illustrate a presentation. PowerPoint makes illustration easy by providing a wide variety of basic shapes that you can combine to create simple or complex illustrations, called *drawing objects*.

Like other objects in PowerPoint, such as graph and text objects, drawing objects can be selected, edited, deleted, sized, moved between foreground and background, and repositioned. Drawing objects, however, can also be manipulated in other ways: they can be given fill colors, snapped to invisible grids, and sized according to the form of the drawing object.

## Examining the PowerPoint Toolbars

**Drawing tool**

A drawing function available from one of three toolbars and used to create and manipulate drawing objects.

Three toolbars provide the *drawing tools* that you use to create drawing objects. These toolbars are the AutoShapes toolbar, the Drawing toolbar, and the Drawing+ toolbar. You can change the shapes of these toolbars, toggle them on and off, and move them about the screen by dragging the toolbar's title bar or border. You use the drawing tools to draw shapes, color and fill shapes, and manipulate drawing objects. Figure 8.1 shows these three toolbars and identifies the tool buttons on each toolbar.

**Figure 8.1**

Toolbars used in PowerPoint drawing.

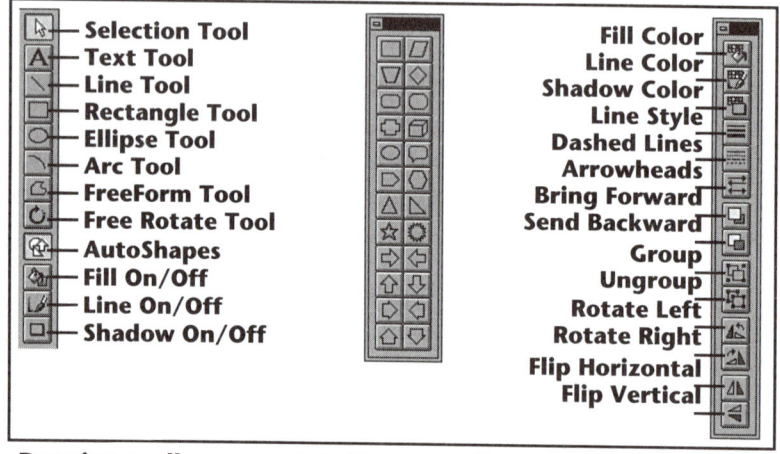

Drawing toolbar          AutoShapes toolbar          Drawing+ toolbar

### The Drawing Toolbar

Tools for drawing various objects, such as squares, rectangles, ellipses, and lines, are available on the Drawing toolbar. You simply click the button for the tool you want. The Drawing toolbar also provides tools for changing the objects that you draw. These tools include the Fill and Free Rotate tools. The AutoShapes button on the Drawing toolbar displays the AutoShapes toolbar.

### The AutoShapes Toolbar

The AutoShapes toolbar buttons produce commonly used shapes, such as squares, plus signs, diamonds, stars, and arrows. You can insert these shapes at any location on a slide and then manipulate them using other toolbar tools. You display the AutoShapes toolbar from the Drawing toolbar, or you can choose **T**oolbars on the **V**iew menu and select this toolbar.

### The Drawing+ Toolbar

The Drawing+ toolbar contains special tools that are used to modify drawing objects. You can change colors, add shadows, change line widths, add arrowhead pointers, move objects between the foreground and background, and flip objects to provide mirror or upside-down images.

You display the Drawing+ toolbar by choosing **T**oolbars from the **V**iew menu or by using the right mouse button to click any open toolbar to produce the Toolbars submenu and then selecting the Drawing+ toolbar.

## Sizing and Positioning Toolbars

You can position toolbars anywhere in the application window by clicking and dragging the title bar or border of the toolbar you want to move. You can resize toolbars by positioning the mouse pointer on the border of a toolbar to display a double-headed arrow and then clicking and dragging the border to change the toolbar's size.

You can add drawing objects to any existing presentation or create a new presentation that will contain drawing objects. In the tutorials in this chapter, you add and modify drawing objects on a presentation prepared for a forum on the issues involving cholesterol-free and fat-free chicken soup.

## Preparing a Presentation for Drawing Objects

The chief nutritionist at Dad's Homebrew has charged that the process for removing the fat and cholesterol from chicken also removes all nutritional value. To answer these charges, Mom's will conduct a forum as a video conference with the participants asking the nutrition experts at Mom's Home Cookin' a variety of questions about the nutritional value of Thik 'N' Thin Chik'N Soup.

The primary objective of the forum is to answer all questions openly and honestly and to squelch the baseless accusations. The presentation you are preparing will combine graphics, text, and drawing objects and will establish the structure of the forum and ensure a fair hearing.

To prepare the presentation for drawing objects, do the following:

❶ Start PowerPoint and a new presentation using the template BANNERS.PPT. The New Slide dialog box appears.

or

If PowerPoint is running, choose **N**ew from the **F**ile menu. Select the **T**emplate option in the New Presentation dialog box and BANNERS.PPT from the Presentation Template dialog box. The New Slide dialog box appears.

❷ Select the slide design Object from the New Slide dialog box, and click OK.

❸ Save the presentation as **FORUM1.PPT**.

❹ From the F**o**rmat menu, choose Slide **C**olor Scheme.

The Slide Color Scheme dialog box appears (see figure 8.2).

**Figure 8.2**
The Slide Color
Scheme dialog
box.

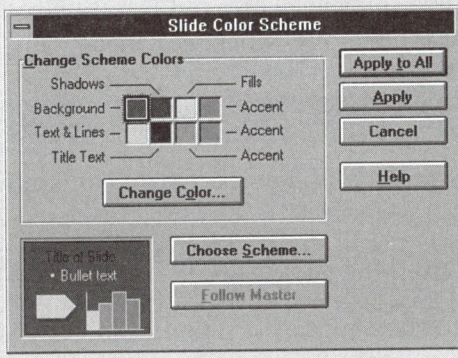

8

(continues)

## Preparing a Presentation for Drawing Objects (continued)

**5** Select Background in the Change Scheme Colors option box, and click the Change Color button.

The Background Color dialog box appears.

**6** In the Color Palette options box, select the lightest gray color, and click OK.

The Slide Color Scheme dialog box reappears.

**7** Select the Fills option, and click the Change Color button.

The Fill Color dialog box appears.

**8** Select the bright yellow color in the Color Palette options box, and click OK.

**9** In the Slide Color Scheme dialog box, click the Apply to All button.

**10** Save the presentation as **FORUM1.PPT**.

You are now ready to create a presentation for the Thik 'N' Thin Chick'N Soup Forum.

### Displaying the Drawing Toolbars

**Dock**

A blank area on any side of a presentation window, used for parking a toolbar.

By default, the Drawing toolbar is displayed in a *dock* at the left edge of the presentation window. Docks are blank areas that are generated by the presence of a toolbar at either side or the top or bottom of a presentation window. When a toolbar is moved from a dock, the dock disappears. If the toolbar is not docked but is parked in the middle of a presentation window, the toolbar is a floating toolbar.

**Floating toolbar**

A toolbar that is parked within a presentation rather than docked.

A *floating toolbar* is easily recognized by the title bar and control button at the top. When you move a floating toolbar into dock, the title bar and control button disappear. You can change the shapes of floating toolbars by clicking and dragging the border of the toolbar.

Displaying the Drawing+ toolbar continuously while you are creating drawing objects keeps these tools readily available, but it is usually more convenient to display the AutoShapes toolbar only when you are actually using it.

## Working with the Drawing Toolbars

To display the drawing toolbars and practice sizing and moving the toolbars, do the following:

**1** Choose Toolbars from the View menu.

The Toolbars dialog box appears (see figure 8.3). The Standard, Formatting, and Drawing toolbar check boxes in the Toolbars option box should be selected. The Color Buttons and Show ToolTips check boxes should also be selected.

**Figure 8.3**

The Toolbars dialog box.

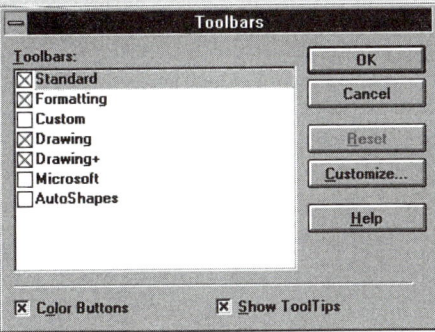

**2** Select the Drawing+ check box if neccessary (as it is in figure 8.3), and click OK.

The Drawing+ toolbar is now displayed; it should be displayed vertically next to the Drawing toolbar.

**3** Position the mouse pointer inside the border of the Drawing+ toolbar but *not* inside one of the toolbar buttons.

**4** Click and drag the Drawing+ toolbar across the screen, positioning the toolbar on the right side of the presentation window.

A new dock appears to contain the toolbar. The presentation window should now have a toolbar in a dock on either side.

**5** Click and drag the Drawing toolbar to the middle of the presentation window.

The dock at the left edge of the presentation window disappears, and a title bar and control menu button appear at the top of the toolbar.

**6** Position the mouse pointer on the right border of the Drawing toolbar so that the pointer changes to a double-headed arrow. Click and drag the border to the right.

The toolbar changes shape from a vertical bar to a series of rectangles to a horizontal bar, depending on how far you drag the border.

**8**

**Note:** *When the shape of a toolbar changes, the size always adjusts to accommodate the number of buttons in the toolbar. The size of the individual buttons does not change in this process.*

## Using the Toolbars

The FORUM presentation will combine graphics, text, and drawing objects. To create the title screen for the forum, do the following:

**1** Dock the Drawing toolbar at the left of the presentation window.

**2** Click the title box, and type the words **Thik 'N' Thin Chik'N Soup**.

**3** Press ⏎Enter, and type the words **Video Conference**, and click anywhere outside the title box.

**4** Double-click the Insert Object icon below the title.

**5** Select Microsoft ClipArt Gallery from the Insert Object dialog box. Click OK.

**6** Select the Video Conference clip art from Microsoft ClipArt Gallery dialog box.

The clip art appears enlarged on the title slide.

**7** Using the lower right corner sizing handle, proportionately reduce the size of the clip-art image until the width of the image is a little less than half the width of the slide.

**8** Position the sized clip-art image in the lower left corner of the title slide.

**9** Click the Ellipse tool button on the Drawing toolbar.

The mouse pointer changes to a plus sign over the presentation window.

**10** Position the mouse pointer in the upper left corner of the gray area of the title slide, about 1/4 inch from the left edge and the yellow title box.

**11** Press and hold down the left mouse button, and drag the mouse pointer toward the lower right corner of the slide.

An ellipse forms, like a large egg in the center of the slide.

**12** When the egg is centered in the gray area of the slide, release the mouse button.

The clip art is obscured by the ellipse, which is shown inside a drawing object box with sizing handles. The presence of sizing handles indicates that the ellipse is currently selected.

If the ellipse is not a solid color and is shown as a dotted white oval, click the Fill On/Off button on the Drawing toolbar to toggle the Fill button on and make the ellipse visible. When the Fill button is toggled off, the drawing object is invisible.

**Note:** *If the ellipse is not centered in the gray area of the slide, you can choose* **U**ndo *from the* **E**dit *menu to remove the ellipse and try again.*

**13** With the ellipse still selected, click the Fill Color button on the Drawing+ toolbar, and select the bright yellow color from the drop-down menu if necessary.

The ellipse changes to bright yellow.

**14** With the ellipse still selected, click the Send Backward button on the Drawing+ toolbar to place this drawing object behind the clip art.

**15** To give depth to the ellipse, with the ellipse still selected, click the Shadow On/Off button on the Drawing toolbar.

**16** To change the color of the shadow, with the ellipse still selected, click the Shadow Color button on the Drawing+ toolbar, and select the color red.

The slide should now resemble that shown in figure 8.4.

**Figure 8.4**
The first slide with text, graphics, and drawing object.

Thik 'N' Thin Chik'N Soup
Video Conference

# Objective 2: Use AutoShapes

AutoShapes are built-in designs that you can use both as starting points for more detailed drawings and as complements to other elements of a design. You select these shapes from the AutoShapes toolbar. Like other objects, AutoShapes can be sized, edited, and moved.

## Opening the AutoShapes Toolbar

**8**

You can open the Drawing toolbar from the Edit menu or from the Toolbars submenu. To open the AutoShapes toolbar by using the Toolbars submenu, do the following:

**1** Position the mouse pointer over any toolbar on the screen.

**2** Click the right mouse button.

The Toolbars submenu appears (see figure 8.5).

## Opening the AutoShapes Toolbar (continued)

**Figure 8.5**
The Toolbars
submenu.

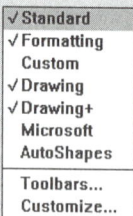

| |
|---|
| √ Standard |
| √ Formatting |
| Custom |
| √ Drawing |
| √ Drawing+ |
| Microsoft |
| AutoShapes |
| Toolbars... |
| Customize... |

**3** Select the AutoShapes toolbar.

Selected and visible toolbars are shown with check marks on the Toolbars submenu.

One of the simplest ways to add impact to a presentation is to use a familiar shape that conveys an impression by its design. Traffic signs are an excellent example. You do not really have to read the word *STOP* to recognize a stop sign on a street corner or the words *Railroad Crossing* to know that the crossed bars are warning motorists of train tracks crossing the road ahead.

## Adding and Sizing an AutoShape

To use a basic shape to convey an impression, do the following:

**1** Select the Balloon Tool button on the AutoShapes toolbar.

The mouse pointer changes to a plus sign.

**2** Position the mouse pointer above the woman's head and a little below the title box area on the slide.

**3** Drag the mouse pointer down and to the right to create a balloon in the space between the woman's head and the title box.

The balloon should be about as wide as the words Video Conference on the slide. Figure 8.6 shows both the placement of the balloon and the text you will be adding in the next tutorial.

**Figure 8.6**
The placement of a balloon on a slide to indicate speech.

**4** Release the mouse button to apply the balloon drawing object.

**5** Adjust the size by using the sizing handles. Reposition the balloon by clicking and dragging the drawing object's border.

**6** Click the Fill Color button on the Drawing+ toolbar, and select the lightest shade of blue.

**7** Click the Shadow Color button on the Drawing+ toolbar, and select Embossed.

The balloon is used to convey the impression of speech in an illustration. The video conference will be led by a moderator—Mom's has hired Ms. Charlestown South Carolina as the hostess of the program—and will combine both sight and sound. The balloon suggests speech on the title screen.

## Adding Text to a Drawing Object

To add text to the balloon, do the following:

**1** Select the Text Tool button on the Drawing toolbar.

**2** Position the mouse pointer in the balloon near the left edge, and click the left mouse button.

**3** Click the Text Color button on the Formatting toolbar, and select the color black.

**4** Type the words **Hello. Mom's Home Cookin**, and press ⏎Enter.

**5** Type the words **welcomes you all to our Forum**, and click anywhere outside the text box.

You may have to adjust either the size of the balloon or the position of the text box so that all the text is contained within the balloon with the balloon shape intact.

### Capturing the Viewer's Interest

**Teaser**

Words or visuals designed to "hook" an audience.

A *teaser* is a few words, an announcement, or a visual designed as a "hook" to capture an audience's interest. The disembodied voice on television that says "Cattle Truck Rams Beer Truck on I-95. Steak and ale cover interstate. Film at eleven," is enticing you to watch the 11 o'clock news by using a teaser.

On a slide, a large arrow pointing right or downward can indicate "next" without actually using the word. Similarly, a basic shape can be combined with text to create a teaser.

**8**

## Using AutoShapes as Teasers

To create a teaser for this presentation, do the following:

**1** Click the Star Tool button on the AutoShapes toolbar.

**2** Draw a large star in the lower right corner of the slide.

**3** Apply a fill color of red and a shadow in black.

**4** Use the Text Tool on the Drawing toolbar to type the word **Starring** on top of the star.

**5** Change the font to Brush Script MT, the font size to 60 points, and the text color to white.

**6** Size the star, and position the text so that the word Starring is contained within the star.

Your slide should now resemble that in figure 8.7.

**Figure 8.7**
The title slide with a teaser that combines an AutoShape and text.

**7** Save the presentation as **FORUM1.PPT** before proceeding to the next objective.

# Objective 3: Use the FreeForm Tool

The FreeForm Tool button on the Drawing toolbar may be a bit confusing at first; but with a little practice, you can make this tool the most valuable in your drawing kit.

## Creating a New Slide and Adding Drawing Objects

As you build the FORUM presentation, you will use a variety of slide designs and objects. An interactive presentation like this provides an excellent opportunity to experiment with different visual effects. To prepare the next slide in this presentation, do the following:

**1** Click the New Slide button on the horizontal scroll bar at the bottom of the presentation window.

❷ Select the slide design Blank from the New Slide dialog box.

The new slide will be slide 2 in the presentation.

❸ Select the Star Tool on the AutoShapes toolbar, and place a small star (about one-half-inch wide from tip to tip) in the upper left corner of the gray bottom portion of the slide. Use the fill color solid yellow.

### Using the FreeForm Tool for Straight Lines

You can use the FreeForm tool in several different ways: as a variable, continuing straight-line drawing tool; as a free-form tool; and as a combination of these. Although the Line tool on the Drawing toolbar can draw a straight line, the Line tool can only draw each line as a single object. The FreeForm tool, however, can produce multiple straight lines in a single drawing object.

**Anchor**

A fixed point in a drawing object in which a portion of the object is locked into position.

The multiple straight lines created with the FreeForm tool are actually a single line that appears to be multiple lines. If you were to insert a series of pins in a random pattern on a bulletin board, tie a string around a starting pin, and then connect the remaining pins by stretching the string between them and looping each one, the string pattern might look as if it were constructed with a bunch of strings, but it is actually one long string. In a drawing object, "pin" locations are known as *anchor* points.

### Drawing Straight Lines with the FreeForm Tool

Figure 8.8 shows slide 2 with the star created in the preceding tutorial and a series of number locations from 1 to 8. The numbers do not appear on your slide but are reference points that will be connected by a series of straight lines in this tutorial.

**Figure 8.8**
Slide 2 with numbered reference points.

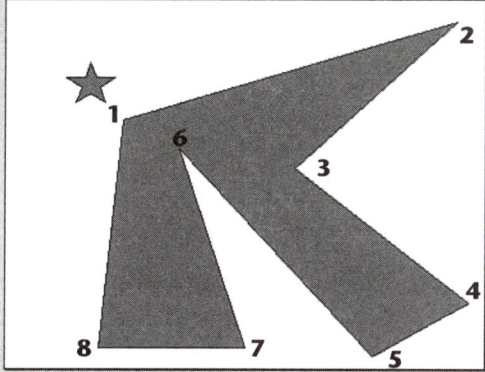

To connect these numbered reference points with a series of straight lines in a single drawing object, do the following:

❶ Remove the AutoShapes toolbar from the screen.

8

(continues)

## Drawing Straight Lines with the FreeForm Tool (continued)

**2** Click the FreeForm Tool button on the Drawing toolbar.

The mouse pointer changes to a plus sign.

**3** Position the mouse pointer on your slide at a point that corresponds to the number 1 in figure 8.8.

**4** Holding the mouse stationary, click the left mouse button.

**5** Move the mouse slightly upward and to the right to a point corresponding to the reference number 2.

A straight line anchored to reference point 1 extends behind the mouse pointer as you move the mouse.

**6** When you reach reference point 2, click the left mouse button again.

You have now anchored the line at this point and can change direction.

**7** Repeat this sequence for the remaining reference points, 3 through 8, pausing at reference point 8 for the next instruction.

**8** Connect reference point 8 with reference point 1, the starting point, by clicking reference point 1 with the left mouse button. If the sizing handles don't appear, press [Esc].

Any area that is totally enclosed by a free-form shape takes the current or default fill color. The enclosed area should now be filled. In addition, the drawing object is marked by a set of sizing handles, indicating that all the lines of the pattern are actually a single drawing object.

**Note:** *If the pattern you drew is not satisfactory, you can delete it by choosing **U**ndo from the **E**dit menu if using the FreeForm tool was your last activity. To delete the pattern later, select the drawing object, and when the sizing handles appear, press ∂    .*

**9** With the drawing object selected, use the Fill Color button on the Drawing+ toolbar to fill the enclosed area with the color yellow if necessary.

**10** Save the presentation as **FORUM1.PPT**.

A city councilman in New York City once said that inside all of us is a frustrated graffiti artist trying to get out. His point was that rather than trying to arrest all the graffiti painters who were decorating New York subways, it was probably better to buy graffiti-proof subway cars. If you are one of those people who have more than a passing interest in subway cars, the PowerPoint FreeForm tool may satisfy the frustrated graffiti artist inside you.

## Using the FreeForm Tool for Random Drawing

To create really weird drawing objects, do the following:

**1** Choose Slide Color Scheme from the Format menu.

The Slide Color Scheme dialog box appears (refer to figure 8.2).

**2** Select the Text & Lines option in the Change Scheme Colors options box, and click the Change Color button.

**3** Select the bright red color, the second box on the first row, in the Text & Line Colors dialog box, and click OK.

**4** In the Slide Color Scheme dialog box, click the Apply button.

You will be applying this color change only to the current slide and not to all the slides in the presentation. When the presentation window returns, the star and the straight-line pattern you created earlier will be bordered in red.

**5** Click the FreeForm tool on the Drawing toolbar.

The mouse pointer changes to a plus sign.

**6** Position the mouse pointer in the upper left corner of the upper yellow panel on the slide, and press and hold the left mouse button.

The mouse pointer changes into a pencil. (OK, it's not a can of spray paint, but this isn't a real subway car either.)

**7** Keeping the left mouse button pressed, draw a graffiti pattern of your own (see figure 8.9 for similar scribbles). Keep artwork inside the upper yellow panel. When you complete your masterpiece, press Esc to stop the drawing.

**Figure 8.9**
Graffiti on a
slide.

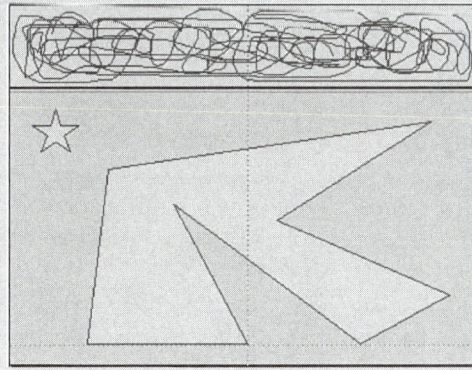

8

If you release the left mouse button at any point and move the mouse, the FreeForm tool reverts to the straight-line pattern you were using in the preceding tutorial. In a sense, the line dribbling out of the pencil is bit like a wad of freshly discarded gum sticking to the bottom of your shoe. In the same way the line is pinned when you click the mouse, everything your shoe touches becomes an anchor point for a new, rubbery strand.

# Objective 4: Edit Lines and Shapes

The lines and shapes you add to a slide as drawing objects are easy to edit. The two primary methods of editing these objects are by changing the size or perspective and by directly changing the object itself.

## Changing Size and Perspective

To change the size and the perspective of drawing objects, do the following:

1 With the sizing handles of the graffiti drawing object visible, position the mouse pointer over the middle sizing handle on the bottom border.

The mouse pointer changes to a vertical double-headed arrow.

2 Click and hold the left mouse button, and drag the lower border upward until the graffiti object outline is about one-quarter-inch wide. Release the left mouse button.

The graffiti drawing object now resembles a rope.

3 Click and drag the graffiti drawing object to the bottom of the slide, leaving a small, thin gray border between the border of the drawing object and the bottom border of the slide.

4 With graffiti drawing object still selected and using the Line Color button on the Drawing+ toolbar, change the line color to bright yellow.

5 Click the star drawing object.

The sizing handles appear.

6 Size and move the star drawing object so that your screen resembles figure 8.10.

Because the straight-line drawing object was created after the star, it is in the foreground, with a portion of the star now hidden.

7 With the star drawing object selected, click the Bring Forward button on the Drawing+ toolbar.

8 Save but do not close the FORUM1.PPT presentation.

# Objective 5: Enhance Objects

**Rotation mouse pointer**
The form the mouse pointer takes when the Free Rotation tool is active.

Adding shadows and patterns and changing colors are techniques often used to enhance objects on a slide. Another way to enhance objects is to change the relative position. You can also enhance drawing objects with the playful use of text. The Free Rotation tool is good to use to enhance your drawing objects. When you use this tool, the mouse pointer becomes the *rotation mouse pointer*. This pointer shape is two arrows revolving around a central dot.

## Enhancing with Shadows and Position

You have learned the basic way to add shadows to an object in previous tutorials, but some other features can add interest to a simple shadow. To add shadows to an object, do the following:

**1** With slide 2 as the active slide, select the star drawing object.

**2** Click the Shadow Color button on the Drawing+ toolbar.

**3** Choose Other Color, and select the bright blue color. Click OK.

**4** Click the Line Style button on the Drawing+ toolbar.

**5** Select the thick black line—third from the top in the Line Style box.

The shadow is now slightly separated from the star, creating a kind of mirrored effect.

**Note:** *If the fill color changes during this process, recolor the fill portion of the star bright yellow.*

**6** With the star drawing object still selected, click the Free Rotate Tool button on the Drawing toolbar. The mouse pointer changes to the rotation mouse pointer.

**7** Position the rotation mouse pointer over the bottom right corner sizing handle of the star drawing object.

**8** Click and hold down the left mouse button, and slowly rotate the sizing handle upward, tilting the star until the bottom right point of the star is aimed approximately at the bottom right corner of the slide.

**9** Release the left mouse button, and click anywhere outside an object area.

The star drawing object is now jauntily tilted.

**10** Select the straight-line single drawing object you created with the FreeForm tool and sent backward earlier in this tutorial.

**11** Click the Shadow On/Off button on the Drawing toolbar.

**8**

Drawing objects are sometimes used to emphasize a particular message. In a presentation, however, the text and the drawing objects should complement each other.

## Enhancing with the Playful Use of Text

To make text and drawing objects work together for mutual enhancement, do the following:

**1** With slide 2 as the active slide, select the Text tool on the Drawing toolbar.

**2** With the mouse pointer in the vertical middle of the slide and aligned with the star drawing object, click the left mouse button.

**3** Click the Font button on the Formatting toolbar, and change the font to Brush Script MT.

**4** Change the font size to 96 points.

**5** Click the Italic button on the Formatting toolbar.

**6** Type the name **Kitty Lytter**.

**7** Use the Free Rotate tool to tilt the name so that it slants upward from the lower left toward the upper right corner of the screen.

**8** Reposition the text box so that the name is contained within the straight-line drawing object (see figure 8.10).

**Figure 8.10**
A jaunty star and name working together on a slide.

**9** Save the presentation as **FORUM1.PPT**, but do not close it.

# Objective 6: Use Guides, Grids, and Rulers

**Cascading menu**
A term used by Microsoft to describe submenus accessed by choosing a secondary menu from main menu choices.

As you create slides, you will move and position the various objects to make the slide visually appealing. PowerPoint provides several tools for aligning and positioning objects on a slide. These tools include the grid, guides, rulers, and the **A**lign *cascading menu,* or submenu, which is accessed from the **D**raw menu.

The method used depends on the nature of the objects to be moved and positioned. You can move a text object or a drawing object that does not contain a fill color by clicking and dragging the border of the object. To move a drawing object that contains a fill color, however, you click anywhere inside the object and then drag it to a new location.

## Using the Grid

**Grid**

An invisible network of criss-crossing lines 1/12 inch apart.

You may have noticed that when you drag an object to a new location, it sometimes jumps, or snaps, into position. That little hop occurs because of an invisible *grid* of criss-crossing lines spaced 1/12 inch apart. When an object is brought close to an intersection of two grid lines, the object is attracted to that point as if it were being pulled by a magnet. The grid can be turned off and on. Objects are snapped to grid locations when the grid is turned on.

The invisible grid helps you align objects on the slide. When drawing objects are similar in appearance but have slight differences in size or perspectives, however, the grid does not align the objects properly. A grid point locks to the edge of a drawing object rather than to an axis. If you want to align objects on an axis, you have to turn off the grid.

### Turning the Grid Off and On

To turn the invisible gridlines on and off, do the following:

**1** With slide 2 the active slide, activate the AutoShapes toolbar, and click the Cube Tool button.

**2** Draw a small cube about 1/4 inch across.

**3** Using the Fill Color button on the Drawing+ toolbar, change the fill color to a soft green—something appropriate for a footlight.

**4** Move the cube on the lower part of the screen by clicking anywhere inside the cube and dragging it to a new location.

**5** Choose the **D**raw menu.

If a check mark appears next to **S**nap to Grid, the grid is turned on.

**6** If the grid is selected, choose the **S**nap to Grid option on the **D**raw menu to deselect the grid.

**8**

## Understanding the Guides

**Guides**

Two straightedges, one vertical and one horizontal, that are used to align objects on a slide.

The guides are two "straightedges," or lines, one vertical and one horizontal, that you can position on a slide. Guides resemble the cross-hairs in a telescopic sight. You can position the guides on a slide and then align objects to the guides. When objects are dragged close to the guides, the objects snap to the guides.

## Using the Guides

The guides must be visible in order to use them. To make the guides visible and to use them on a slide, do the following:

**1** Select **G**uides from the **V**iew menu.

The horizontal and vertical guides appear centered on-screen.

**2** In the workspace area between the presentation window and the slide itself, point to the vertical guide, and click and hold down the left mouse button.

A meter reading appears on-screen indicating the current position of the vertical guide.

**3** Move the vertical guide back and forth, observing the changes in the meter reading, and then center the guide on the slide at the 0.00 meter reading.

**4** Drag the horizontal guide up and down with the pointer, and then center the guide on the slide at 0.00 meter reading.

**5** Move the cube drawing object near a guide, and watch the object snap to the guide.

Depending on how you position the object, the edge or the center will snap to the nearest guide. Leave the guides visible for the next tutorial.

**Note:** *To remove the guides, deselect **G**uides on the **V**iew menu.*

### Understanding the Rulers

**Rulers**

Two rulers, vertical and horizontal, that appear at the top and left side of the window.

You use the vertical and horizontal *rulers* to align objects precisely on a slide. Located, respectively, at the left side and the top of the presentation window, the rulers appear either as drawing rulers or text rulers, depending on the selected object—drawing or text. A moving hairline on the drawing rulers shows the current pointer position relative to the center of the slide, and the text rulers display tab markers relative to the left corner of the slide.

## Using the Rulers

You turn the rulers on and off through the **V**iew menu. To select and display the rulers, do the following:

**1** Select **R**uler from the **V**iew menu.

A check mark appears next to **R**uler, and the rulers appear on-screen.

**2** Select the cube object.

**3** Without holding down a mouse button, move the pointer around the screen, and observe the hairlines' movement on the two rulers.

The hairlines show the precise location of the pointer.

**4** Select the text box.

The rulers turn dark except in the areas corresponding to the currently selected text box.

When you have several objects to align, the **A**lign choice on the **D**raw menu eliminates the need to select and move the objects one at a time. Using **A**lign, you can align a group of objects on center or on the top, bottom, left, or right borders.

## Using the Align Cascading Menu Choice

The design for slide 2 calls for a row of footlights across the bottom of the screen to simulate a stage. To create and align a group of objects, do the following:

**1** With the guides visible on-screen, move the vertical guide to position 0.00 and horizontal guide to position 3.31 at the bottom of the slide.

**2** Select the cube object, and position it at the intersection of the guides so that the guides run through the center of the cube object.

**3** With the cube object selected, click the Copy button on the Formatting toolbar.

**4** Click the Paste button on the Formatting toolbar.

**5** Click and drag the duplicate cube object to the right, watching the hairline on the top ruler. When the hairline is on the number 2, release the duplicate cube object.

**6** Click anywhere on the screen outside of an object area to deselect the duplicate cube object.

**7** Click the Paste button.

**8** Again using the top ruler, click and drag the new cube object to a position corresponding to the number 4 on the ruler, and then deselect the object.

**9** Create two more duplicate cube objects, locating each at positions 2 and 4 on the left side of the slide, and deselecting each in turn.

**10** Holding down ⇧Shift, select each of the five cube objects in turn, and then release ⇧Shift.

The five cubes are now selected as a group; all the cubes now have sizing handles.

**11** Choose **A**lign from the **D**raw menu.

The Align cascading menu appears (see figure 8.11).

**8**

(continues)

**Using the Align Cascading Menu Choice (continued)**

**Figure 8.11**
The Align
cascading menu.

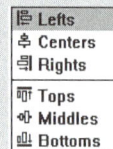

⓬ Choose the Middles menu item.

You could also align the cube objects in a row by choosing Tops or Bottoms.

**Note:** *The top half of the Align cascading menu applies to column alignment and the bottom half to row alignment. If you select any of the column items for the cube objects, all your cubes will wind up on top of each other.*

# Objective 7: Understand PowerPoint's Color Capabilities

No discussion about illustrating a presentation would be complete without a brief explanation of PowerPoint's color capabilities. Throughout this book, you have seen references to a presentation's color scheme; and in the beginning of this chapter, you used the Slide Color Scheme dialog box from the Format menu (refer to figure 8.2).

The color scheme is a basic set of eight colors that are assigned to a presentation or to individual slides. The eight elements of a slide to which colors are assigned are the background, shadows, fills, text and lines, title text, and three accent colors.

The background color is the underlying color of your slide. You can put any object of any color on top of a slide, but the underlying color remains and is visible if you move that object.

Lines and text colors are used for drawing objects and text characters. This color usually contrasts with the background color so that the object stands out clearly. Lines and text colors set the tone for a slide. Depending on the combinations, pastels are warm, harvest colors are earthy, blacks and grays are somber, and bright contrasting colors are gaudy or fun.

The title text color should also contrast with the background. The shadow color is often a darker shade of the background color, but unusual colors can create interesting effects.

Fill colors, the colors that are used to fill areas enclosed by drawn lines, should contrast with both the background and the text and line colors. Accent colors are those used for secondary slide features, such as designs that appear in the background.

**Hue**
A color.

**Saturation**
The intensity of a color.

**Luminance**
The amount of black or white added to a color.

When you click one of the color buttons on a toolbar, you get a menu that gives you the option of selecting Other Color and choosing a color from an Other Color dialog box. You can select any of these colors, but if you do not see what you like or if none of the choices is just right, you can mix your own. In fact, if your monitor has sufficient resolution, you can create millions of custom colors.

When you mix your own colors, you can change the hue, saturation, and luminance. *Hue* refers to the color itself; blue, orange, purple, and red are all hues. *Saturation* refers to the intensity of the color, from the lightest to the most intense. *Luminance* changes the amount of black or white that is added to a color.

## Mixing Your Own Color

Mixing your own colors is easy. To create a custom color, do the following:

**1** With slide 2 the active slide, select the star object.

**2** Click the Fill Color button on the Drawing+ toolbar.

The Fill Color drop-down menu appears.

**3** Click Other Color.

The Other Color dialog box appears (see figure 8.12).

**Figure 8.12**
The Other Color dialog box.

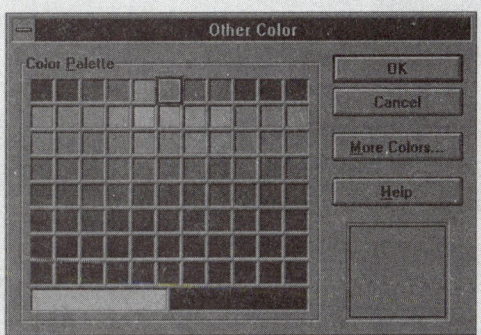

**4** Click the **M**ore Colors button.

The More Colors dialog box appears (see figure 8.13).

**Figure 8.13**
The More Colors dialog box.

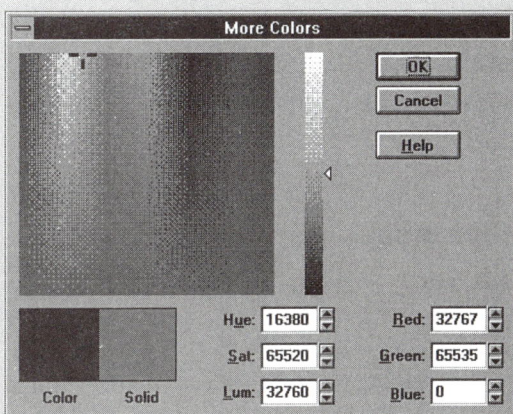

8

(continues)

**Mixing Your Own Color (continued)**

The current hue, saturation, and lumination have numeric values.

**Note:** *The changes you see on your screen may differ from those described here because of differences in computer equipment.*

**5** Set the Hue value to 9600.

The color changes from full yellow to a yellow-orange.

**6** Change the saturation to 65200.

The intensity of the color changes to a little less than before; that is, the color is little less yellow-orange.

**7** Change the luminance to 34000.

This choice adds a bit more white to the color.

**8** Click OK in this and the Other Color dialog boxes.

The custom color now fills the star object.

**9** Save and close FORUM1.PPT.

# Chapter Summary

In this chapter, you have learned how to access the drawing toolbars and how to add drawing objects to your slide. You worked with AutoShapes, and you practiced using the FreeForm tool to create straight lines and random sketches. You discovered how easily you can edit drawing objects and add special effects that enhance drawing and the text objects. You learned to use guides, grids, and rulers in the precise positioning of objects on a slide. You used the Align feature. The chapter also explores the use of colors on a slide and illustrates the mixing of custom colors.

# Checking Your Skills

### True/False Questions

For each of the following statements, circle *T* or *F* to indicate whether the statement is true or false.

T  F  **1.** Two drawing toolbars and two AutoShapes submenus provide drawing tools for enhancing a presentation.

T  F  **2.** The drawing object shaped like an ellipse most likely was created with the Oval tool.

T  F  **3.** The drawing object shaped like an irregular star most likely was created with the Star tool on the AutoShapes toolbar.

T  F  **4.** The guides are a network of criss-crossed lines spaced 1/12 inch apart and used to align drawing objects.

T  F  **5.** The appearance of a ruler depends on whether a text or a drawing object is selected.

## Multiple-Choice Questions

In the blank provided, write the letter of the correct answer for each of the following questions.

___ **1.** If you want to use special tools to modify a drawing object, you most likely will use the tools that are available _____.

   **a.** on the Drawing toolbar

   **b.** on the Drawing+ toolbar

   **c.** from various menu options

   **d.** on the AutoShapes toolbar

___ **2.** AutoShapes are _____.

   **a.** vehicle designs

   **b.** buttons on the Drawing toolbar

   **c.** predesigned drawing objects

   **d.** basic designs used in bulleted lists

___ **3.** The FreeForm tool is particularly useful _____.

   **a.** for creating the appearance of multiple lines

   **b.** in mixing AutoShapes and straight lines

   **c.** when several rows of straight lines are required

   **d.** for building grids

___ **4.** The quickest way to arrange a series of drawing objects in a row according to the center point of each object is to use _____.

   **a.** the grid

   **b.** the guides

   **c.** the ruler

   **d.** the Align submenu from the Draw menu

___ **5.** When you add black or white to a color, you are changing the _____.

   **a.** luminance

   **b.** hue

   **c.** saturation

   **d.** scheme

8

### Fill-in-the-Blank Questions

In the blank provided, write the correct answer for each of the following questions.

1. You can position toolbars anywhere in the application window by clicking and dragging either the toolbar _____ or the area inside the border of the toolbar not occupied by a button.

2. When a floating toolbar is moved into a _____, the toolbar title bar and control menu button automatically disappear.

3. AutoShapes can be used as _____ to entice viewers to the next slide.

4. A single drawing object can give the appearance of multiple straight lines even though it is a single continuous line with _____ at selected points.

5. The _____ are two lines, one vertical and one horizontal, that can be positioned anywhere on a slide and then used to position a drawing object.

# Applying Your Skills

### Review Exercises

In the review exercises that follow, you will be completing slide 2. The completed slide is shown in figure 8.14. Your task is to add the individual elements called for in each project.

**Figure 8.14**
The completed slide 2.

### Exercise 1: Adding a Title

Add the title lines shown in figure 8.14 to slide 2 of the presentation FORUM1.PPT. Try copying and pasting the text object from the title slide and then making the appropriate changes. To make the title line more effective, select an appropriate title color. Save the file as **CHP8_EX1.PPT**.

### Exercise 2: Adding Ms. Lytter

Insert the appropriate clip-art image, Business Woman, and then position the clip-art image using the guides to align the figure as shown in figure 8.14. **Hint**: Use the sizing handles to adjust her size. Save the file as **CHP8_EX2.PPT**.

**Exercise 3: And Here's Chuck the Chicken**

Add the text lines announcing the special appearance of Chuck the Chicken. You may use any font, size, and color you think appropriate. This illustration in figure 8.14 uses Arial, 32-point for the lead line, and Impact, 36-point for the name line. Use AutoShapes to add the arrow and select a contrasting fill color. Save the file as **CHP8_EX3.PPT** .

## Continuing Projects

### Project 1: Illustrating a Complicated Process

In Chapter 6, you created an advertising presentation, ADV2.PPT, that showed the processing steps required to remove the fat and cholesterol from chicken. You added WordArt in Chapter 7 and saved the presentation as ADV3.PPT. The advertising executives have asked you to draw a diagram that illustrates the processing steps and times required to produce no-fat, no-cholesterol chicken. Using the drawing tools and such color as you think necessary, draw and add this diagram to ADV3.PPT. Save the new presentation as **ADV4.PPT** .

**Hint:** You can draw pots and pipes if you like and have the time, but boxes and lines will be satisfactory.

### Project 2: Mapping Out a Presentation

You are planning a fund-raiser for your boss' favorite charity at your house and think that a PowerPoint presentation would be a neat way to extend the invitation to the guests. Your presentation will include an announcement slide, a description of the type of party, a list of anything the guests are expected to bring, and a map that shows the directions. Choose the appropriate template, color scheme, and clip-art images that will fit the occasion. Use the drawing tools to construct your map.

Save the presentation as **PARTY1.PPT** .

**8**

# CHAPTER 9

# Communicating with Graphs

A presentation is the visual communication of concepts, processes, and plans. You have seen how a simple graph can make a presentation clearer and more effective. In this chapter, you learn the elements of a graph and the different types of graphs that are available and appropriate; and—most important—you learn how to use graphs to communicate. In addition, the chapter explores some of the many features of Microsoft Graph, a subprogram that is distributed with PowerPoint.

## Objectives

By the time you have finished this chapter, you will have learned to

1. Understand Graphs

2. Use Datasheets

3. Select a Graph Type

4. Enhance a Chart

5. Insert a Graph into a Slide Using External Data

6. Create Your Own Default Datasheet

## Objective 1: Understand Graphs

Graphs enable you to make complex data easy to read and understand, especially when you have multiple comparisons, trends, and relative values. Not every graph is appropriate for every set of data, however.

### Understanding the Basic Chart Types

Graphing programs like Microsoft Graph, included with PowerPoint 4.0, have built-in chart types and variations, such as 2-D and 3-D charts. Each chart type illustrates data in a certain way.

**Line chart**
A chart consisting of lines, usually for illustrating trends over time.

**Doughnut chart**
Similar to a pie chart, but charts multiple categories in separate rings of the pie chart.

**Area chart**
Emphasizes each value's contribution to the whole.

**Radar chart**
A chart that shows the values of items relative to each other and to a center point.

**Scatter chart**
A variation of a line chart in which a second series of values replaces the time increments on the horizontal axis.

**Legend**
The name and its indicator that identify a category of items on a chart.

**Legend box**
A box on a chart that contains the legends.

Line charts, best suited for illustrating trends over a period of time, are probably the best known chart type. A *line chart* places even increments, such as months, on the horizontal axis and item values on the vertical axis. A line connects the value points to show trends over time. Bar and column charts compare different sets of data. The *bar chart* uses horizontal rows to compare the values of a series of items, usually at a particular point in time. A bar chart places categories of items on the vertical axis and the values of the items on the horizontal axis. A *column chart* uses columns to make the comparisons and show changes in the values over a period of time. The column chart places items on the horizontal axis and values on the vertical axis.

The *pie chart* illustrates the relationship of the parts to the whole for a single category of parts by displaying the whole as a circle and the values as wedges. The less familiar *doughnut chart* is similar to a pie chart, but the doughnut chart places the proportionate values in rings for multiple categories. Both of these chart types show the value of each element's contribution to the whole.

When you need to emphasize the relative value of each element's contribution to the whole over a period of time, the *area chart* is the best choice.

Two lesser known charts for specialized data reporting are the *radar chart* and the scatter chart. A radar chart shows the changes in values of items in a series relative both to the same items in another series and to the other items within the same series. Each item category of the radar chart radiates from a center point with the values for each item in that category placed on the line as a data marker. Separate lines connect all the data markers in the same item series. The *scatter chart*, sometimes known as an XY graph, is similar to a line chart but uses another set of values instead of time increments. Scatter charts show the relationship between the values in two different series of items.

Although many more chart types exist, the types discussed are generally considered the basic charts. Unless you are developing charts for specialized disciplines, such as statistics and engineering, this basic group will serve most of your needs.

The terms *2–D* and *3–D* indicate dimensional representations of the charts. For example, a 3-D column chart uses three-dimensional columns to illustrate the same data as the ordinary column chart. The difference is one of perspective, and the added value may be related more to attractiveness than actual depth.

### Understanding the Elements of Chart Structure

Whether you use Microsoft Graph or another graphing program to create a chart, you will encounter a number of terms that refer to specific parts of the chart. All the parts or elements of a chart have specific names, and although not all elements appear on every chart, charts have many common elements (see figure 9.1).

**Figure 9.1**
A column chart illustrating the various chart elements.

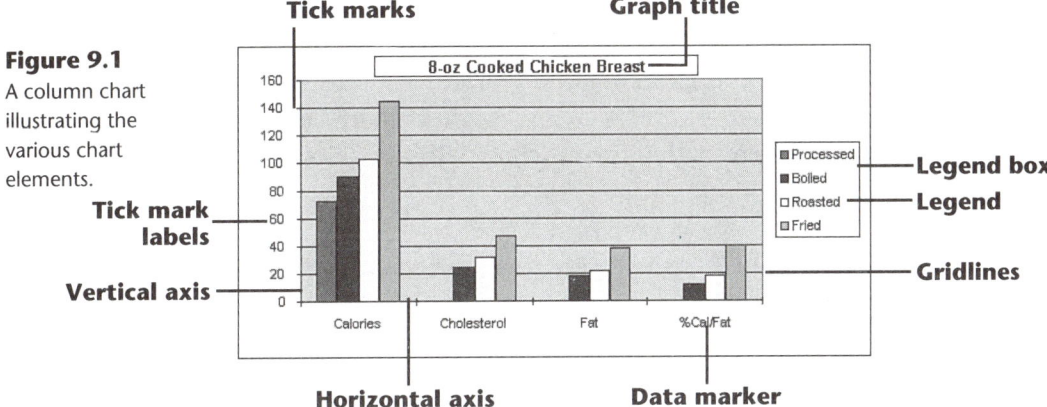

**Axis**
An imaginary line that aligns items in a category or their values.

The *axis* is a term for an imaginary line that aligns either the items in a category or the values of items. Bar and column charts have both a *vertical* and a *horizontal axis*. On a bar chart, the items are aligned on the vertical axis, and the values are on the horizontal axis; on a column chart, the items are aligned on the horizontal axis, and the values are on the vertical axis. The axis that aligns the values is the measuring stick of the graph. On a bar chart, for example, the horizontal axis is the measurement in values for the items listed on the vertical axis.

**Tick marks**
Markers that evenly divide values on any axis.

*Tick marks* are small lines that divide an axis into units. When the axis aligns the items in a category, the tick marks usually designate the divisions between the categories. When the axis aligns the values of the items, the tick marks designate incremental values. One common place you see tick marks is on a ruler. The small lines that designate values, such as 1/8-inch marks between 1 and 2, are tick marks.

**Tick mark label**
A name that identifies a specific tick mark.

A *tick mark label* is a name that identifies a specific tick mark. On the axis that aligns the values, a tick mark label usually consists of numbers.

**Data point**
A point on an axis that corresponds to the specific value of an item.

A *data point* is a point on an axis that corresponds to the specific value of an item. Although the *data marker*—a bar on a bar chart, a column on a column chart, a line on a line chart, and so on—is positioned at the data point to show the specific value, *a data label*, which states that value, is optional.

**Data marker**
A mark on an axis that identifies a data point.

The *legend* on a chart is a name and its corresponding indicator; these items identify a category of items on a chart. Indicators include broken lines, colored lines, and patterns. Legends are sometimes contained within *legend boxes*.

**Data label**
The printed item name or value for a data point.

On many charts, the *gridlines* can be displayed or hidden. Gridline spacing is determined by the values of the items, although some graphing programs enable you to set precise measurements in terms of inches, meters, or decimal values. When used, gridlines are primarily a background for the displayed data.

**Graph title**
The title of a graph or chart.

A *graph title*, the heading that names or describes the chart, is optional in PowerPoint, but using a title generally makes it easier for a viewer to identify the chart.

**9**

**Note:** *You must know how to use the Microsoft Excel 5.0 ChartWizard in order to complete the tutorials in this chapter.*

## Identifying Charts and Chart Elements

You can use the Microsoft Excel 5.0 ChartWizard not only for creating charts but also for examining the various chart types and chart elements that are available. To experiment with different charts, do the following:

**1** Enter the following data into an Excel worksheet:

**Minimum Daily Requirements Provided in One Serving, Chicken Soup**

|  | Mom's | Dad's | LI Red |
|---|---|---|---|
| **Protein** | 29.2 | 31 | 31 |
| **Vitamin A** | 25 | 20 | 20 |
| **Vitamin C** | 2.0 | 0 | 1.0 |
| **Thiamin (B1)** | 1.8 | 1.0 | 1.4 |
| **Calcium** | 1.2 | 2.4 | 1.8 |
| **Potassium** | 4.0 | 5.2 | 4.8 |
| **Sodium** | 5.0 | 8.7 | 9.1 |
| **Iron** | 8.0 | 3.0 | 5.0 |
| **Phosphorus** | 15 | 12 | 15 |
| **Magnesium** | 20 | 10 | 15 |
| **Zinc** | 10 | 10 | 10 |
| **Copper** | 30 | 20 | 25 |
| **Total Carb.** | 3.0 | 5.8 | 4.6 |
| **Dietary Fiber** | 4.0 | 4.0 | 6.2 |

The spreadsheet now contains the percentages of the minimum daily requirements for vitamins and minerals for Mom's Thik 'N' Thin Chick'N Soup and two competing brands.

**2** Select only the item names and values for Mom's; then click the ChartWizard button on the Standard toolbar. Use the ChartWizard to work through the remaining steps in this tutorial.

**3** Create a pie chart.

**4** Using the data for both Mom's and Dad's, create a doughnut chart.

**5** Using all the data, create a bar chart.

**6** Convert the bar chart to a column chart.

Experiment with 3-D charts.

**7** Using all the data, create a line chart.

**8** Using all the data, create a radar chart.

**9** Save the worksheet as **NUTRINT.XLS**.

# Objective 2: Use Datasheets

In earlier chapters, you learned how to input data into datasheets to create charts. This section shows you how to plan a datasheet and how to make changes to a chart based on your data.

**Measurement scale**
The incremental values on the axis that align data units based on a unit of measurement.

**Timeline**
Incremental time values on an axis.

When planning a datasheet, you should have some idea of what type of chart you feel would best convey the information. A chart typically displays data points along a *measurement scale*, an axis divided into proportional units based on some unit of measurement. The unit of measurement may be length, quantity, or percentages. When divisions involve time, the measurement scale is referred to as a *timeline*.

Data points are derived from the values you record for a list of items. Here is a list of items:

Chicken

Stock

Mixed Vegetables

Rice

Seasonings

The list contains the basic ingredients for chicken soup. Mom's makes a big deal out of rating the quality of its soup according to the percentage of ingredients compared to other brands. A typical comparison is shown in table 9.1.

**Table 9.1    Percentage of Ingredients in a Variety of Chicken Soups**

|  | Mom's | Dad's | LI Red |
|---|---|---|---|
| Chicken | 12% | 10% | 8% |
| Stock | 32% | 40% | 36% |
| Mixed Vegetables | 47% | 40.4% | 45.7% |
| Rice | 8% | 8% | 10% |
| Seasonings | 1% | 1.6% | 2.3% |

9

**Category**
A group of related items.

**Data series**
A collection of values for a category, all pertaining to a single subject.

In charting terminology, a *category* is any group of related items. In the preceding list, you have three categories of items: Mom's, Dad's, and LI Red. Each item in any category has its own value. All the values for any category are referred to as a *data series*.

When you plan a datasheet, you have to decide whether you want your data series in rows or columns. In most cases, entering your data series in rows is probably the best option. Of course, if you make the wrong decision, you can use Microsoft Graph to reformat your chart from rows (the default setting) to columns.

One reason to reformat into columns might be that you really want to show the relationship of each ingredient to a particular brand of soup rather than compare the quantities in different brands. Although a bar or column chart would be suitable for the latter comparison, a doughnut chart might be more appropriate for the former comparison.

Using the Microsoft datasheet is much like using a spreadsheet in another program; however, you should keep in mind certain factors when creating a datasheet for a chart:

- The datasheet that appears when you create a chart in PowerPoint always contains some sample data. You can type over the existing data or clear the contents of all cells before you enter your data. If you elect to clear the cells, be sure to clear both the contents and the formatting. If you delete just the existing data, the cell is not cleared but still retains a zero value.

- The numbers you display in your data can be formatted in a variety of ways, just as in Excel and other spreadsheet programs. For consistency, it is probably better to select **N**umber from the F**o**rmat menu to format all the cells that are being used for data points.

## Creating a Datasheet for a Chart

Your company feels that the best way to start the forum is to present some key facts about Thik 'N' Thin Chik'N Soup in a series of charts. The idea is to present a quick overview of the nutritional content of the soup to establish a framework for discussion.

To create a datasheet for a chart, do the following:

❶ Load the FORUM1.PPT presentation that you created in Chapter 7, and save it as **FORUM2.PPT**.

❷ Add a new slide to the end (slide 3) of the presentation, selecting the Text & Graphics design.

This slide will have a title, text on the left, and a chart on the right.

**3** Choose Slide Color Scheme from the Format Menu.

**4** Change the Text & Lines color to dark gray, and click OK.

**5** Create the text information for slide 3 using the slide illustrated in figure 9.2 and information from table 9.1 as your guide.

**Figure 9.2**
Slide 3 prepared for a chart.

**6** Double-click the graph object.

Remember to think through what you want to do. What type of chart do you think will best display this data? Assume that a pie chart would be best.

**7** Type the values into the datasheet in Microsoft Graph as they are shown in figure 9.3.

**Figure 9.3**
A datasheet with category, items, and values entered correctly.

| FORUM2.PPT - Datasheet | | | | | | |
|---|---|---|---|---|---|---|
|  | A | B | C | D | E | F |
|  | Chicken | Stock | Vegs. | Rice | Seasons |  |
| 1 Mom's | 12% | 32% | 47% | 8% | 1% |  |
| 2 |  |  |  |  |  |  |
| 3 |  |  |  |  |  |  |
| 4 |  |  |  |  |  |  |

**8** Select the 2-D Pie Chart as the chart type. Click anywhere outside the Data sheet dialog box.

**9** Save the presentation as **FORUM2.PPT**, but do not close the presentation.

# Objective 3: Select a Chart Type

**9**

In the preceding tutorial, the pie chart appeared to be the best choice. The choice, although satisfactory, really lacks a clear and convincing appeal (see figure 9.4). Because the purpose of a chart is to communicate, you should always consider what type of chart best communicates this information to the audience.

**Figure 9.4**
Slide 3 with a simple pie chart.

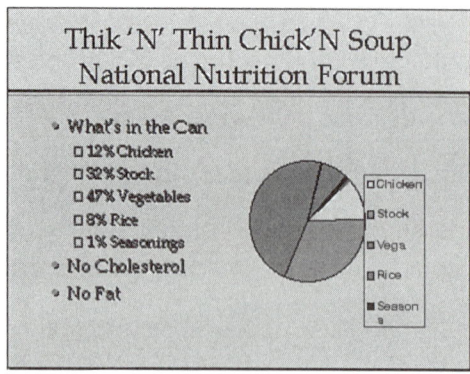

Thik 'N' Thin Chick'N Soup
National Nutrition Forum

- What's in the Can
  - □ 12% Chicken
  - □ 32% Stock
  - □ 47% Vegetables
  - □ 8% Rice
  - □ 1% Seasonings
- No Cholesterol
- No Fat

□ Chicken
□ Stock
□ Vega
□ Rice
■ Season s

**Pie chart**
Chart showing the proportion of parts to the whole.

**Bar chart**
A chart that uses horizontal rows to compare the values of a series of items.

**Column chart**
Similar to a bar chart, but uses vertical columns instead of bars.

Microsoft Graph has 14 basic chart types, with a wide variety of variations on each type. With so many types available, you may not always know the best type of chart to use, but you can narrow the selection by considering the nature of the data you want to illustrate:

- If you need to compare items in a single category but want to show the relationship of the parts to the whole, one of the *pie charts* will probably do.

- If you are comparing items in single or multiple categories, a *bar chart* or column chart may serve best.

- If you want to emphasize a change in comparison over a period of time, a *column chart* is the best choice.

- If the data is time sensitive, a *line chart* would seem appropriate.

Although the preceding suggestions offer general guidelines, the best way to determine what type of chart best fits the message you want to deliver is to experiment with different chart types using the same data. For example, you can use the data you just entered and change the chart to a bar chart. Once you have a bar chart, you can change the formatting of the data—by row or by column—on the chart itself.

## Changing a Chart Type

Whether you want to change a chart type completely or merely edit a chart, you can do so quickly by double-clicking the chart on the slide. To modify a chart, do the following:

**1** Double-click the chart object on slide 3.

The Microsoft Graph window appears with the chart object selected.

**2** Choose **C**hart Type from the F**o**rmat menu.

The Chart Type dialog box appears (see figure 9.5).

**Figure 9.5**

The Chart Type dialog box.

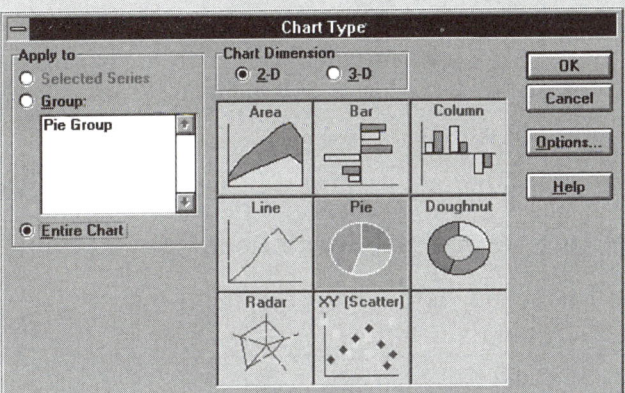

❸ Click the **3**-D button in the Chart Dimension option box, and click OK.

❹ Use the sizing handles to stretch the legend box to a little less than the width of the chart box.

❺ Drag the legend box to the bottom of the chart object box beneath the pie chart.

❻ Using the sizing handle at the top of the legend box, compress the legend box so that the legends are pushed close together.

❼ Click outside of the chart object to return to PowerPoint.

❽ Save **FORUM2.PPT**, but do not close the presentation.

# Objective 4: Enhance a Chart

Up to this point, this chapter has covered the mechanics of creating a chart: the use of Microsoft Graph to generate charts in PowerPoint and the use of Excel to create charts that can be imported. Creating charts, however, is a little like using WordArt: just because you *can* do something does not mean that you *should*.

A gaudy chart, just like gaudy WordArt, can negate the message you want to convey. On the other hand, you can add to your charts many interesting and subtle effects that will enhance your message.

One of the points that Mom's likes to emphasize is the amount of chicken meat contained in each can of soup. Mom's has more meat than any other competing brand has. Flatly stating this fact at a nutrition conference might be a bit tacky, but you can subtly call attention to this fact.

**9**

## Enhancing a Chart

Among the ways you can enhance your chart are to change fonts, colors, and backgrounds and to add titles and data labels where appropriate. To enhance a chart, do the following:

**1** Double-click the chart on the slide to activate Microsoft Graph.

**2** Choose **T**itles from the **I**nsert menu.

The Titles dialog box appears (see figure 9.6).

**Figure 9.6**
The Titles dialog box.

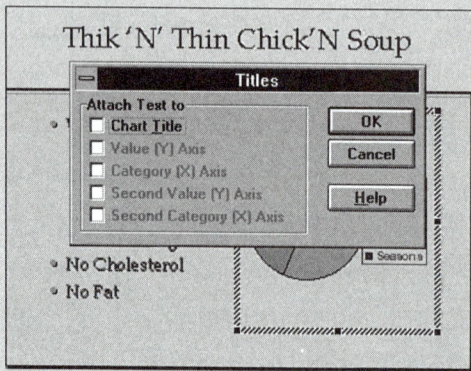

**3** Select Chart **T**itle in the Attach Text To box.

This choice turns the option on for all future charts created.

**4** Click OK.

The Microsoft Graph workspace reappears with the word Mom's highlighted in a text box.

**5** Position the mouse pointer after the word Mom's and type **Thik 'N' Thin Chik'N Soup**; then click anywhere outside the text box.

**6** Position the pointer over the wedge of the pie that represents the chicken portion, and click to select only that wedge.

**7** Click and drag the wedge about two-thirds of the way out of the pie. Leave the wedge selected.

**8** Choose Selected Data **P**oint from the **F**ormat menu.

The Format Data Point dialog box appears.

**9** Click the Data Labels tab (see figure 9.7).

**Figure 9.7**
The Format Data Point dialog box with the Data Labels tab selected.

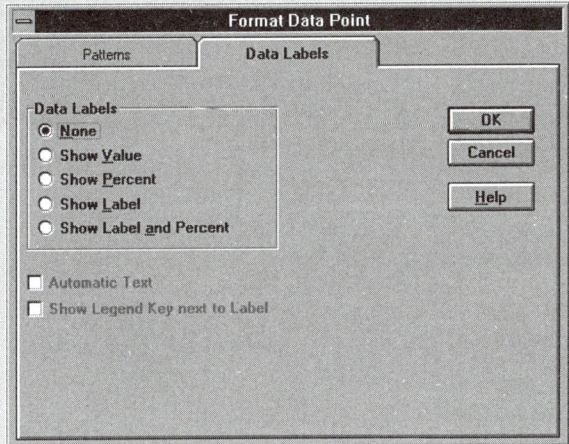

⓾ Click the Show Label **a**nd Percent button in the Data Labels option box, and click OK.

The label and percent appear next to the wedge in a text box.

⓫ Select the word Chicken in the text box containing the label and the percent.

⓬ Choose **F**ont from the **Fo**rmat menu.

The Format Data Labels dialog box appears with the Font tab selected (see figure 9.8).

**Figure 9.8**
The Format Data Labels Font dialog box.

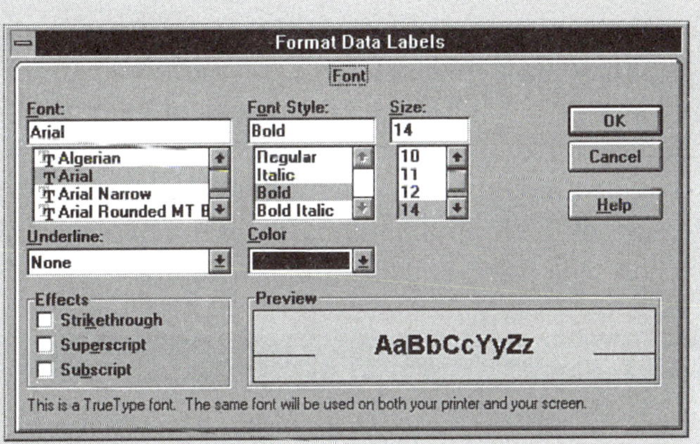

⓭ In the **S**ize list box, change the font size to 12 points, and click OK.

⓮ Move the text box containing the label and percent below and slightly to the right of the extracted wedge that represents the chicken.

When completed, the slide and chart should resemble the slide illustrated in figure 9.9.

**9**

(continues)

## Enhancing a Chart (continued)

**Figure 9.9**
The completed slide 3 with enhanced chart.

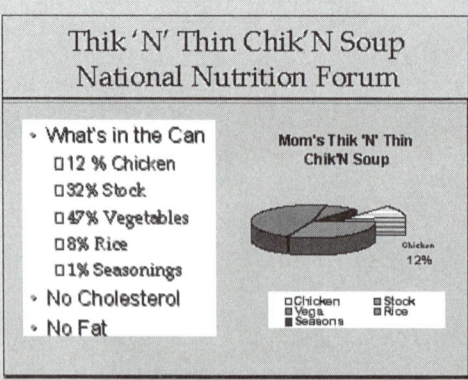

⓯ Save but do not close **FORUM2.PPT**.

# Objective 5: Insert a Graph into a Slide Using External Data

**Caution**
If you have to close your PowerPoint application to create the spreadsheet, be sure to save the FORUM2.PPT file first.

In addition to creating a chart in Microsoft Graph and importing charts from Excel and other programs, you can insert a graph directly into a slide using data created either in a word processing program or in a spreadsheet from Excel, Lotus, Symphony, or Multiplan.

For example, if you use a word processing program to create a table in which the data elements are separated by tabs or commas, you can use that table to insert a graph into a slide. You must save the file containing the table in ASCII format. For spreadsheet programs, generally all that is required is for PowerPoint to import the data. PowerPoint does not import formulas from spreadsheets—only the current results of the formulas. In many cases, however, you can import formats, such as boldface or italic, and alignment with the values.

## Inserting a Graph into a Slide

To insert a graph into a slide using external data, do the following:

❶ Create the following spreadsheet in Excel, Lotus, or Multiplan, and save the file as **CHICKEN.XLS** (or another appropriate extension).

**Calories and Fat in Chicken Processed and Conventional**

|           | Calories | Cholesterol | Fat   | %Cal/Fat |
|-----------|----------|-------------|-------|----------|
| Processed | 72       | 0.005       | 0.001 | 0        |
| Boiled    | 90       | 24          | 18    | 12       |
| Roasted   | 103      | 32          | 22    | 18       |
| Fried     | 145      | 47          | 38    | 40       |

**2** Make FORUM2.PPT the active file in PowerPoint; then add a fourth slide, choosing Graph as the design for the new slide.

**3** Double-click the graph icon on the slide.

**4** Clear the contents of the datasheet.

**5** With the upper left corner cell as the active cell on the datasheet, choose **I**mport Data from the **E**dit menu.

The Import Data dialog box appears (see figure 9.10).

**Figure 9.10**
The Import Data dialog box.

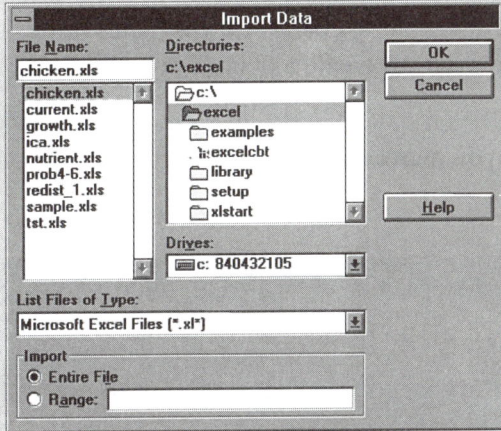

**6** Select the CHICKEN file you created in the spreadsheet program.

**Note:** *You need not import a complete spreadsheet when generating a chart. You can select the Range option in the Import options box and enter either a cell range, or if using Excel, a range name.*

**7** Click OK.

The imported data appears in your datasheet. Take a few minutes to clean up the datasheet, removing any words or values you do not want to appear on your chart (see figure 9.11).

**Figure 9.11**
The datasheet with data imported from a spreadsheet file.

**FORUM2.PPT - Datasheet**

|   |   |   | A | B | C | D |
|---|---|---|---|---|---|---|
|   |   |   | Calories | Cholesterd | Fat | %Cal/Fat |
| 1 |   | Processed | 72 | 0.005 | 0.001 | 0 |
| 2 |   | Boiled | 90 | 24 | 18 | 12 |
| 3 |   | Roasted | 103 | 32 | 22 | 18 |
| 4 |   | Fried | 145 | 47 | 38 | 40 |

**8** Select the Column chart type, and return to the PowerPoint presentation window.

**9** Save but do not close **FORUM2.PPT**.

**9**

If an Excel spreadsheet contains an embedded chart based on the data that is being imported, the chart data will not be imported into the datasheet. The chart type used in Excel, however, may carry over to Microsoft Graph and become the default for the current chart.

# Objective 6: Create Your Own Default Datasheet

Each time the datasheet appears, it contains default data. If you create many charts, this default data may become annoying. You can create a blank worksheet for the default if you prefer to start each chart-making session from scratch. However, if you need to create many charts of the same type—for example, you need several line charts showing sales trends in various area branches—you may want to create a default line chart that contains your basic line chart settings.

This step will save you a great deal of time in preparing repetitive charts for your report.

## Creating a Default Chart

To create a default chart, do the following:

**❶** Double-click the chart object that you want to use as a default.

**❷** When the Microsoft Graph window opens, choose **O**ptions from the **T**ools menu.

The Graph Options dialog box appears (see figure 9.12).

**Figure 9.12**
The Graph Options dialog box.

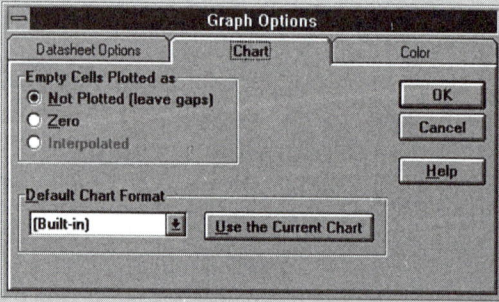

**❸** Click the Chart tab.

**❹** Click the **U**se the Current Chart button in the **D**efault Chart Format box, and click OK.

**❺** Save and close the **FORUM2.PPT** presentation.

# Chapter Summary

This chapter discusses the basic chart types and the elements that form the structure of a chart. You learned more about how to use datasheets and how to enter data for a particular chart type. You discovered new ways to enhance a chart and to communicate information using charts. You created a spreadsheet in another program and used that spreadsheet to insert a graph into a slide. Finally, you learned how to create your own default worksheet.

# Checking Your Skills

## True/False Questions

For each of the following statements, circle *T* or *F* to indicate whether the statement is true or false.

T  F  **1.** The axis that aligns values on a graph is the measuring stick of the graph.

T  F  **2.** Legends on a chart usually correspond to the data labels.

T  F  **3.** The most important part of a chart is the gridlines.

T  F  **4.** On a bar chart, the items are aligned on the vertical axis and the values are aligned on the horizontal axis; the opposite is true on a column chart.

T  F  **5.** Microsoft Graph has 14 basic chart types, with a wide variety of variations on each type.

## Multiple-Choice Questions

In the blank provided, write the letter of the correct answer for each of the following questions.

___ **1.** You want to illustrate magnitude of each item's contribution to the whole. The chart type you would most likely use is a _____.

   **a.** pie chart

   **b.** line chart

   **c.** column chart

   **d.** area graph

___ **2.** The chart type that best compares the value of one item to other items and shows changes in values over a period of time is the _____.

   **a.** bar chart

   **b.** column chart

   **c.** area graph

   **d.** line chart

**9**

___ **3.** A specific position on an axis that corresponds to the specific value of an item is known as a _____.

    **a.** data marker

    **b.** data point

    **c.** data label

    **d.** gridline

___ **4.** A table written in a word processing program can be used to create a chart in PowerPoint if the table _____.

    **a.** is formatted as a table in Word for Windows 6.0

    **b.** uses a standard row and column format

    **c.** has the data elements separated by tabs or commas and the file is in ASCII format

    **d.** contains no formulas or formatting

___ **5.** When planning a chart for a slide, the first thing you should consider is _____.

    **a.** what chart type would look best

    **b.** what chart type would best convey the information clearly

    **c.** how to enter the data in your datasheet

    **d.** the color scheme

## Fill-in-the-Blank Questions

In the blank provided, write the correct answer for each of the following questions.

**1.** _____ visually identify evenly divided values on any axis.

**2.** A _____ on an axis corresponds to a specific value of an item.

**3.** Among the ways a chart can be enhanced is by changing fonts, colors, and backgrounds and adding titles and _____ labels where appropriate.

**4.** In some cases when you are using a spreadsheet file to insert a chart into a slide, the _____ along with the values is imported.

**5.** If you are creating many charts of the same type, you may want to create a _____ chart that contains your basic line chart settings.

# Applying Your Skills

## Review Exercises

### Exercise 1: Enhancing a Slide

Use the techniques you learned in this chapter to enhance slide 4 in the FORUM2.PPT presentation (see figure 9.13). Adding a title would seem to be the most obvious, but how about the category names? With the slide in the current form, no one really knows what this slide represents.

**Figure 9.13**
The incomplete slide 4 in the FORUM2 presentation.

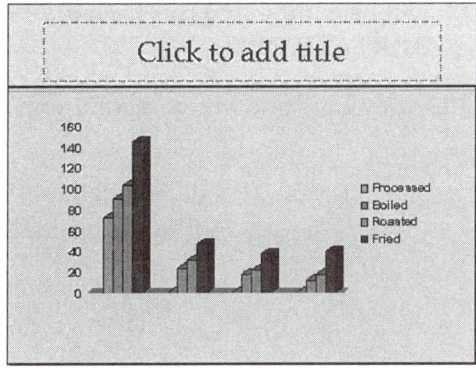

### Exercise 2: Finding an Error in Logic

You have just discovered that the data values in the chart on slide 4 are not the same. The values in the first three columns refer to grams, but the values in the fourth column, %Cal/Fat, show the percentage of calories derived from the fat content of the chicken. Eliminate the last column, and create a new chart with valid data. Save the file as **FORUM3.PPT**.

### Exercise 3: Using Imported Data to Create a Chart

Use the NUTRINT.XLS worksheet that you created in Objective 1 of this chapter to create a chart for a new slide that you add to FORUM3.PPT. You will have to be creative in designing the slide because you have so much information. You also have the option of creating a logical division so that the information is displayed over two slides. Use your best judgment, but keep in mind that you want to communicate facts clearly and in an appealing manner.

## Continuing Projects

### Project 1: Creating Charts to Explain Data Differently

Using the ADV3.PPT presentation you completed in Chapter 8, develop a pie chart that shows the relationship of the individual time elements to the total time required to process the chicken. Next, create another slide using the same data but showing the process over a timeline on a line chart. If you completed Continuing Project 2 in Chapter 6, add these new charts after the linked chart you created using the data in your Excel spreadsheet. Save the presentation as **ADV4.PPT**.

**9**

**Project 2: Overlaying Events to Create Perspective**

In Continuing Project 2 in Chapter 7, you completed a presentation using the HERSTORY.PPT file. If you print an outline of the presentation, you will notice the correlation between certain historical events happening throughout the world and events in the company history of Mom's Home Cookin'. Create two categories—history and herstory. Plot the actual historical events in the history category and the company events in the herstory category. Using your imagination, create a chart that graphically depicts the interrelationship of the two. Insert the chart into an appropriate point of the presentation. Be prepared to justify your placement. (You will be completing this presentation in Chapter 10). Save the presentation as **HERTALE.PPT**.

**Hint:** The items in both categories have one thing in common.

# Creating a Professional Presentation

This chapter builds on the knowledge and skills you have learned in previous chapters and shows you how to give your presentations professional quality. The text discusses the effects of color schemes in different formats and shows you how to change a color scheme quickly and easily. You learn some of the finer points of giving a presentation, such as using on-screen drawing, creating branched presentations, and other changes that add impact to handouts. The chapter also shows you how to prepare a presentation for distribution.

## Objectives

By the time you have finished this chapter, you will have learned to

1. Make Good Decisions about Colors, Formats, and Media
2. Change a Color Scheme
3. Perfect Your Presentation Skills
4. Use On-Screen Drawing
5. Create Branched Presentations
6. Print Presentations, Speaker's Notes, and Handouts
7. Use the PowerPoint Viewer

## Objective 1: Make Good Decisions about Colors, Formats, and Media

When you set the options for a software program, you tend to use colors you feel comfortable with, personal choices that reflect your own taste. Some people prefer to use black type on a white screen in a word processing program, for example, but others may prefer chartreuse letters on a purple background.

**Medium**

The means by which a presentation is displayed—a computer video screen, overhead projector, or television screen.

Presentations, however, are a shared experience. In addition to choosing colors appropriate to the type of presentation, you must also pay special attention to the *medium* used to display the presentation—computer monitor, transparencies on an overhead projector, LCD (Liquid Crystal Display), or television screen.

If you know in advance how you will be displaying your presentation, you can adjust the colors as needed. For example, for overhead projectors and *LCD projection panels*, you will want to use darker colors because light colors will look washed out or faded in the high-intensity lights used to project the image on a screen or wall.

**LCD projection panels**

A flat-screen LCD device, typically used with an overhead projector, that creates computer-directed, electronic transparency images.

If you will be using a television monitor to display your images, you should stick to the more basic colors—blues, greens, reds, yellows, black—because subtler hues do not display well on many television systems, particularly projection-type television systems. You will also want to avoid fine-dot patterns, because television resolution is generally not as good as that of the higher resolution computer monitors.

Different computer monitors and their corresponding video display cards also have significant differences. What may be a vibrant yellow on the computer monitor in your office may be a muddy brown on the computer monitor rented for a seminar at a hotel.

**Service bureau**

In connection with PowerPoint, a producer of 35mm slides, transparencies, and photoprints of slides for a presentation.

If you are planning to use color transparencies or slides, you can use a *service bureau*, such as Genigraphics Corporation, a producer of professional slides and transparencies for businesses, or Elegant Digital Images, Inc., to generate your slides. PowerPoint enables you to save your presentations in a form these service bureaus can use. Service bureaus can produce high-quality slides, transparencies, or even photoprints, but you may find significant variations in the final colors produced by different bureaus.

When selecting a service bureau, send out only a few slides to selected companies for comparison. This trial will give you an opportunity to evaluate the samples and make the right decision for your full presentation.

Can you avoid all problems? Of course not. But if your next raise, bonus, or pat on the back depends on a professional presentation, you can certainly minimize the obvious disasters. Following are some suggestions:

- Start by picking the appropriate template type for your presentation. PowerPoint provides templates in four categories: 35mm slides, black-and-white overheads or transparencies, color overheads, and video screens.

- If you plan to use a television monitor or LCD to display your slides, use color overheads for your template category.

- If at all possible, conduct a trial run with the actual or equivalent equipment you will use. This way, you can make adjustments before the presentation.

- If you are traveling to a different location, a portable computer with PowerPoint installed is probably essential. If your trial run on the remote equipment would please only Andy Warhol fans, you can make adjustments on your portable computer.

**10**

# Objective 2: Change a Color Scheme

You can change color schemes at any time—even after you have created a presentation. If you are on the road expecting to use a computer but you end up having to use a television monitor, you can make whatever changes you need very quickly.

Another reason for changing color schemes is to differentiate between similar presentations. For example, you can create one basic presentation and then add customized slides for specific audiences; you may have one set for sales, one for marketing, and one for advertising. By changing the color scheme for each audience, you can instantly tell that you are running the correct presentation.

## Changing a Color Scheme

The process for changing the color scheme of a presentation enables you to choose new colors and to view a sample of your choices at the same time. To change a color scheme for a presentation, do the following:

**1** Load the presentation SOUP3.PPT.

**2** Choose Slide **C**olor Scheme from the F**o**rmat menu.

The Slide Color Scheme dialog box appears (see figure 10.1). You have used this dialog box previously to change scheme colors on a slide. In this tutorial, you use the Choose **S**cheme option.

**Figure 10.1**
The Slide Color Scheme dialog box.

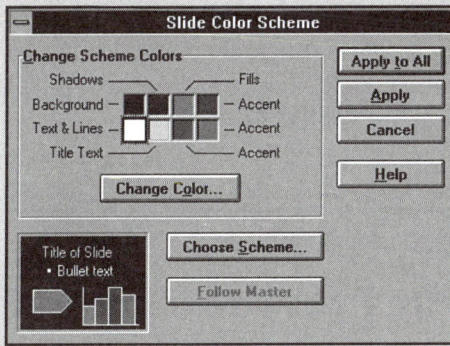

**3** Click the Choose **S**cheme button.

The Choose Scheme dialog box appears (see figure 10.2).

(continues)

## Changing a Color Scheme (continued)

**Figure 10.2**
The Choose
Scheme dialog
box.

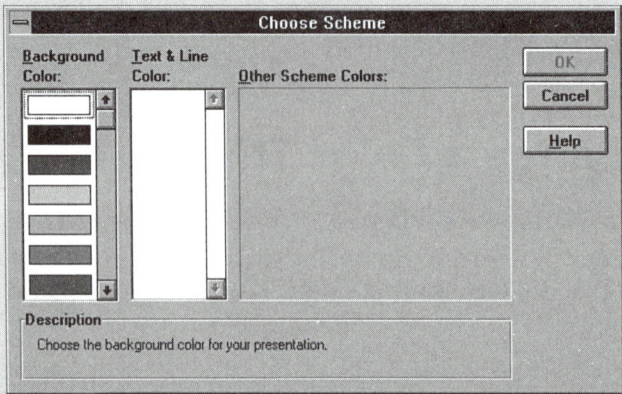

To change the color scheme, you have to select a background color first.

**4** Scroll through the **B**ackground Color list box to view the various background colors that are available, and select a color.

When a background color is selected, a new list of colors appears in the **T**ext & Line Color list box.

**5** Scroll through the **T**ext & Line Color list box, and select a color.

The sample slides that appear in the **O**ther Scheme Colors preview box shows the results of applying the new colors. You can select as many variations as you want in order to see how the new colors look.

**6** When you find a combination that you like, click OK.

**7** In the Slide Color Scheme dialog box, click the Apply **t**o All button.

PowerPoint displays a message stating that all the slides in the presentation are being updated with the new color scheme.

**8** If you don't like your new color scheme, you don't have to go through the same process to return to the original color scheme. Simply choose **U**ndo from the **E**dit menu.

# Objective 3: Perfect Your Presentation Skills

Nothing quite beats practice for giving a professional presentation. You want to appear confident, and you want your presentation to be smooth and seamless. Fortunately, PowerPoint provides a number of features that help you produce a polished presentation.

When you are designing a presentation on your computer, you rely heavily on the mouse. In fact, some activities in PowerPoint can be done only with a mouse. However, you can issue only two commands with a mouse when giving a presentation: you can click the left mouse button to show the next slide, and you can click the right mouse button to show the preceding slide. When giving a computer-controlled presentation, use the keyboard for commands.

The keyboard commands are not only more versatile, but because PowerPoint often provides multiple keyboard commands to achieve the same action, you can use the command that is most convenient or comfortable for you. These actions and the keyboard commands that initiate them are summarized in table 10.1.

| Table 10.1   Keyboard Commands Used in Giving Presentations | |
| --- | --- |
| **Action** | **Keyboard Commands** |
| Show next slide | Spacebar |
| | N |
| | → |
| | ↓ |
| | PgDn |
| Show preceding slide | ← |
| | ↑ |
| | PgUp |
| Go to a certain slide | Type the number of the slide you want to go to, and press ↵Enter. |
| Switch between the presentation and a white screen | W |
| | , (comma) |
| Switch between the presentation and a black screen | B |
| | . (period) |
| Display or hide the mouse pointer | A |
| | = (equal sign) |
| Pause or resume an automatic slide show | S |
| | + (plus sign) |
| End a slide show | Esc |
| | Ctrl+Break |
| | - (hyphen) |

Rather than use all the keyboard commands that are available for any action, you should decide which keyboard commands are most comfortable for you to use and then practice with this group.

**Practicing Keyboard Commands for a Slide Show**

Use table 10.1 as your reference and the file SOUP3.PPT as your presentation; try the different keys available for each activity as you work through the following steps:

**1** Starting with the first slide of SOUP3.PPT, choose **S**lide Show from the **V**iew menu.

**2** Select **A**ll from the Slides options and **M**anual Advance from the **A**dvance options; then click **S**how.

**3** Advance from slide 1 to slide 2.

**4** Return to slide 1.

**5** Go directly to slide 11.

**6** Switch to a white screen.

**7** Switch back to the presentation.

**8** Switch to a black screen.

**9** Switch back to the presentation.

**10** Move the mouse slightly so that the mouse pointer appears.

**11** Hide the mouse pointer.

**12** Display the mouse pointer.

**13** End the slide show.

**14** Repeat this tutorial, practicing each step until you feel comfortable using the keyboard and your key selection.

# Objective 4: Use On-Screen Drawing

Although the keyboard is best for controlling the presentation, the mouse is the only tool for creating on-screen marks. Frequently, when giving a presentation, you may want to underline or check off certain points. You do this by changing the mouse pointer to a pen and then using the pen to make your marks. The marks you make during a presentation are not permanent.

Using the pen to make check marks, circle a topic, or even underline a point will seem a little awkward at first, but with practice, you will be able to make passable annotations. (For more information about using the pen, refer to "Using the Freehand Annotation Tool" in Chapter 4.)

## Practicing Screen Drawings

To practice drawing with the pen, do the following:

**1** Start the presentation SOUP3.PPT, and advance to slide 4, "Objectives."

**2** Move the mouse slightly so that the mouse pointer appears.

**3** Click the Freehand Annotation icon in the lower right corner of the screen.

The mouse pointer changes to a pen.

**4** Using the pen, underline the words `Test Market`.

**5** Put check marks before items 1, 2, and 3.

**6** Circle the word `East`.

**7** Draw an asterisk in front of item 4.

**8** Draw an arrow pointing to items 5 and 6.

**9** Draw a curving arrow from item 7 back to item 4.

**10** Draw a left parenthesis grouping items 8 and 9.

**11** Go to the next slide, and then return to slide 4.

The marks you made previously on this slide have disappeared.

**12** Repeat steps 2 through 11 until you feel comfortable using the drawing pen.

# Objective 5: Create Branched Presentations

Presentations frequently take divergent paths. You may be giving a presentation on a business expansion plan to the directors of your company, and someone asks to see more of the advertising plans. Another director wants to know more about the marketing plan, and another wants to know how the product is produced.

If you have these presentations prepared and think that they might be requested, you can create branching options in your main presentation. One way to create these options is to set the branching option on the slide where the question is most likely to come up, but a more professional approach is to set all your branching options on one slide. Then if you need to branch, you can simply go to that slide and select the appropriate option.

## Adding Branching Options to Your Presentation

Adding a branching option to a slide is one way to run another presentation and then return to the main presentation. To add branching options to your presentation, do the following:

**1** In the Slide view with SOUP3.PPT as your main presentation, make slide 13 your active slide.

**2** Choose **O**bject from the **I**nsert menu.

The Insert Object dialog box appears (see figure 10.3).

**Figure 10.3**
The Insert Object dialog box.

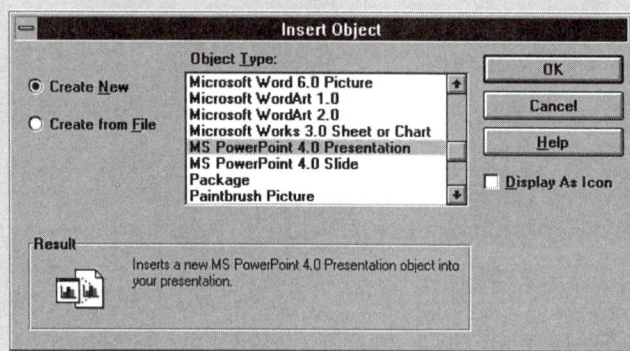

**3** Select MS PowerPoint 4.0 Presentation from the Object **T**ype list box.

**4** Click the Create from **F**ile option.

A text box and a **B**rowse command button appear.

If you know the name of the file you want, you can type the name in the text box.

**5** Click the **B**rowse button.

The Browse dialog box appears (see figure 10.4).

**Figure 10.4**
The Browse dialog box.

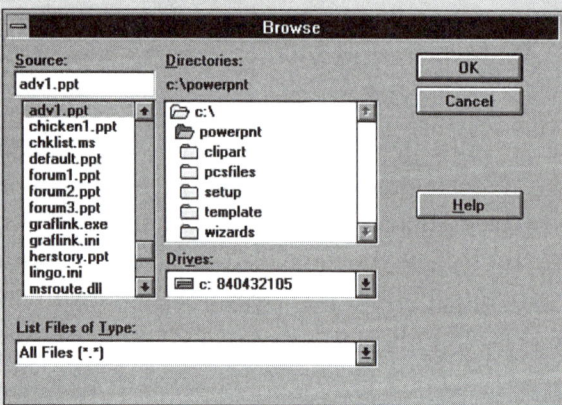

**6** Select the ADV1.PPT presentation, and click the OK button.

**10**

**7** Select the **D**isplay As Icon box in the Insert Object dialog box, and click OK.

An icon with a presentation name appears on slide 13 of the SOUP3 presentation.

**8** Click and drag the icon to the lower left corner of the slide.

**9** With the icon still selected, chose Colors and **L**ines from the **F**ormat menu.

**10** Select for the icon a **F**ill color that contrasts with the background color of the slide.

If the background is blue, for example, a white fill color is appropriate.

**11** With the icon still selected, choose Pla**y** Settings from the **T**ools menu.

The Play Settings dialog box appears (see figure 10.5).

**Figure 10.5**
The Play Settings dialog box.

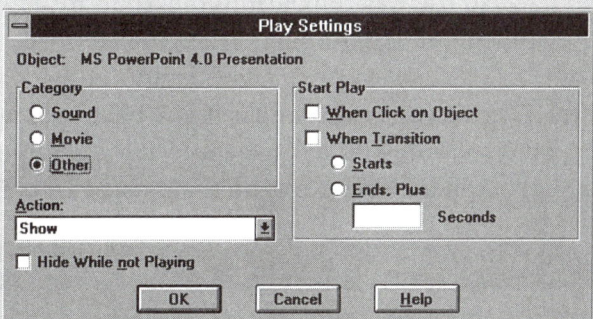

You can set a variety of features in this dialog box, which enables you to select several different methods of starting the branched presentation, including having it start automatically after a certain time period.

**12** With the **W**hen Click on Object box selected, click OK.

**13** Save the presentation as **SOUP4.PPT**.

You can add more presentation icons to this slide if desired. For example, you could add the HERSTORY.PPT presentation as an icon so that HERSTORY would also be available.

**14** Run the SOUP4.PPT slide show, and go to slide 13.

**15** Click the ADV1.PPT icon.

The ADV1 presentation starts.

**16** Press Esc to end the ADV1 presentation.

You return to slide 13 in the SOUP4 presentation. You can then continue this presentation by advancing to the next slide.

# Objective 6: Print Presentations, Speaker's Notes, and Handouts

Although you can print a copy of your entire presentation, you generally will print only selected parts. You may create a file to transmit by modem to a service bureau, which can then print slides, or you may have access to a desktop film recorder, which enables you to print your own slides. You can print overhead transparencies directly and indirectly. You can get transparency film that can be used in black-and-white and color inkjet and laser printers. If your printer is limited to one color, your transparencies will be limited to one color, of course.

If you are creating or printing a slide show for a particular medium, such as film, paper, or video display, you probably will want to size your slides for that medium. You size slides in the Slide Setup dialog box from the File menu.

**Aspect ratio**
A dimensional change in a visual, that is necessitated by a change in medium or orientation.

When you select an option in the Slides Sized For drop-down list box, PowerPoint automatically sets the correct *aspect ratio* for certain selections. The aspect ratio refers to the way dimensions of a slide are adjusted proportionally for a particular medium. For example, changing an image from a Portrait oriented print to a 35mm slide uses 2:3 aspect ratio so that the content will fill the slide area in Landscape orientation. If you have ever seen a 70mm motion picture film on television with a blank space at the bottom and top of the screen, you have seen an example of an unadjusted aspect ratio.

> **Tip**
>
> You determine the aspect ratio by dividing the height and width by the largest common denominator (7.5/2.5 = 3; 10/2.5 = 4).

PowerPoint creates and prints slides in Landscape orientation. The default size is 7.5 inches tall by 10 inches wide, and the default aspect ratio is 3:4. If you are creating and printing slides that will be reduced to 35mm film, PowerPoint adjusts the size to 7.5 inches tall by 11.25 inches wide, an aspect ratio of 2:3 that will allow the slide to fill the full 35mm film image area. If the aspect ratio is not adjusted for film, you will see blank areas to the left and right of the image on film.

## Choosing the Components to Print

The actual printing of different components of the presentation is done from the Print dialog box. In this box, you can select what you want to print: slides with and without builds, outlines, notes pages, and handouts with 2, 3, and 6 slides per page.

You also have other options in the Print dialog box. You can choose to print all the slides in a presentation, the current slide, or selected slides (from one slide to a range of slides). You can choose automatic scaling to fit the size of paper in your printer; choose to print pure black and white, which turns all color fills to

**10**

white and text and lines to black; and choose to print to a file, which generates either a PostScript file, which can create 35mm slides, or printer files for computers and printers that do not have PowerPoint installed.

### Printing from the Handout Master

Handouts consist of printed information that you provide to your presentation audiences. For instance, you can print small pictures of each of your slides, along with captions or other information, and provide a blank space where audience members can make their own notes.

**Handout Master**
A view in which a handout template can be created or modified.

Just as PowerPoint has a Slide Master and an Outline Master, which enable you to create overall designs for your presentation, PowerPoint also has a *Handout Master*, which you use to design your handouts. As you create audience handouts in the Handout Master, you can add art and text to your handouts.

The Handout Master screen opens with small boxes that indicate where the pictures of the slides in your presentation will be printed. You can add new art and text outside of these outlined boxes. You set the number of slide outline boxes appearing on the Handout Master in the Print dialog box.

## Setting Slide Sizes and Printer Setup Options

After you have set your options for your presentations, you probably will not have to change them often. When you do need to make changes, however, do the following:

**❶** Choose **S**lide Set**u**p from the **F**ile menu.

The Slide Setup dialog box appears (see figure 10.6).

**Figure 10.6**
The Slide Setup dialog box.

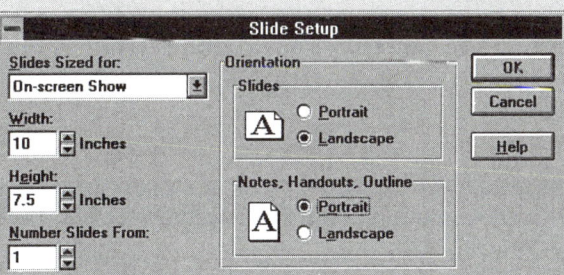

**❷** In the **S**lides Sized For drop-down list, select the choice that fits your project.

The selections are On-screen Show, Letter Paper, A4 Paper, 35mm Slides, and Custom. If you select Custom, you can set your own height and width in the **H**eight and **W**idth boxes.

**❸** Select the orientation, **P**ortrait or **L**andscape, in the Slides box under Orientation.

(continues)

## Setting Slide Sizes and Printer Setup Options (continued)

In the Portrait mode, the image is taller than it is wide; in the Landscape mode, the image is wider than it is tall. Portrait mode is often used for speaker's notes, handouts, and Outline view printouts. Landscape is most often used for printed transparencies. You can select different orientations for each category.

**4** Type the beginning slide number in the **N**umber Slides From box.

Although you probably want most of your presentations to begin with number 1, some situations call for different numbering. For example, rather than have one long presentation, you might have a series of short presentations that are given in order, much like chapters in a book. You also may have a standard opening or logo sequence for your company in a library of repeated presentation segments, and you want new presentations to pick up at that point.

**5** To complete your setup, click OK.

# Objective 7: Use the PowerPoint Viewer

**Play list**
A list of presentations in the order in which the Viewer will run them.

The PowerPoint Viewer is its own application. You can use the Viewer to run a presentation on any computer that has Microsoft Windows Version 3.1 or later, whether or not PowerPoint is installed on that computer. If you want to distribute copies of your presentation, you can include and distribute the Viewer with your presentation. You can open the Viewer and select a presentation, or you can set the Viewer to begin a specified presentation immediately. You can also create a *play list*, which the Viewer will use to run several presentations consecutively.

## Using the PowerPoint Viewer to Open a Presentation

Two reasons to use the Viewer yourself are that you are in a hurry to review a presentation you do not need to edit or that you want to give a quick presentation. To use the PowerPoint Viewer, do the following:

**1** Save and close any presentation that may be open in PowerPoint.

**2** Exit PowerPoint.

**Note:** *Although ending your PowerPoint session is not necessary to use the Viewer—you could simply switch to the Windows Program Manager—this tutorial is also intended to show that the Viewer can be used without PowerPoint loaded.*

**10**

**3** In the Program Manager, double-click the PowerPoint Viewer icon (see figure 10.7). The icon may be installed in the Microsoft Office group on your system. If this group is minimized, restore the group to access the icon.

**Figure 10.7**
The PowerPoint Viewer icon in the Microsoft Office group.

**PowerPoint Viewer icon**

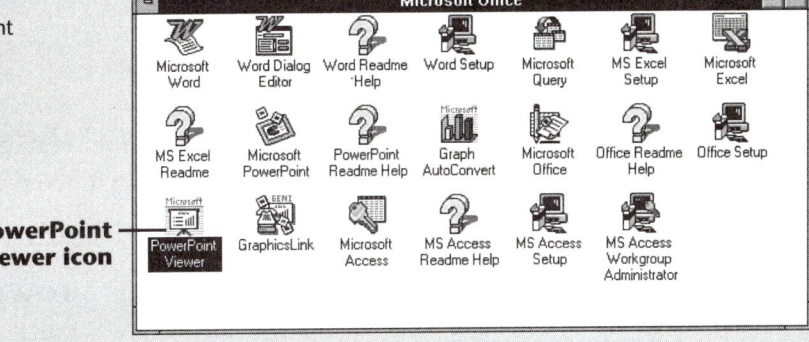

The PowerPoint Viewer dialog box appears (see figure 10.8)

**Figure 10.8**
The Microsoft PowerPoint Viewer dialog box.

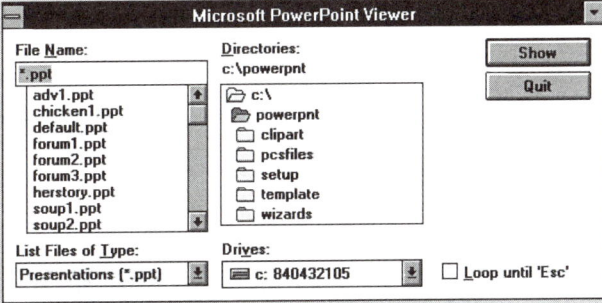

**4** Select the SOUP4.PPT file.

**5** Click the Show button.

The presentation begins. Use the keyboard commands you learned earlier in this chapter to advance and end the presentation. When the presentation ends, the Microsoft PowerPoint Viewer dialog box returns.

**6** Click the Quit button to end the Viewer session.

You can write a Windows play list in any word processor that can save an ASCII file. Once you have a play list, you run it from PowerPoint by choosing **O**pen from the **F**ile menu and selecting the list file, or by using the Viewer.

**Note:** *The following examples assume that the presentation files and the list file are in the same drive and directory.*

## Creating a Windows Play List

To create a play list, do the following:

**1** In any word processor, open a new document.

**2** Type **adv1.ppt**, and press ⏎Enter.

The name of each presentation must be on a separate line. You can use a single file name or multiple file names, typing one file name per line.

**3** Type **forum3.ppt**, and press ⏎Enter.

**4** Save the file as a text (ASCII) file with an extension of LST: **FOWL.LST**. Save the LST file in the same directory as your presenation files.

You now have created the file FOWL.LST. The key to this file is the LST extension.

**5** Close your word processor.

You can run the file directly from the Viewer, or you can choose the **R**un command from the **F**ile menu in the Program Manager.

## Using the Viewer to Run a Play List

To run a play list from the Program Manager and the File menu, do the following:

**1** With the Program Manager the active window, choose **R**un from the **F**ile menu.

The Run dialog box appears.

**2** In the **C**ommand Line box, type the path and file name to open the Viewer, followed by the path and file name of the LST file. Your command line should resemble, but not necessarily be identical to, this:

```
c:\powerpnt\pptview.exe a:\fowl.lst
```

The c:\powerpnt\pptview.exe is the path to the executable file—PPTVIEW.EXE on drive C. The a:\fowl.lst tells the executable file to use the file FOWL.LST on drive A.

**3** Press ⏎Enter.

The Viewer runs the shows you have listed in the FOWL.LST file.

**10**

Microsoft allows you to distribute the Viewer program, PPTVIEW.EXE without any additional license so that other people can watch the presentations on their computers even if they do not have a copy of PowerPoint themselves.

PowerPoint provides a separate disk, labeled *Viewer*, with the installation disks. The following tutorial tells you how to make a copy of the Viewer disk.

## Distributing Your Presentations with the Viewer

To create a set of distribution disks for your presentation, do the following:

**1** Make a copy of the Viewer disk that is distributed with PowerPoint. Label the disk *Viewer*.

Keep the original with your other PowerPoint disks in case you need to add or remove files in the future.

**Note:** *If you need to make many copies of this disk, you may want to create a special VIEWER directory on your computer system and copy the contents of the Viewer disk to that directory. You should put nothing else in that directory but the Viewer disk contents. To make your own Viewer disks, format a 1.44M or a 1.2M disk, and copy the contents of the VIEWER directory to the formatted disk.*

**2** Format a second disk, and copy your presentations to that disk or disks. Label the disk(s) *Presentation disk(s)*.

Do not put your presentation files on your Viewer disk.

**Note:** *If the presentation contains branches to another presentation, set the slide timings for each presentation separately, and then save the presentations with the* **U***se Slide Timings option button selected. Copy all the presentations, including the branched-to presentations, to your distribution disks.*

**3** With your distribution disks, provide a copy of the following instructions (substituting the name of your LST file for the FOWL.LST file in the example):

   A. **Start Windows, and in the Program Manager, run VSETUP on the Viewer disk.**

   B. **Specify the directory on your hard drive where the Viewer will be installed.**

   C. **Use the File Manager to copy the presentation files on the remaining disks to a directory on your hard drive.**

   D. **With the Program Manager the active window, choose Run from the File menu.**

   **The Run dialog box appears.**

(continues)

---

**Distributing Your Presentations with the Viewer (continued)**

    **E. In the Command Line box, type the path and file name to open the Viewer, followed by the path and file name of the LST file. Your command line should read**

        **c:\powerpnt\pptview.exe a:\fowl.lst**

    **F. Press Enter.**

    **The Viewer runs the shows in FOWL.LST file.**

This example assumes that the presentation files and the list file are in the same drive and directory.

---

# Chapter Summary

In this chapter, you have learned that effective color schemes are often media dependent. You learned how to change color schemes quickly and how to handle any accompanying problems. You practiced using keyboard commands to run a smooth and professional presentation. You also practiced on-screen drawing to gain proficiency in this often difficult task. You created a branched presentation and practiced branching during a presentation. Additional printing features are explained, including the capability to print files for service bureaus. You also learned how to use the Viewer and how to prepare disks for distribution.

# Checking Your Skills

### True/False Questions

For each of the following statements, circle *T* or *F* to indicate whether the statement is true or false.

T F **1.** In PowerPoint, the term *medium* refers to a color scheme that can be used for both video and transparency displays.

T F **2.** An LCD is a computer-controlled display device that records transparency images.

T F **3.** Darker colors are probably better for transparencies.

T F **4.** When clicked, the Freehand Annotation icon branches to another presentation.

T F **5.** Multiple branches may be added to any presentation.

## Multiple-Choice Questions

In the blank provided, write the letter of the correct answer for each of the following questions.

10

___ **1.** A dimensional perspective for slide images in a particular medium is _____.

   **a.** dependent on the color scheme for that medium

   **b.** known as the aspect ratio

   **c.** based on a Landscape default orientation

   **d.** set in the Printer dialog box

___ **2.** One of the keyboard commands for switching between a blank white screen and a presentation slide is _____.

   **a.** ⟨.⟩ (period)

   **b.** ⟨A⟩

   **c.** ⟨B⟩

   **d.** ⟨W⟩

___ **3.** One of the keyboard commands that pauses a presentation with automatic timing is _____.

   **a.** ⟨P⟩

   **b.** ⟨A⟩

   **c.** ⟨S⟩

   **d.** ⟨W⟩

___ **4.** The term *Play Settings* refers to the _____.

   **a.** timing set between slides in a presentation

   **b.** category of a PowerPoint object

   **c.** transition effects between slides in a presentation

   **d.** settings used to start a branched presentation

___ **5.** Aspect ratios of slides are determined by _____.

   **a.** dividing the height by the width

   **b.** dividing height and width by the largest common denominator

   **c.** dividing the width by the height when the height is the largest common denominator

   **d.** whether the presentation is for a 35mm or 70mm slide

### Fill-in-the-Blank Questions

In the blank provided, write the correct answer for each of the following questions.

1. Professional slides can be produced by an outside _____.

2. PowerPoint provides _____ in four categories, which correspond to the display media.

3. To go to any particular slide while giving a presentation, you simply type a _____ and press ⏎Enter.

4. As opposed to images in the Landscape mode, an image printed in the _____ mode is taller than it is wide.

5. The Microsoft PowerPoint _____ can be freely distributed with your presentation files.

# Applying Your Skills

## Review Exercises

### Exercise 1: Changing a Color Scheme
The ADV1.PPT presentation appears washed out in color transparencies. Change the color scheme to one you feel will project better images.

### Exercise 2: Printing Audience Handouts
The big day has arrived, and you now must give the presentation SOUP4.PPT to the company directors. Create a set of audience handouts based on the speaker's notes that you created earlier. The format is up to you, but fewer slides on a page would probably be better.

### Exercise 3: Adding Branching to a Presentation
At the last minute, your boss tells you that several of the directors are also interested in the history presentation, HERSTORY.PPT, and the forum preparations. Add two more icons to the "Recommendations" slide in the SOUP4.PPT presentation. Run through the presentation, practicing the keyboard commands—especially those for going to the "Recommendations" slide from any point in the presentation and then returning to where you left off.

## Continuing Projects

### Project 1: Creating Presentation Distribution Disks
Your boss wants to take a copy of the HERSTORY.PPT presentation to the next national sales meeting. Create a set of distribution disks that will enable your boss to give the presentation on a computer at the meeting location. A copy of PowerPoint will not be available at that location.

**Project 2: Preparing a Professional Presentation**

In Continuing Project 2 in Chapter 4, you added notes and timing to a presentation that you created on an activity that interested you. You also practiced your delivery. Return to that presentation, and prepare the color scheme for an LCD format. Make any other changes or refinements that you think will make the presentation more professional. Print a set of audience handouts. Practice your delivery using the full set of keyboard commands. Finally, prepare a set of distribution disks so that you can give the presentation on any computer.

**10**

# Working with Windows

**Graphical user interface**
An easy-to-use method of combining graphics, menus, and plain English commands so that the user communicates with the computer.

Microsoft Windows is a powerful operating environment that enables you to access the power of DOS without memorizing DOS commands and syntax. Windows uses a *graphical user interface* (GUI) so that you can easily see on-screen the tools you need to complete specific file and program management tasks.

This appendix, an overview of the Windows environment, is designed to help you learn the basics of Windows.

## Objectives

By the time you have finished this appendix, you will have learned to

1. Start Windows

2. Use a Mouse in Windows

3. Understand the Windows Desktop

4. Understand the Program Manager

5. Get Help

6. Get Comfortable with Windows

7. Exit Windows

## Objective 1: Start Windows

Many computers are set to open in Windows. If your computer does not automatically open in Windows, however, you can easily access the program.

### Starting Windows

To start Windows from the DOS command prompt, follow these steps:

1. Type **win**.

2. Press `⏎Enter`. Windows begins loading. When it is loaded, you see the Program Manager window open on-screen.

**Window**

A rectangular area on-screen in which you view program icons, applications, or documents.

The Program Manager *window* includes many different elements, such as the menu bar, title bar, and icons. (You open windows, start applications, and select items by selecting the appropriate icon.) Your Program Manager window may look different from the window used in this book's illustrations. For example, you may have different program group icons across the bottom of the Program Manager window (see figure A.1).

**Figure A.1**

The first time you start Windows, a group window may be open on the desktop.

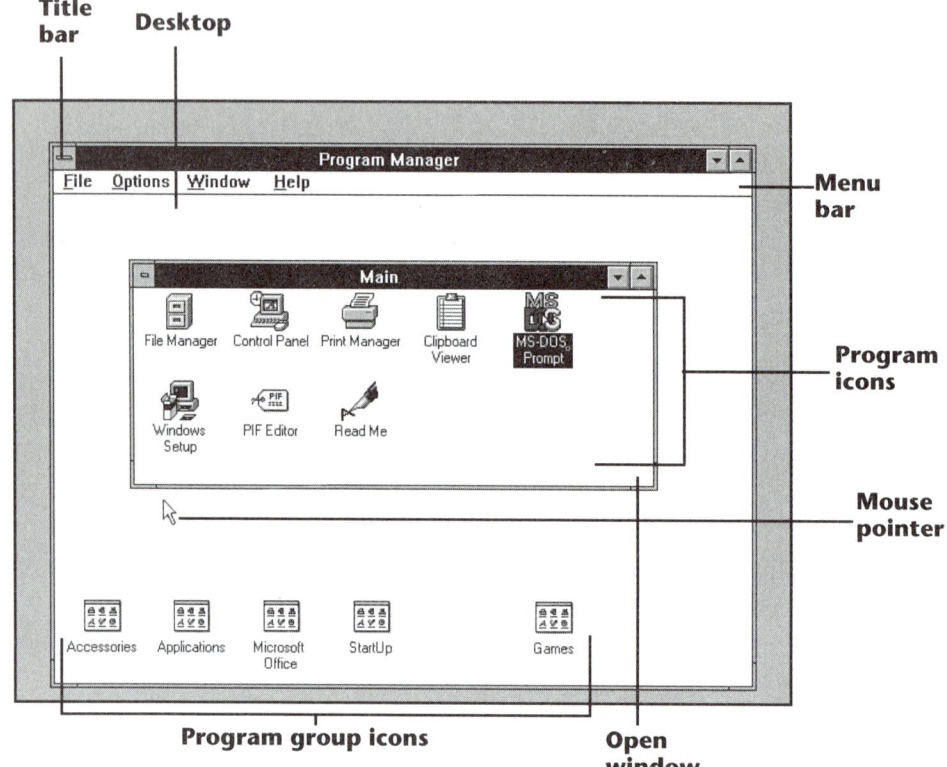

# Objective 2: Use a Mouse in Windows

**Mouse**

A pointing device used in many programs to make choices, select data, and otherwise communicate with the computer.

Windows is designed for use with a *mouse*. Although you can get by with just a keyboard, using a mouse is much easier. This book assumes that you are using a mouse.

In the Windows desktop, you can use a mouse to

- Open windows
- Close windows
- Open menus
- Choose menu commands
- Rearrange on-screen items, such as icons and windows

**Mouse pointer**
An on-screen symbol that indicates the current location of the mouse.

**Mouse pad**
A pad that provides a uniform surface for a mouse to slide on.

The position of the mouse is indicated on-screen by a *mouse pointer*. Usually, the mouse pointer is an arrow, but it sometimes changes shape depending on the current action.

On-screen the mouse pointer moves according to the movements of the mouse on your desk or on a *mouse pad*. To move the mouse pointer, simply move the mouse.

There are three basic mouse actions:

- *Click*. To point to an item and press and release quickly the left mouse button. You click to select an item, such as an option on a menu. To cancel a selection, click an empty area of the desktop.

- *Double-click*. To point to an item and then press and release the left mouse button twice, as quickly as possible. You double-click to open or close windows and to start applications from icons.

- *Drag*. To point to an item, press and hold down the left mouse button as you move the pointer to another location, and then release the mouse button. You drag to resize windows, move icons, and scroll.

  **Note:** *Unless otherwise specified, you use the left mouse button for all mouse actions.*

---

**If you have problems...** If you try to double-click but nothing happens, you may not be clicking fast enough. Try again.

---

# Objective 3: Understand the Windows Desktop

**Desktop**
The background of the Windows screen, on which windows, icons, and dialog boxes appear.

Your screen provides a *desktop*, the background for Windows. On the desktop, each application is displayed in its own window (hence the name Windows). All windows have the same set of elements that enable you to move, resize, and manipulate the window.

If you have multiple windows open, they may overlap on the desktop, just as papers on your desk can be stacked one on top of the other. You may have one or more windows open when you start Windows.

**Icon**
A picture that represents a group window, an application, a document, or other element in a GUI-based program.

## The Title Bar

Across the top of each window is its title bar. At the right side of the title bar are the Minimize button for reducing windows to icons and the Maximize button for expanding windows to fill the desktop. At the left side of the title bar is the control menu *icon*, a box with a small hyphen in it. The control icon activates a window's control menu (see figure A.2).

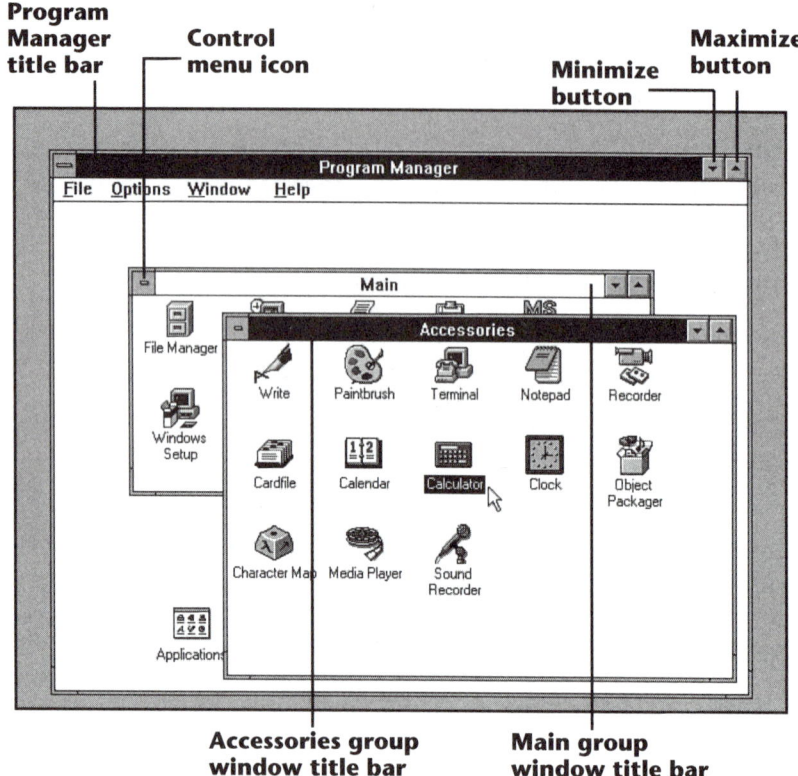

**Figure A.2**
Every open window has a title bar, used to identify the contents of the window.

**Program Manager title bar**

**Control menu icon**

**Minimize button**

**Maximize button**

**Accessories group window title bar**

**Main group window title bar**

## Menus

Menus enable you to select options to perform functions or carry out commands (see figure A.3). The control menu, for example, enables you to control the size and position of its window.

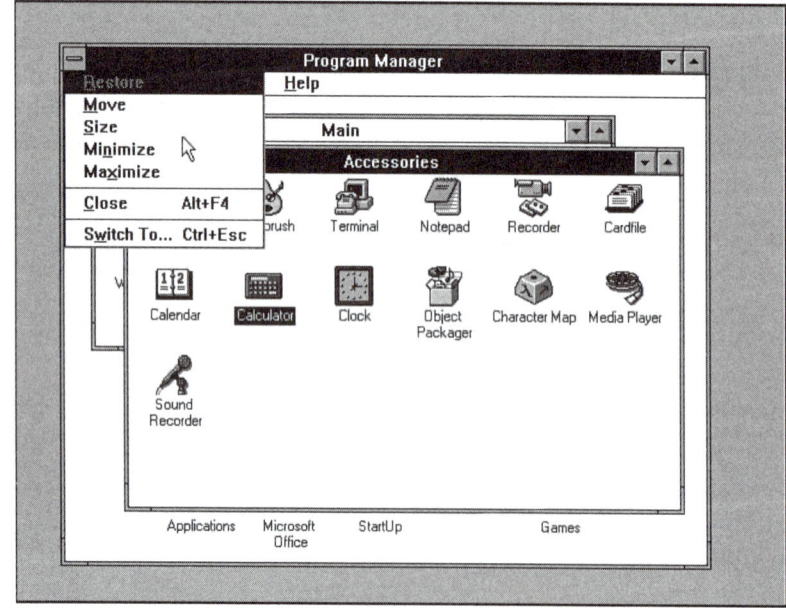

**Figure A.3**
Menus, like the control menu shown here, enable you to choose commands without remembering DOS syntax, switches, or parameters.

## Dialog Boxes

**Dialog box**
A window that opens on-screen to provide information or to ask for the additional information.

Some menu options require you to enter additional information. When you select one of these options, a *dialog box* opens (see figure A.4). You either type the additional information into a text box, select from a list of options, or select a button.

**Figure A.4**
In a dialog box, you provide additional information that Windows needs to complete the command.

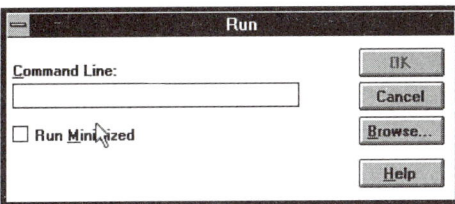

## Buttons

Buttons are on-screen areas with which you select actions or commands. Most dialog boxes have at least a Cancel button, which stops the current activity and returns to the preceding screen; an OK button, which accepts the current activity; and a Help button, which opens a Help window (see figure A.5).

**Figure A.5**
The Search dialog box of the Help features, with buttons you click to select topics and perform actions.

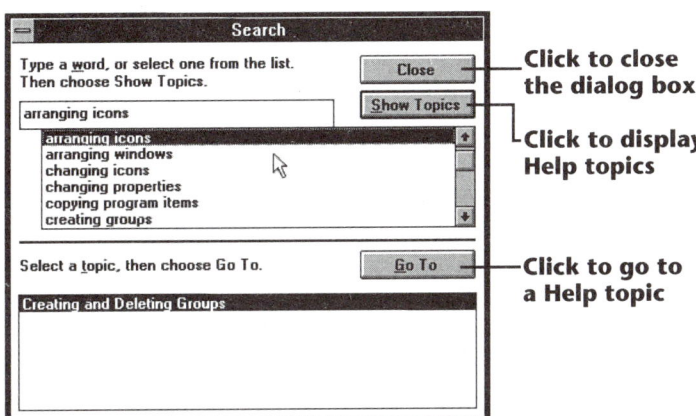

# Objective 4: Understand the Program Manager

The Program Manager is the central Microsoft Windows program. When you start Microsoft Windows, the Program Manager starts automatically. When you exit Microsoft Windows, you exit the Program Manager. You cannot run Microsoft Windows if you are not running the Program Manager.

**Program group**
Application programs organized into a set that can be accessed through a program group window.

The Program Manager does what its name implies—it manages programs. You use the Program Manager to organize programs into groups called *program groups*. Usually, programs in a group are related, either by function (such as a group of accessories) or by usage (such as a group of programs used to compile a monthly newsletter).

Each program group is represented by a program group icon (see figure A.6).

**Figure A.6**
When you double-click a program group icon, a group window opens on-screen.

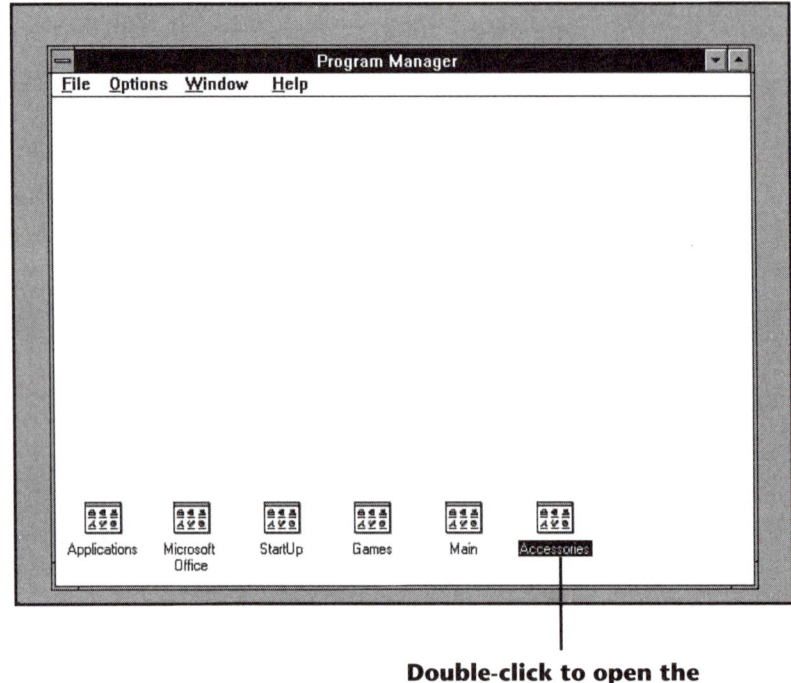

**Double-click to open the
Accessories group window**

In each program group window, you see the icons for each program item in the group (see figure A.7).

**Figure A.7**
When you double-click a program icon, the program starts.

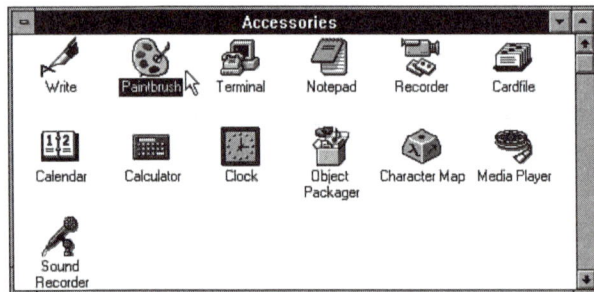

# Objective 5: Get Help

Almost every Windows application has a Help menu. From the Help menu, you can start a Help program to display information about many aspects of the program.

To display Help information, take one of the following actions:

**Context-sensitive**
Pertaining to the current action.

- Press F1. The Help program starts, and a *context-sensitive* Help window opens on-screen.

- Choose **H**elp from the menu bar, and choose one of the Help menu commands.

**Note:** *To choose a menu item, point to it with the mouse pointer; then click the left mouse button.*

### Displaying Help for a Topic

To display Help for a particular topic, follow these steps:

1. Choose **H**elp from the menu bar.

2. Choose **C**ontents from the Help menu. A Help window opens; it displays the main topics for which Help is available (see figure A.8).

**Figure A.8**
The Help window groups topics into How To and Commands categories.

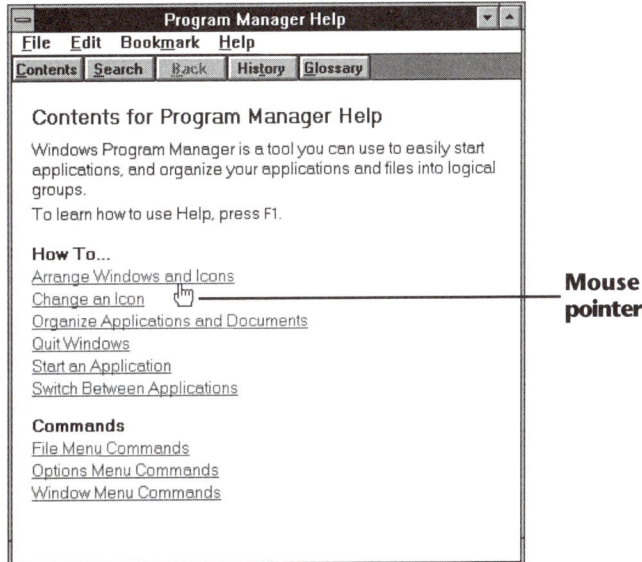

3. Choose the topic for which you want additional information. Windows displays the Help information.

### Closing the Help Window

To close the Help window, take one of the following actions:

- Choose **C**lose from the Help window's Control menu.

- Choose E**x**it from the Help window's File menu.

- Double-click the Control menu button.

---

**If you have problems...** To open the control menu, click the control menu button at the far left end of the window's title bar.

---

# Objective 6: Get Comfortable with Windows

To be comfortable using Windows, you need to know how to control your Windows desktop, which in large part means controlling the windows themselves.

You can open, close, move, and resize all the windows that appear in Windows, including the Program Manager.

## Opening a Window

To open a window, double-click the appropriate icon (see figure A.9). When you double-click a program group icon, you open a group window. When you double-click a program icon, you start that program.

**Figure A.9**
You can continue opening windows until the desktop is full or until you run out of memory.

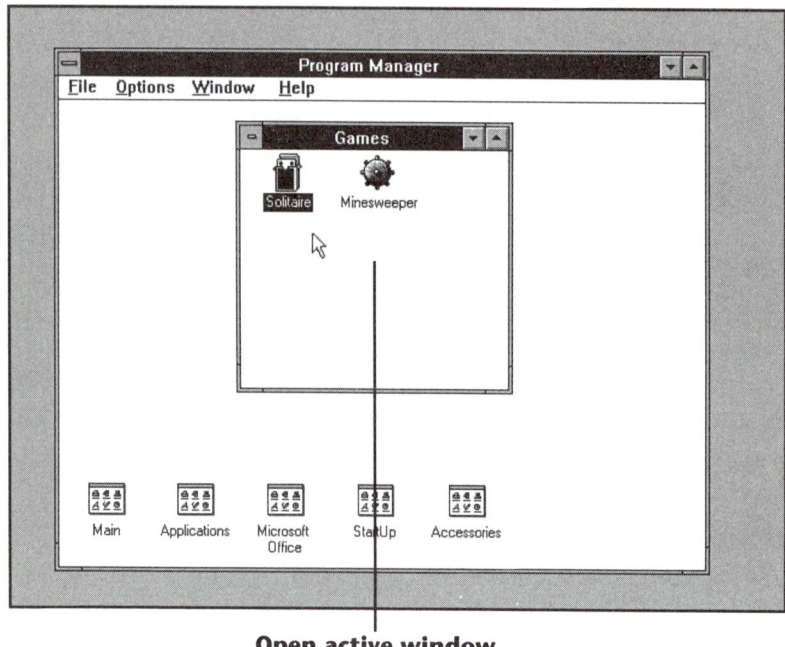

Open active window

---

**If you have problems...** If a control menu opens instead of a window, you are not double-clicking fast enough. Try again, or choose Restore from the control menu.

---

Don't worry if your screen looks different from the screens used to illustrate this book. Your desktop may be organized differently. You still can perform all the same tasks.

**Note:** *You can also use the control menu to open a window. Click the icon once to display the control menu. Then click* **R***estore.*

## Changing the Active Window

**Active window**
The window in which you are currently working.

No matter how many windows are open on the desktop, you can work only in the *active window*.

You can tell which window is active in two ways:

- The active window is on the top of other open windows on the desktop.

- The title bar of the active window is highlighted (see figure A.10).

**Figure A.10**
Four windows are open. The Games group window is the active window.

**Highlighted title bar of active window**

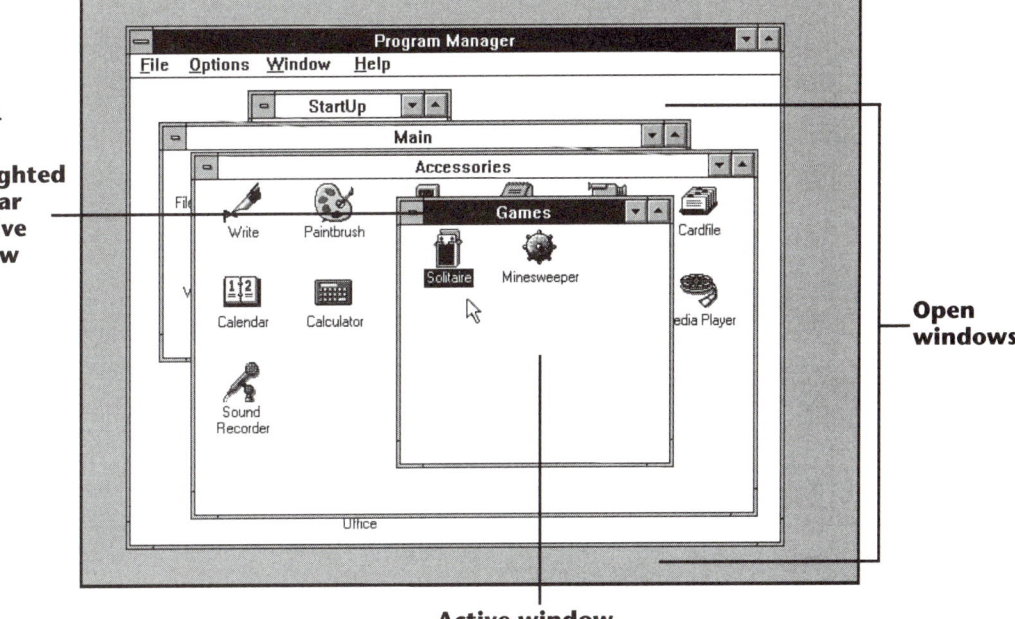

**Open windows**

**Active window**

To make a window active, click anywhere in it. The window moves to the top of the desktop, and its title bar appears in a different color or shade.

---

**If you have problems...** If the window you want to make active is hidden behind another window, click **W**indow on the menu bar to open the Window menu. From the list of available windows, choose the one you want to make active.

---

## Resizing a Window

You can change the size of any open window by dragging its borders with the mouse.

To resize a window, follow these steps:

**1.** Point to the border you want to move.

   **Note:** *When you are pointing to the border, the mouse pointer to a double-headed arrow.*

**2.** Press and hold down the left mouse button, and drag the border to its new location. As you drag, you see the border move along with the mouse pointer.

**3.** Release the mouse button. The window adjusts to the new size (see figure A.11).

   **Note:** *To change the height and width of the window simultaneously, drag one of the window's corners.*

**Figure A.11**
To resize a window, drag one of its borders.

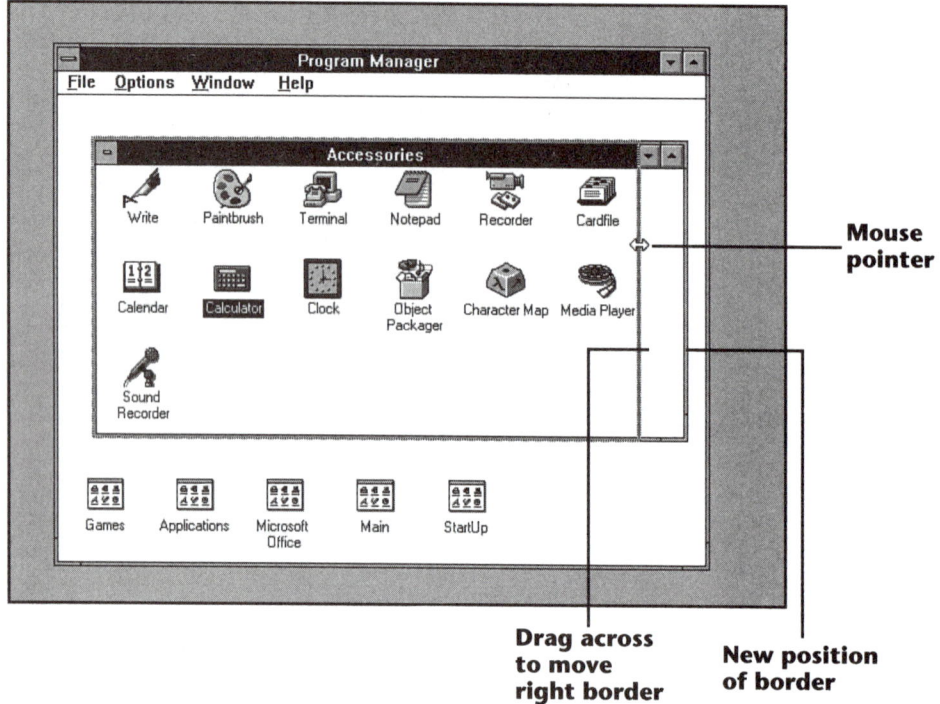

**Mouse pointer**

**Drag across to move right border**

**New position of border**

---

**If you have problems...** If nothing happens when you try to change a window size, you probably are not pointing at a border. Make sure that the mouse pointer changes shape to a double-headed arrow before you drag the border.

---

## Moving a Window

You can move a window to a different location on the screen by dragging it with the mouse.

To move a window, follow these steps:

1. Point to the window's title bar.

2. Press and hold down the left mouse button, and drag the window to the new location. You see the borders of the window move with the mouse pointer (see figure A.12).

3. Release the mouse button.

---

**If you have problems...** If nothing happens when you try to move a window, you are probably not pointing to the window's title bar. Make sure that the mouse pointer is within the title bar before you drag the window.

---

## Maximizing a Window

You can maximize a window to fill the entire desktop. Maximizing a window gives you more space in which to work.

**Figure A.12**
You can move a window to any location on the desktop.

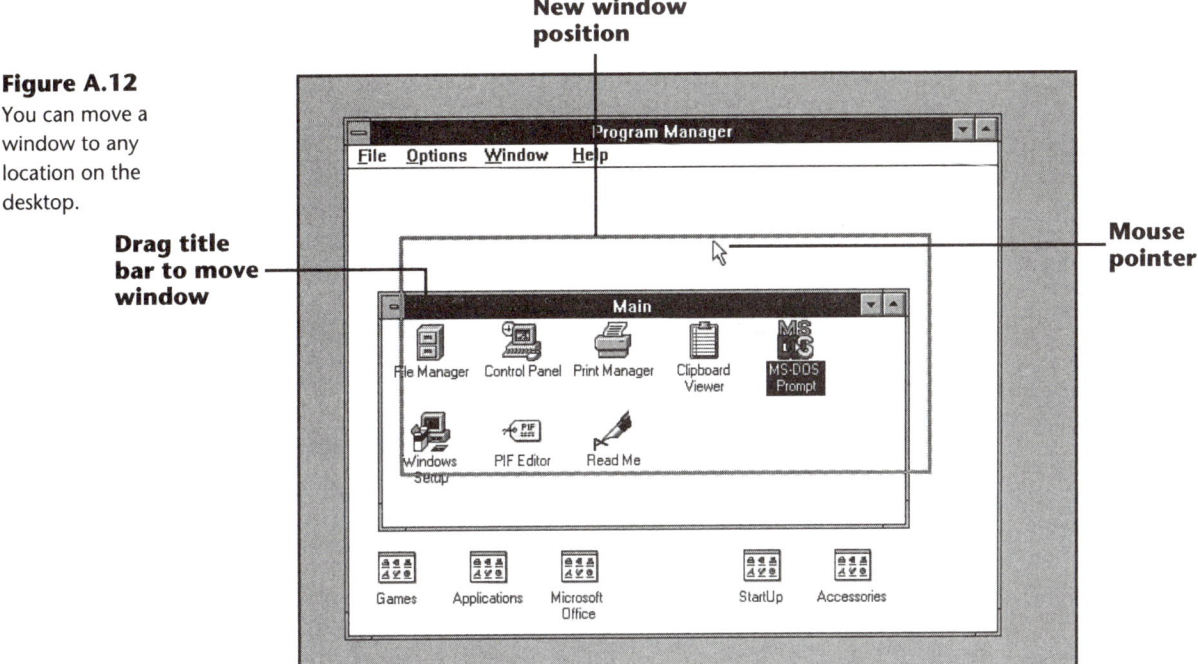

**Maximize**
To increase the size of a window until it covers the desktop.

To *maximize* a window, do one of the following:

- Click the Maximize button at the far right of the window's title bar. This button has an arrowhead pointing up.

- Choose **M**aximize from the window's control menu (see figure A.13).

**Figure A.13**
Each window has a Maximize button at the right end of its title bar.

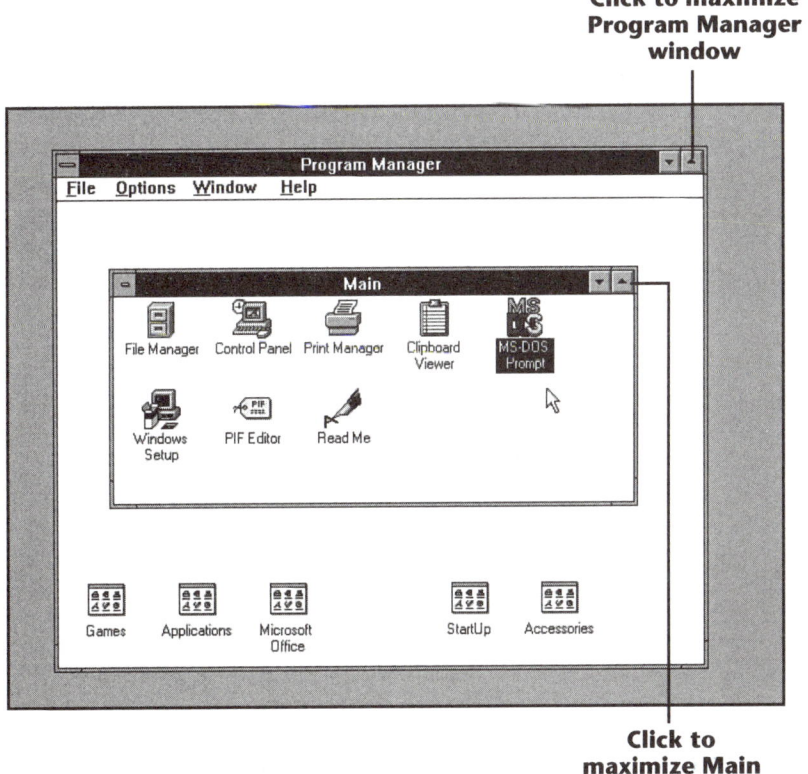

## Minimizing a Window

**Minimize**
To reduce a window to an icon.

You can *minimize* a window that you are not currently using.

To minimize a window, take one of the following actions:

- Click the Minimize button on the title bar. This button has an arrowhead pointing down (see figure A.14).

**Figure A.14**
Each window has a Minimize button, which you can use to minimize the window to an icon.

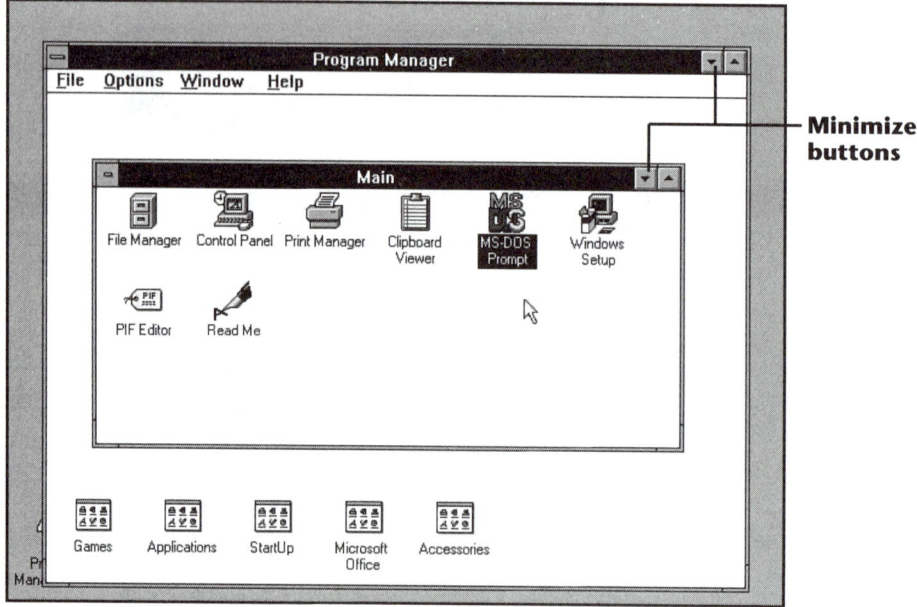

- Choose Mi**n**imize from the window's control menu.

  **Note:** *Program group windows, such as the Main group, are reduced to program group icons at the bottom of the Program Manager. Application, utility, or document icons are positioned at the bottom of the desktop, behind any active windows. The application that has been minimized is still active; it is just out of the way.*

## Restoring a Window

**Restore**
To return a window to its most recent size and position on the desktop.

You can *restore* a window that has been maximized or minimized to its most recent size and location.

To restore a window to its most recent size, take one of the following actions:

- Click the Restore button, which replaces the Maximize button on the title bar. The Restore button has arrowheads pointing up and down (see figure A.15).

- Choose **R**estore from the window's control menu.

**Figure A.15**
When you maximize a window, the Restore button appears at the left end of the title bar in place of the Maximize button.

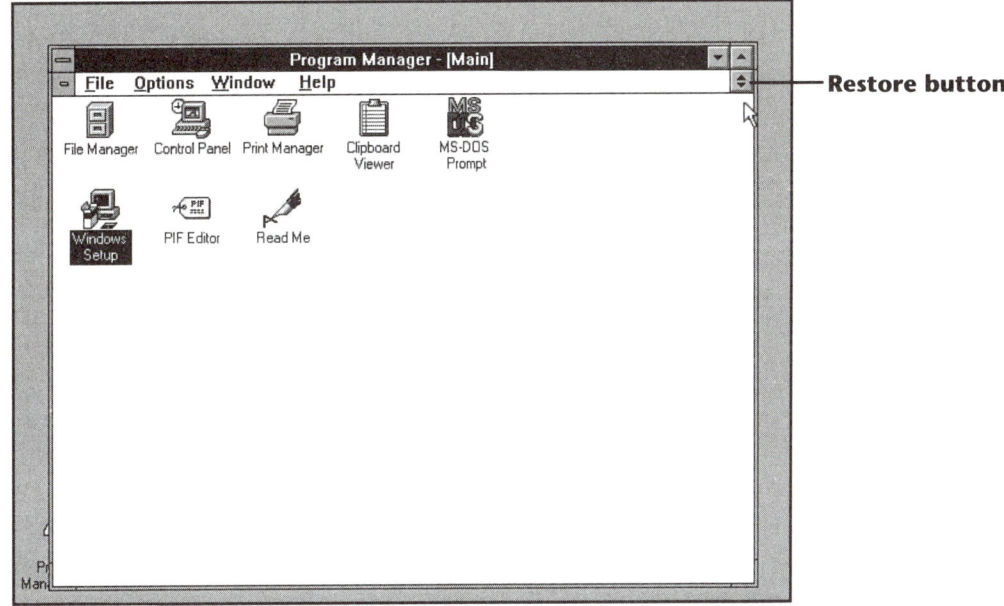

Restore button

**If you have problems...** If you try to restore the window but nothing happens, the window has not been maximized or minimized. You cannot restore a window unless it has been maximized or minimized first.

## Arranging the Windows on Your Desktop

Sometimes a desktop becomes so cluttered with open windows that you cannot tell what you are using. When that happens, you can choose either to *tile* or to *cascade* the open windows on-screen so that you can see them all.

To arrange the windows on the desktop, follow these steps:

**1.** Choose **W**indow from the menu bar to display the Window menu.

**2.** Choose one of the following:

- **T**ile, to arrange the windows on-screen so that none are overlapping (see figure A.16).

- **C**ascade, to arrange the windows on-screen so that they overlap (see figure A.17).

**Tile**
To arrange open windows on the desktop so that they do not overlap.

**Cascade**
To arrange open windows on the desktop so that they overlap, but at least a portion of each window is displayed.

**Figure A.16**
The windows are tiled on the desktop.

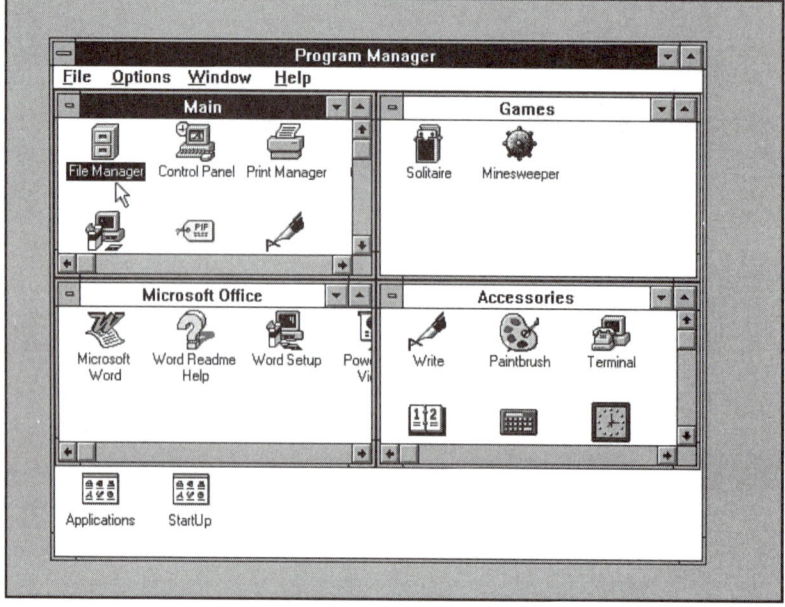

**Figure A.17**
The windows are cascaded on the desktop.

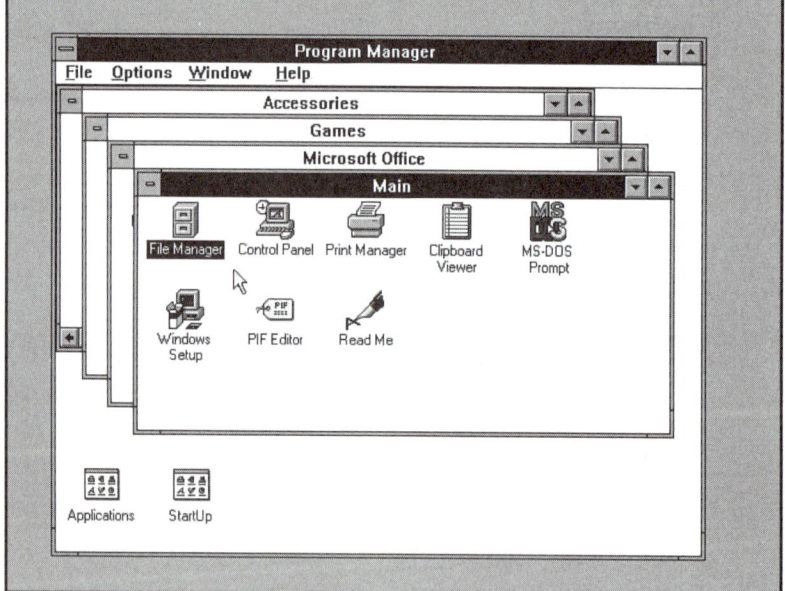

## Closing a Window

To close a window, take one of the following actions:

- Choose **C**lose from the window's control menu.

- Choose **C**lose from the window's **F**ile menu.

- Double-click the control menu button. (To open the control menu, click the control menu button at the far left end of the window's title bar.)

---

**If you have problems...** If the Exit Windows dialog box appears, you clicked the control menu box for the Program Manager rather than the control menu box for the window you want to close. Click Cancel.

---

# Objective 7: Exit Windows

You should always exit Windows before turning off your computer. To exit Windows and return to the DOS command prompt, follow these steps:

**1.** Close all open windows and applications.

**2.** Point to File in the menu bar, and click the left mouse button.

**3.** Point to Exit Windows, and click the left mouse button. Windows prompts you to confirm that you want to exit.

**4.** Point to OK, and click the left mouse button. Windows closes, and the DOS command prompt is displayed.

**Note:** *As a shortcut, simply double-click the control menu button at the far left of the Program Manager title bar. Windows asks you to confirm that you want to exit. Click OK.*

# Sending and Routing Presentation Files on Mail Systems

Presentations often involve a number of people, particularly in team environments where several individuals are cooperating in the creation of a presentation. Even in workgroup environments, several individuals may be contributing sections of the presentation based on each person's expertise.

In some situations, having others in the company review and add their comments to a presentation may be helpful. Although any presentation can be sent to others on disk, exchanging presentation files electronically is much faster and often more convenient.

To send and route presentations electronically, you must have Microsoft Mail or a compatible mail program installed on all computers in the routing network that will be exchanging files. A quick way to determine whether mail is installed on your system is to access the File menu in Word for Windows and see whether the Send command is present. If so, then your system has Microsoft Mail.

You can send a presentation to one person or to several people at once, or you can route the presentation so that it is transmitted to one individual after another in a particular order.

## Sending a Presentation to Another Individual

To send a presentation to another individual, do the following:

1. Make the presentation you want to transmit your active presentation.

2. Choose Send from the File menu.

   The Send dialog box appears.

3. Select the name of the recipient.

4. Click the Send button.

   A copy of the presentation is transmitted.

# Routing a Presentation to Multiple Individuals

You can send one or more copies of a presentation to a group of individuals or route them to the members of a group in a particular order. To route a presentation, do the following:

1. Make the presentation you want to transmit your active presentation.

2. Choose Add **R**outing Slip from the **F**ile menu; or if you are editing an existing routing slip, choose **E**dit Routing Slip from the **F**ile menu.

   The Routing Slip dialog box appears.

3. Click the **A**ddress button.

4. Select the names of the recipients. If you want the recipients to receive the presentation in a certain order, use the Move Up and Move Down arrows to rearrange the list order.

5. Click Add and then OK.

   The recipients have been added to the routing slip.

6. Type the subject of this transmission in the **S**ubject text box.

7. Type any message you want to send with the presentation in the **M**essage text box.

8. Do one of the following in the Route to Recipients option box:

   a. Select the **O**ne After Another option button to route one copy of the presentation to each recipient in turn.

   b. Select the All At **O**nce option button to send multiple copies to all recipients at once.

9. Click the **R**oute button.

   Confirm in the message box that you want to route the presentation.

# Glossary

**Alignment.** The positioning of text in a text box on a slide, such as centered, right, left, and justified, that affects the entire paragraph.

**Anchor.** A fixed point in a drawing object in which a portion of the object is locked into position.

**Area graph.** Graph emphasizing the magnitude of each value's contribution to the whole, rather than the rate of change over time.

**ASCII.** A 7-bit standard code that produces an electronic file consisting primarily of alphanumeric characters.

**Aspect ratio.** A dimensional change in a visual that is demanded by a change in medium or orientation.

**AutoContent Wizard.** A tool that guides a planner through the steps of a proposed presentation.

**Axis.** An imaginary line that aligns either items in a category or the value of items. When aligning values, the axis becomes the measuring stick of the graph.

**Balance.** A general matching of like elements on a slide so that no one element overwhelms another.

**Bar chart.** Chart that places categories of items on the vertical axis, and the value of the items on the horizontal axis.

**Cascading menu.** A term used by Microsoft to describe submenus accessed by choosing a secondary menu from main menu choices.

**Category.** A group of related items.

**Choose.** To initiate a command or option.

**Clip art.** Small pictures or illustrations.

**Column chart.** Similar to a bar chart, but with items on the horizontal axis and values on the vertical axis.

**Data label.** The printed item name or value that appears at or corresponding to a data point.

**Data marker.** A mark on an axis that identifies a data point.

**Data point.** A point on an axis that corresponds to the specific value of an item.

**Data series.** A collection of values for a category, all pertaining to a single subject.

**Datasheet.** A miniature spreadsheet that appears in a Datasheet dialog box and is used to produce graphs.

**Dock.** A blank area on any side of a presentation window for parking a toolbar.

**Doughnut chart.** Similar to a pie chart but allowing for multiple categories by placing each category in a separate ring of the pie chart.

**Drawing object.** An illustration created with PowerPoint drawing tools.

**Drawing tool.** A drawing function available from one of three toolbars and used to create and manipulate drawing objects.

**Electronic slide show.** A presentation created and displayed on a computer.

**Embedded objects.** Objects that are a permanent part of the presentation.

**Floating toolbar.** A toolbar that is parked within a presentation rather than docked.

**Graph title.** The title of a graph or chart.

**Grid.** An invisible network of criss-crossing lines 1/12 inch apart.

**Gridline.** Criss-crossed lines running at right angles to each other and evenly spaced on their particular axis.

**Group.** A collection of objects on a slide that are linked so that they can be treated as a single object.

**Guides.** Two straightedges, one vertical and one horizontal, that are used to align objects on a slide.

**Handles.** Small, black sizing boxes located between and on the corners of a highlighted border or frame of an object.

**Handout Master.** A view in which a handout template can be created or modified.

**Harmony.** The complementary relationship of various elements on a slide; the use of elements appropriate to the theme or content of the presentation.

**Horizontal axis.** Item categories or values placed horizontally in respect to each other.

**Hue.** A color.

**Import.** To bring a document or selection created in one computer program into another computer program.

**LCD.** Liquid Crystal Display. A low-power display technology used in laptop computers and small, battery-powered electronic devices.

**LCD projection panel.** A flat-screen LCD device, typically used with a slide projector, that creates computer-directed, electronic transparency images.

**Legend.** The name and its corresponding indicator that identify a category of items on a chart.

**Legend box.** A box on a graph that contains the legends.

**Line chart.** Places even increments, such as months, on the horizontal axis and item values on the vertical axis. A line connects the value points to show trends over time.

**Link.** The connection between a source document and a picture of the source that appears on a slide. Updates to the original will be reflected on the slide when updated. Linked objects are not actually stored in a presentation.

**Location tab.** A selection in the Advanced Search dialog box for entering drive and directory information.

**Luminance.** The amount of black or white added to a color.

**Master slide.** The slide that provides formatting of the basic slide elements for all slides in a presentation.

**Measurement scale.** The incremental values on the axis that align the values of times.

**Medium.** The means by which a presentation will be displayed—a computer video screen, overhead projector, or television screen.

**No-do bar.** Angled line across a simple picture indicating that the action depicted is not allowed. (The no-smoking sign shows a cigarette crossed out by a no-do bar.)

**Notes Pages view.** A view in which speaker's notes are attached to each slide.

**Objective.** The goal of a presentation; another way of defining a problem or premise.

**Outline Master.** A view in which an outline template can be created or modified.

**Outline view.** A view of a presentation in which the text is shown in outline form.

**Overheads.** Black-and-white or color transparencies that are projected by a transparency projector.

**Permanent text.** Text on a master slide that is reproduced on all slides in a presentation.

**Pick a Look Wizard.** A tool for changing the appearance of a presentation.

**Pie chart.** Chart that shows the proportion of parts to the whole for a single series of values in the same category by displaying the whole as a circle and the values as wedges.

**Placeholder.** A designated location on a slide in which titles, text, art, graphs, charts, or other objects can be inserted.

**Play list.** A list of presentations in the order in which the PowerPoint Viewer will run them.

**Presentation.** A collection of slides that are displayed in a timed sequence to convey information.

**Presentation type.** A classification of a presentation according to the situation or circumstances.

**Radar chart.** A chart that shows the value of items relative both to each other and to a center point.

**Rehearsal.** A two-step process that entails learning the material and practicing delivery.

**Rotation mouse pointer.** The form the mouse pointer takes when the Free Rotation tool is active.

**RTF.** A method used by many word processing programs to format text documents that retain certain minimal attributes.

**Rulers.** Two rulers, vertical and horizontal, that appear at the top and left sides of the window.

**Saturation.** The intensity of a color.

**Scatter chart.** A variation of a line chart in which a second series of values replace the time increments on the horizontal axis.

**Select.** To highlight a menu item as a possible choice.

**Service bureau.** In connection with PowerPoint, a producer of 35mm slides, transparencies, and photoprints of slides for a presentation.

**Slide Layout.** A slide design that contains placeholders for text and graphics objects.

**Slide Master.** A view in which a slide template can be created or modified.

**Slide view.** A view of a presentation in which individual slides are displayed one at a time.

**Spelling Checker.** A subprogram that checks the spelling of titles and text used on slides.

**Summary tab.** A selection in the Advanced Search dialog box for entering summary information.

**Supplementary materials.** Additional materials provided by PowerPoint to assist in a presentation.

**Teaser.** Words or visuals designed to "hook" an audience.

**Template.** A pattern for a slide or presentation.

**Text object.** A term used to describe text in a text box. This text is actually a graphic object.

**Theme.** The specific and overall purpose of the presentation that is consistently supported by all of the elements.

**Tick mark.** A visual marker that evenly divides values on any axis.

**Tick mark labels.** A numeric or time name that identifies a specific tick mark.

**Timeline.** Incremental time values, such as seconds, minutes, months, and years on an axis.

**Timestamp.** A selection in the Advanced Search dialog box for entering information about the last time a presentation was saved.

**Tone.** The voice of a presentation. The active voice is generally better than the passive voice in a sales presentation.

**ToolTip.** A small yellow box that displays the name of a tool when the mouse pointer is over that button.

**Transition effects.** The visual way in which one slide replaces another.

**Vertical axis.** Item categories or values placed vertically relative to each other.

**View.** The perspective from which you look at a presentation.

**Wizard.** A utility that asks a series of questions and produces a presentation based on the answers.

**WordArt.** Subprograms used to create special effects with text.

# Index

# Notes

# Notes

# Notes

# Notes

# Notes

# Notes